Flawed by Design

THE EVOLUTION
OF THE CIA, JCS, AND NSC

AMY B. ZEGART

Flawed by Design

THE EVOLUTION
OF THE CIA, JCS, AND NSC

STANFORD UNIVERSITY PRESS

STANFORD, CALIFORNIA

Stanford University Press
Stanford, California

© 1999 by the Board of Trustees
of the Leland Stanford Junior University

Printed in the United States of America
CIP data appear at the end of the book

For Craig

Contents

Figures

Tables

Acknowledgments

This project has been a collaborative endeavor. Above all, I thank Condi Rice, whose unwavering support, probing intellect, and passion for Stanford athletics made my time in Palo Alto so special. I also owe a tremendous debt of gratitude to the rest of my dissertation dream team: Steve Krasner, for his uncanny ability to find every hole in my argument; Terry Moe, whose work and encouragement first inspired me to tackle bureaucracies; and David Brady, for his unending supply of bad food and good advice.

I benefited greatly from a summer stint on the staff of President Clinton's National Security Council. A special thanks to all those who made it possible, and particularly to Bob Fauver, Will Itoh, Sandy Kristoff, Bob Manzanares, and Kent Wiedemann.

A number of legislative and executive branch officials generously shared their insights in personal interviews. I am especially grateful to Brent Scowcroft and the late McGeorge Bundy, both of whom laughed at my jokes and challenged my approach. Ty Cobb and Paul Stevens opened up their files as well as their memories, providing a treasure trove of clippings and unclassified documents. Their help went above and beyond the call of duty. Many others have asked to remain anonymous; some spent hours helping me frame the right questions, while others revealed candid and extremely personal stories in an effort to flesh out the answers. You know who you are. I hope you know how much you are appreciated. Thanks also to those who made my Washington fieldwork possible: Barry Blechman and the staff at DFI International, for giving me a home base; Dayna Bender, Joanne Lawson, and Rebecca Rubin, for giving me a home; and Janne Nolan for giving help whenever I needed it and the best writing advice I ever got: "Bang that sucker out."

Unfortunately, this book did not emerge full-blown, like Athena from the head of Zeus. Fortunately, I have benefited from the help of colleagues who generously took red pen to my green ideas. I am grateful to Nora Bensahel, Rui de Figueiredo, and Scott Sagan for going through multiple rounds of revisions and for providing a constant stream of articles and suggestions. I owe a special debt to Jack Rakove, who breathed life into early American history for me. I also thank Jenna Bednar, Matt Dickinson, Dan Drezner, Peter Feaver, John Ferejohn, Alex George, Chappell Lawson, and Barry Weingast for their constructive criticisms.

Thanks also to the Olin Institute at Harvard University and to the Political Science departments at the University of Virginia, Princeton University, and Yale University for enabling me to present various parts of the work in progress. There is nothing like good-natured grilling to spark sudden insight.

One of the great joys of graduate school was the opportunity to teach world-class undergraduates. In particular, I thank Lisa Dawe, Robert Franklin, Jason Koepp-Herthel, Wendy Kula, Anja Miller, Peppie Stephenson, Carrie Wendell, and my magical Thursday-night Poli Sci 35 section. In teaching them, I learned just how much students can inspire their teachers.

Many people worked hard to make this book a reality. I'm not sure who deserves more gratitude—those who supported the project knowing nothing about it or those who supported it knowing all about it. The National Science Foundation funded my research early on with a Doctoral Fellowship. Muriel Bell at Stanford University Press has earned a place in my heart for her faith and assistance in bringing this project to fruition. Thanks also to my colleagues at McKinsey & Company, who enabled me to take a leave of absence to put on the finishing touches. I can only hope the return was worth the investment.

My family has long lived with my obsessive interest in political science. There can be no better measure of love than that. Thanks to my parents, Shelly and Kenny Zegart, for their forbearance and their unconditional support. My son, Alex, had to hear parts of the book read aloud to him in the womb and managed to kick approvingly at all the right moments. Archie Epps has always, always been there for me. And then there is my husband, Craig Mallery. I spent five years digging through Stanford's libraries. Without a doubt, he is the best thing I ever found there.

A.B.Z.

Abbreviations

CIA	Central Intelligence Agency
CIG	Central Intelligence Group
CINCs	Commanders in Chief (of unified and specified commands)
CSIS	Center for Strategic and International Studies
DCI	Director of Central Intelligence
DIA	Defense Intelligence Agency
DMV	Department of Motor Vehicles
EOP	Executive Office of the President
EPA	Environmental Protection Agency
FBI	Federal Bureau of Investigation
ICC	Interstate Commerce Commission
JCS	Joint Chiefs of Staff
NIA	National Intelligence Authority
NIE	National Intelligence Estimates
NIMA	National Imagery and Mapping Agency
NRO	National Reconnaissance Organization
NSA	National Security Agency

NSC   National Security Council
NSDD   National Security Decision Directive
OCB   Operations Coordinating Board
ONI   Office of Naval Intelligence
OPC   Office of Policy Coordination
ORE   Office of Reports and Estimates
OSS   Office of Strategic Services
PAC   Political Action Committee
SDI   Strategic Defense Initiative

Flawed by Design

THE EVOLUTION
OF THE CIA, JCS, AND NSC

Introduction

Everyone knows that national security agencies are important.[1] No president, however skilled, can by himself amass the information and expertise necessary for advancing American national interests abroad. The Founders recognized this executive need almost immediately. In July 1789, before establishing any other Cabinet department, they passed legislation creating a Department of Foreign Affairs. Modern presidents face an even more complex and threatening world: in today's global village of instant communications, nuclear weapons, and increasing interdependence, American chief executives have little choice but to rely on a broader executive branch foreign policy apparatus. Forging American national security policy is a team game.

But organization is never neutral. As any Washington taxi driver can point out, government organization has serious implications for policy outputs. It matters who has the information, who has the jurisdiction, who has the last word. It matters whether intelligence is collected by diplomats or spies, whether international negotiations are conducted through the Department of State or through back channels in the White House. Senator Henry M. Jackson (D-Wash.) put it well in 1959 when he remarked before the National War College, "Organization by itself cannot assure a strategy for victory in the cold war. But good organization can help, and poor organization can hurt" (Jackson 1959). When it comes to selecting, shaping, and implementing U.S. foreign policy, the devil often lies in the details of agency design.

Though the precise systematic relationship between organizational structure and policy outcomes is admittedly murky, we know it exists. Examples abound. Many observers argue that fundamental weaknesses in the organization of the Joint Chiefs of Staff (JCS) contributed to the 1983 terrorist bombing of a Marine barracks in Beirut and to numerous operational failures during the U.S. invasion of Grenada.[2] In perhaps the most telling episode of that assault, one Army officer had to use his AT&T card at a local pay phone to call in air support for his troops; interservice coordination was so poor that the Army and Air Force did not even operate on the same radio frequencies (Locher 1985, 365). Similarly, many of the excesses, problems, and scandals of the Central Intelligence Agency (CIA) appear to have organizational roots. The CIA was able to expand into illegal domestic operations and foreign subversion in part because no one was watching. Congress never set up an oversight mechanism when it created the agency in 1947 and had little incentive to do so until it heard public outcries in the 1970s. On a more positive note, key features of the National Security Council (NSC) staff—its small size, insulation from Congress, and responsiveness to presidential needs and interests—have enabled it to play a decisive role in issues ranging from the Cuban missile crisis to the establishment of diplomatic relations with China. If there is any doubt about the significance of agency design, we need only ask: Would there have been a Bay of Pigs without the CIA? An Iran-Contra without the NSC staff?

Fleshing out a broader, more theoretical connection between agency structure and foreign policy outcomes is no easy task, and I do not presume to provide the magic answer in this book. What I do hope to offer is a critical first step, a theoretical approach to understanding national security agencies in their own right. What factors shape initial agency design? What forces drive agency change over time? These are the central questions I address. Indeed, I am convinced that we cannot ever hope to develop a compelling theory of agency *influence* without first devising a theory of agency *origins*. Any systematic examination of how agency design shapes policy hinges on isolating the determinants and hallmarks of agency design over time.

Unfortunately, existing work in political science provides little help. U.S. foreign policy agencies in general and national security agencies in particular have been vastly understudied in the discipline. The omission is both substantive and theoretical. Though political scientists have focused on many empirical aspects of the Cold War, the American national security apparatus has not been one of them. We know far more about mobile nuclear missile silos than we do about the original setup of the National Security Council system, the Central Intelligence Agency, or the Joint Chiefs of Staff. More important, these agencies are absent from the larger theoretical debates in the fields of both international relations and American politics. At best, aside from normative discussions of agency function (Allison and Szanton 1976; George 1980; Sorensen 1987), existing theory remains silent about the origins and evolution of national security agencies. At worst, it ignores such questions altogether. U.S. national security organizations have fallen between the cracks of international relations and American politics.

The crux of the problem is that national security agencies are too domestic for students of international relations and too foreign for students of American politics. International relations theory, for its part, focuses on international issues and outcomes, but generally does not have a well-developed understanding of domestic-level organization. To be sure, foreign policy agencies are not completely ignored here. Looking within the state, domestic-level approaches to international relations tell us that bureaucracies (Hilsman 1967; Allison 1971; Halperin 1974), as well as regime types (Doyle 1983; Levy 1988; Owen 1994; Shultz 1996), national values (Hartz 1955), decision-making psychology (Janus 1972; Jervis 1976; George 1980), economic systems (Lenin [1917] 1939; Chomsky 1972; Weisskopf 1974), and a host of other factors influence foreign policy. The problem is that these arguments share little besides an inside-the-state level of analysis. One theory's noise is another's critical variable. Without a common research agenda, these approaches have tended to produce ad hoc studies of the foreign policy–making process, leading to more theoretical disarray than progress. Moreover, almost all of this work treats national-level factors as independent variables.[3] Seeking to explain international outcomes, it takes domestic components or conditions as given.

That's the good news. For the vast majority of international relations theorists, how American foreign policy agencies arise and evolve is not a burning question. The field's dominant paradigm, realism, focuses on relations *between* states, not on what occurs inside them. Ironically, realism reveals more about domestic national security agencies by what it doesn't say than by what it does say.

Realists tell us that for all intents and purposes, states behave as rational unitary actors. In an anarchic international system, power rules the day, and states have little choice but to protect themselves. We need not consider any domestic-level factors such as foreign policy agencies or individual leaders to understand why alliances form, why wars occur, or why international organizations arise. In fact, it is precisely by ignoring these subnational influences that realists can offer such a general theory of international politics.[4]

But for realists to be right, national security agencies must be well designed to serve the needs of the state. They must be structured to translate national objectives into national policies and to carry those policies out faithfully. The pressures of the international system—the constant threat of war and the absence of world government—compel states to design agencies that optimally promote national survival. Indeed, realists can treat states as unitary rational actors only by assuming that domestic-level processes are unproblematic. Though Kenneth Waltz (1979) tells us that assumptions need not be true, they do need to come close. If, as realists claim, systemic factors drive state behavior, then individual government agencies cannot act independently or capriciously. They cannot be selfish or partisan. National interest, not self-interest, must determine their behavior.

Realism's unspoken claims about domestic national security agencies can be formulated into some specific testable hypotheses about agency origins and evolution (Figure 1). Simply put, it is the threat of war between states, not political wrangling between the branches of American government, that determines the creation and evolution of American national security organizations.

As we shall see, this approach may be theoretically elegant, but it is empirically wrong. When the military services cannot communicate with each other during battle; when military lines of authority become so convoluted that no one can be held accountable for success or failure; when intelligence experts cannot predict North Korea's invasion of the South, Iran's fundamentalist revolution, the Soviet Union's collapse, or India's testing of a nuclear device; when spies target American citizens on American soil in violation of the law, something, surely, is amiss. The truth is that international fac-

Agency origins

Proposition 1: An agency's original design is determined by international, not domestic, factors.

Proposition 2: National security agencies are optimally designed to serve the national interest.

Agency evolution

Proposition 3: Agencies evolve in response to changes in the international system.

Proposition 4: Congressional oversight does not matter; agencies are well designed at the outset and are responsive to ongoing changes in the international system.

Proposition 5: An individual agency's evolution can be explained by systemic-level factors — by the state's place in the international system, by the distribution of power among states, and by the security imperatives these two factors generate.

FIGURE 1. *The Realist Model: Propositions*

tors such as the onset of the Cold War may catalyze the development of new agencies, but they hardly determine the final shape those agencies take. Nor do they ensure the agencies' responsiveness over time. If anything, American history tells us that government agencies are sticky. Once they arise, they become very difficult to change. One need only glance at the CIA to see this point. The Cold War is long over, yet this Cold War organization remains undaunted and largely unaltered. In short, a realist approach misses more than it captures. Although realism offers some valuable insights into international organizations and outcomes, it has a thin understanding of domestic-level organization because it discards domestic politics. And domestic politics is the key to the puzzle of agency origins and evolution.

When we turn to the field of American politics, we find some help but no complete answers. Though American politics has a good handle on domestic-level organization, the field pays almost no attention to foreign policy. It is fair to say that American politics is the study of American *domestic* politics.

Theories of bureaucracy are particularly bad on this count. Capture theory (Stigler 1971; Peltzman 1976; Becker 1983) makes no

bones about its domestic regulatory focus. Developed principally by
Chicago economists, the approach seeks to explain why, as a rule,
"regulation is acquired by the industry and is designed and operated
primarily for its benefit" (Stigler 1971, 114). More recently, the rising tide of bureaucracy studies rooted in transaction cost economics
and labeled the new institutionalism also confines its discussion of
bureaucracy to domestic regulatory agencies such as the Federal
Trade Commission (Weingast and Moran 1983), the Interstate
Commerce Commission (ICC) (Gilligan, Marshall, and Weingast
1989; Rothenberg 1994), and the Environmental Protection Agency
(Moe 1989). Employing such concepts as collective action and principal-agent analysis, new institutionalist accounts start at the
ground level, with conflict, with institutions, and with self-interest.
Interest groups are key in this account: they are self-interested, powerful, and fundamentally concerned with the structure of government agencies. Because interest groups are out for themselves, and
because legislators have electoral incentives to do their bidding,
bureaucracy is built in a piecemeal fashion. The system lacks any
overarching, rationalizing architecture. The bureaucratic whole is
not more than the sum of the parts. To new institutionalists,
"American public bureaucracy is not designed to be effective" (Moe
1989, 267). More specifically, a strict new institutionalist approach
makes the claims shown in Figure 2.

These propositions work well in explaining how regulatory agencies such as the Interstate Commerce Commission arise and evolve.
But not all agencies look like the ICC. New institutionalism's
bureaucratic universe does not mirror the empirical one. In fact, it
turns out that foreign policy agencies look quite a bit different. As a
result, new institutionalism's broad theoretical claims do not apply
broadly to the foreign policy arena. Though it is more helpful than
realism, new institutionalism does not offer a perfect model for
understanding national security agencies.

Thus, much of what I set out to do is to translate and transform
new institutionalism to work in the foreign policy realm. Doing so
yields two striking results. For one thing, we find that *national security agencies arise and evolve in fundamentally different ways than
their domestic policy counterparts* traditionally studied in American politics. In domestic policy, interest groups and their legislative
supporters take the lead in shaping agency design and operations.
The action takes place mostly in Congress. But in national security

Agency origins

Proposition 1:   Congress drives initial agency design.

Proposition 2:   Agencies reflect conflict between contending interest groups and their legislative champions. As a result, agencies are not well designed to promote national interests.

Agency evolution

Proposition 3:   Congress drives agency evolution.

Proposition 4:   Congress oversees the bureaucracy; legislators have strong incentives and powerful tools to keep a firm watch.

Proposition 5:   An individual agency's evolution can be explained by changes in the interest group environment, the composition of congressional committees, and congressional preferences.

FIGURE 2.   *A Strict New Institutionalist Model: Propositions*

affairs, presidents and bureaucrats are the primary players, battling over agency structure far away from the Capitol steps. This is no small finding: it suggests that the politics of bureaucratic structure takes place even in the absence of interest groups. It seems that politics does not disappear when societal interests do.

The foreign policy/domestic policy distinction holds for the evolution of agencies as well. Domestic policy agencies may develop in step with the changing constellation of interest groups (Moe 1989) or with the shifting preferences of relevant congressional committees (Weingast and Moran 1983) or majority parties (Kiewiet and McCubbins 1991), but national security agencies generally do not. Rather, the trajectory of a national security agency is a function of three related factors. They are, in order of descending importance: (1) the structural choices made at an agency's birth; (2) the ongoing interests of bureaucrats, presidents, and to a lesser degree legislators; and (3) exogenous events, which are rare.

Because legislation is difficult to pass in the American system of separated powers, agency mandates, procedures, and structures that manage to become incorporated in law generally endure. Thus enabling legislation plays a pivotal role in shaping an agency's developmental course. Initial agency design makes possible certain paths and rules out others. Founding moments loom large. Not everything, however, is predetermined. Once an agency arises, the interests and capabilities of political actors come into play. Presidents, bureaucrats, and legislators are not free to do whatever they want. But they do have an array of tools that—if the incentives are high enough—they can use to shape agencies to their liking. For each of these players, deciding whether to tolerate or transform an agency depends on what options are available, on what opposition is expected, and on what rewards are to be gained. Enacting legislation may determine the range of possible developmental paths for a given agency. However, it is the rational self-interests of political players that determine which particular course the agency will follow. On top of all this, international and domestic events can provide exogenous shocks that shift the interests and capabilities of relevant actors. Taken together, these factors suggest that the evolution of national security agencies is neither automatic nor unpredictable.

Perhaps more important, viewing national security agencies through a modified new institutionalist lens challenges the realist claim about optimal agency design. We find that *national security organizations are not rationally designed to serve the national interest—and for perfectly rational reasons.*[5] By this I mean two things. First, in a very literal sense, the major actors involved in creating key foreign policy agencies did not consider broad national needs. Instead, agencies such as the Joint Chiefs of Staff and the Central Intelligence Agency grew out of political conflicts and compromises among self-interested players. In the American political system, only presidents have incentives to think of the national interest—and they can rarely get the kind of national security agencies they desire. As Richard Neustadt (1960) observed many years ago, presidents operate from a position of weakness. They are single individuals with limited political resources, saturated political agendas, and many potential opponents, both inside and outside of the executive branch. To understand why national security organizations are poorly equipped to promote national aims, we must understand the incentives, interests, and capabilities of political actors. We must see how those most central to the creation and development of our foreign policy apparatus have proposed agency designs with selfish aims in mind. We must begin by realizing that agencies arise out of politics.

Second, it is fair to say that U.S. national security agencies have not served national interests as well as they could have. At some base level, the modern American national security apparatus has not performed up to par since its inception after World War II. We do not need a theory of optimal agency design to reach this conclusion. We know when an organization's performance is suboptimal. Consider the U.S. Postal Service. Surely we do not need to conjure up an ideal plan of the perfect postal system to recognize an imperfect one. It does not take much expertise to conclude that sending a letter across town should take less than three weeks.

My argument proceeds in two steps. First, I lay the theoretical groundwork. In Chapter 1 I develop a modified new institutionalist framework for understanding the origins and evolution of national security agencies. I do so by analyzing new institutionalism's theoretical foundations and central arguments; by delineating key differences between national security and domestic regulatory agencies; and by raising some critical questions about domestic politics and the national interest. It turns out that national security agencies differ in some crucial ways from their domestic policy counterparts. In domestic affairs, interest groups are rampant, information about agency activities is easy to obtain, policy issues lie in the purview of the legislative branch, and agencies are only loosely connected to one another. This is not the case in foreign affairs. There, interest groups are scarce and weak, information about agency activities is very difficult to get, presidents exercise unique and powerful prerogatives, and agencies unavoidably interact with one another. Placing the new institutionalist logic in this new context allows us to devise an alternative National Security Agency Model. The model's propositions are outlined in Figure 3.

In step 2 I illustrate these propositions with empirical case studies of the National Security Council system, the Joint Chiefs of Staff, and the Central Intelligence Agency. My choice of case study methodology and the particular cases was not haphazard. The inherently small number of national security organizations and the need for a close, rigorous reconstruction of political history to examine new institutionalist propositions made the case study method a natural. As for the specific cases, this trio was in many ways ideal. All three agencies were originally formed at the same time, by the same cast of characters, to meet the same emerging Soviet threat, yet they subsequently developed along very different trajectories. Examining them together allowed me to control for key independent variables (such as the international environment) while still maintaining a

Agency origins

Proposition 1:   The executive branch drives initial agency design.

Proposition 2:   Agencies reflect conflict between contending bureaucrats and the president. As a result, agencies are not well designed to promote national interests.

Agency evolution

Proposition 3:   The executive branch drives agency evolution.

Proposition 4:   Congress exercises only sporadic and ineffectual oversight; legislators have weak incentives and blunt tools.

Proposition 5:   An individual agency's evolution can be explained by three factors. They are, in order of descending importance: initial agency structure, the ongoing interests of relevant political actors, and exogenous events.

FIGURE 3.   *The National Security Agency Model: Propositions*

large variance in outcomes. In addition, the NSC system, JCS, and CIA appeared to be tough cases for a new institutionalist account. If any organizations should be well designed to promote American national interests, it is these Cold War policy-making, military, and intelligence agencies. Finally, these organizations are among the most important national security agencies in the United States. Any theory about American governmental agencies worth its salt must account for them.

Chapters 2 through 7 lay out in detail how the NSC system, JCS, and CIA were not created with the national interest in mind. Established by the National Security Act of 1947, these agencies were creatures of conflict and compromise. They arose from one of the most bitter bureaucratic battles in American history. Other than Harry Truman, nobody in the executive or legislative branches sat around thinking about ideal or optimal agency organization. The War and Navy departments, the intelligence bureaucracy, and the Congress were all too busy guarding their own interests to worry about national ones.

Once formed, these agencies developed along divergent paths for similar reasons. The National Security Council system underwent a rapid and radical transformation. Almost overnight, the formal statutory National Security Council—which included major Cabinet secretaries and the president—became eclipsed by an informal, presidentially appointed NSC staff. The Joint Chiefs of Staff, by contrast, remained mired in its original, ineffective design for nearly forty years. Only in 1986, when a rare political aligning of the stars made reform possible, did the Joint Chiefs get the capabilities to offer truly joint advice and conduct joint operations well. The Central Intelligence Agency followed a schizophrenic path: while the agency's covert side grew much like the NSC staff, its coordination and analysis side stagnated like the JCS.

These evolutionary trajectories have imposed substantial costs. Even a generous assessment finds two of the three agencies did not perform as well as they should have. During the Cold War, when it counted most, the Joint Chiefs and the CIA fell short. Riven by parochial service interests, the JCS proved unable to offer presidents coherent military advice or to conduct effective joint military operations. From Korea to Vietnam to Grenada, military operations were routinely plagued by coordination problems, by unclear lines of command, and by unnecessary loss of life. Similarly, the Central Intelligence Agency never succeeded in centralizing intelligence. Instead of exerting discipline over the far-flung intelligence community, the CIA only added to the crowd, producing its own reports and developing its own independent collection capabilities. In addition, the agency pursued a series of illegal and quasi-legal activities that eventually triggered citizen outcries and congressional intervention.

In sum, though the case studies do not and cannot "prove" the National Security Agency Model, they do provide strong supporting evidence for it. They show how and why national security agencies have served the interests of the few, not the many.

CHAPTER I

Toward a Theory of National Security Agencies

All government agencies are not created equal. We need not look very far to know that the CIA hardly looks and acts like the Department of Motor Vehicles; few Americans fear their local DMV clerk will take matters into his own hands. The name of the bureaucratic game is diversity. As James Q. Wilson writes, "Bureaucracy is not the simple, uniform phenomenon it is sometimes made out to be" (Wilson 1989, ix).

Rather than embrace this diversity, political science has relegated explanations of American bureaucracy to two extremes. At one end of the spectrum, realist theories of international relations argue that at least one set of U.S. agencies—those that formulate and implement foreign policy—are rationally suited to promoting the national interest. These agencies are well designed and well equipped to translate national goals into policies. At the very least, as Stephen Krasner (1978) argues, foreign policy agencies pose no obstacles for policy making—they do not impede leaders from pursuing national objectives over the long term. At most, these agencies work so well that they do not matter; structural realists can treat states as unitary rational actors only by assuming that domestic-level agencies do their jobs well (Waltz 1979; Gilpin 1981). Rather than explain American bureaucracy by looking within, to societal interests, realists look without, to the pressures of the international system. In the absence of world government and the looming presence of potential war, political leaders have good reason to design good agencies.

At the other end of the spectrum, new institutionalist theories of American politics suggest just the opposite. They view government agencies as ineffective, inefficient, and incapable of serving any broadly based national interest. By this account, all agencies look pretty much alike, and for the same reason: they are constructed and shaped by competing interest groups that are out for themselves. Though groups are not the only actors, they are the dominant ones, driving members of Congress to structure agencies in certain ways. To understand why agencies look and behave the way they do is to understand what interest groups are involved, what they want, and what kind of power they can bring to bear. American bureaucracy, in short, is a creature of politics (Moe 1989; Moe and Wilson 1994; Rothenberg 1994).

Neither picture is perfect. Realism misses the mark entirely, while new institutionalism needs some serious tweaking to capture the ways in which American national security agencies arise and evolve. In this chapter I argue: (1) Realists are wrong in suggesting that national security agencies are optimally designed to serve the national interest. Even if interest groups and legislators are not prominent players on the political scene, politics still drives the making of government agencies. Presidents have national interests at heart and they sometimes figure prominently in the process of agency development, but they do not necessarily prevail. In fact, presidents rarely get the kind of national security agencies they want or need. (2) New institutionalist theories of American bureaucracy have the right idea but the wrong actors. Formulating their claims with domestic policy agencies in mind, they miss crucial differences between domestic and national security agencies. These differences suggest that though the general approach offers a valuable theoretical foundation for understanding agency origins and evolution, it over-plays the role of interest groups and Congress while underplaying the importance of bureaucrats and presidents. For national security agencies, there *is* such a thing as politics without interest groups. These agencies arise and develop out of battles between self-interested bureaucrats and nationally minded presidents.

My argument proceeds in four steps. I start by outlining new institutionalism's analytic core, key concepts, and particular claims in the domestic policy realm. Second, I lay out the fundamental ways in which national security agencies differ from most domestic policy agencies. As we shall see, these differences have serious implications for new institutionalist theory, calling its basic assertions into question. With these national security agency differences in hand, I revisit new institutionalist theory and offer four alternative propositions about the origins and evolution of national security organizations. Third, I relax the strict foreign policy/domestic policy dichotomy, taking a closer look at differences *among* national security agencies. In doing so, I offer a fifth and final proposition that explains why individual national security agencies evolve along different developmental paths at different rates. Last, I address two principal questions raised by the propositions: why presidents cannot forge the kind of national security agencies they want and why bureaucratic actors have any say in the design and development of other agencies at all. Answering these questions brings politics more centrally into the equation and reveals some compelling reasons why American national security agencies are not and cannot be designed to serve any broad-based conception of national interest.

Theoretical Foundations: New Institutionalism and Domestic Policy Agencies

CORE ASSUMPTIONS

New institutionalism is actually less a theory than a collection of analytic concepts. The rubric encompasses a vast set of arguments that examine everything from asset specificity in private firms to the origins of regulatory agencies. Yet all of these arguments are grounded in rational choice, and all of them have a common theoretical core. For one thing, new institutionalists make some rather traditional microeconomic assumptions about the nature of actors and the units of analysis. The approach assumes that individuals are self-interested rational maximizers. It also assumes that collective outcomes—including organizational design—have roots in individual behavior. From these traditional assumptions new institutionalism makes a very untraditional claim: institutions matter. New institutionalism treats institutions as both dependent and independent variables. Its central research questions ask where institutions come from and how, in turn, institutions shape the world around them. Within economics, the theory goes inside the black box of the firm to explain why firms arise. Likewise, in political science, it asks how political institutions such as congressional committees arise and how they influence political outcomes. In doing so, new institutionalism addresses problems that are largely overlooked by other approaches—such problems as transaction costs, principal-agent relationships, and collective action. In the new institutionalist world, uncertainty is rampant, information is never complete, and opportunism is always possible. Though these problems can never be eliminated, they can be mitigated—by designing institutions in certain ways.[1]

POLITICAL ACTORS: LEGISLATORS, PRESIDENTS, AND BUREAUCRATS

Within political science, new institutionalist arguments share an additional set of assumptions about how political actors behave. Indeed, there is nothing much new here about new institutionalism. The approach fits well with standard conceptions of principal political players.

Congress is the clearest case. Almost every analysis of Congress begins by assuming that legislators always work to maximize their chances for reelection. Reelection may not be their only aim, but it is their paramount one—in David Mayhew's words, "the goal that must be achieved over and over if other ends are to be entertained" (Mayhew 1974, 16). This leads to all sorts of behavior, not all of it good. Members focus on delivering particularized benefits to the districts back home; cater to the preferences of organized interests that have the money, votes, and information to deliver electoral gains; take stands on issues without doing anything about them; and oversee government agencies only when they stand to gain in the eyes of constituents. Legislators do not have to be bad people with evil intentions to do these things. The "electoral connection" compels all members to design congressional institutions and to behave in ways that serve particular interests at the expense of general governance. As Gary Jacobson notes, the reelection motive itself produces a Congress that is "inordinately responsive without being responsible" (Jacobson 1987, 73).

The standard view of presidents also focuses on motivations, incentives, and the structure of the American political system. But presidents appear quite different from members of Congress. Unlike legislators, the chief executive is elected by a national constituency and cares about making his or her mark in history (Neustadt 1960; Fiorina 1981; Moe 1985). By and large, presidents do not listen to or care much about organized interest groups (Light, 1991; Peterson 1992a, 1992b). They do not have to. Instead, all presidents, Democratic and Republican alike, have strong incentives to concentrate on broader national concerns. This is what the public expects of them. From inflation to earthquake relief to war, the chief executive is held responsible for the state of the nation. Consequently, he or she has good reasons to get things done, to make government work, to think in terms of the national interest. Presidents are the closest embodiment of national interest in the American political system (Moe and Wilson 1994).

Bureaucrats, finally, have interests of their own and some powerful weapons to pursue them. Whether this means ensuring their organization's survival, maintaining professional norms, or advancing certain policy goals, agencies often behave in ways that legislators and presidents never intended (McCubbins and Page 1987; Wilson 1989; Rothenberg 1994). Whatever the specific aim, bureaucrats tend to enjoy two distinct advantages over other political actors: information and expertise (Weber 1946, 196–244). Presidents and legislators may come and go, but civil servants do not. They are unelected experts who are hired to develop sophisticated policy knowledge and who are placed on the front lines of policy formulation and implementation. Even those who argue that Congress "controls" the bureaucracy concede that control is inherently problematic. As Mathew McCubbins, Roger Noll, and Barry Weingast (McNollgast) write:

> A consequence of delegating authority to bureaucrats is that they may become more expert about their policy responsibilities than the elected representatives who created their bureau. Information about cause-effect relations, the details of existing policies and regulations, the pending decision agenda, and the distribution of benefits and costs of agency actions is costly and time-consuming to acquire. As in all agency relations, it may be possible for the agency to take advantage of its private information. (McNollgast 1987, 247)

Out for themselves, bureaucrats possess the interests, information, and expertise to make life difficult for elected officials.

NEW INSTITUTIONALISM MEETS POLITICS:
TWO VARIANTS

Using these common beliefs about rational choice, institutions, and the nature of specific political actors, new institutionalism has sparked an array of work in American politics that has focused largely on congressional institutions and on domestic policy agencies. Arguments can be divided roughly along two lines. The first line looks primarily at Congress. Coming to new institutionalism from social choice theory, these scholars were initially concerned with how Congress arrives at stable majority outcomes.[2]

More recently, work along this line has focused on congressional-bureaucratic relations. The specifics vary but the basic argument is the same: Congress controls the bureaucracy. Why? Because legislators have both the electoral incentives and the capabilities to keep domestic policy agencies in line. Simply put, members of Congress care about interest groups, and interest groups often care about what government agencies do. What's more, legislators devise oversight mechanisms that minimize political costs while maximizing electoral gains. Whether they do so by writing administrative procedures into law at the outset (McNollgast 1987), by engaging in constant "police patrol" surveillance of agency activities (Aberbach 1990), by responding to oversight fire alarms triggered by constituents' complaints (McCubbins and Schwartz 1984), or by some combination of these methods (McCubbins 1985; McCubbins and Page 1987; Bawn 1994), legislators oversee only as much and as intensely as they must to derive net political benefits.

The second basic variant of the new institutionalism takes a more systemic view of political institutions and gives the theory a more political cast. These authors move away from Congress-centered questions and explanations to emphasize the substantive origins of domestic policy agencies. Theoretically, they look to a range of political actors—presidents, bureaucrats, courts, interest groups—to explain political outcomes. In doing so, they find a much greater role for distinctly political factors and processes—factors such as elections, separation of powers, political uncertainty, and authority (Wood 1988, 1990; Derthick 1990; Moe 1990b, 1991; Rothenberg 1994).

For domestic policy agencies, this means trouble. The rational desires of interest groups, legislators, and presidents lead to irrational agency structures. In Terry Moe's words, new institutionalism suggests that "American public bureaucracy is not designed to be effective" (Moe 1989, 267). Two features of American democracy create a bureaucracy that is unavoidably flawed at birth. First, the American separation-of-powers system requires political compromise—and compromise allows agency opponents to sabotage aspects of structural design. Second, elections inject uncertainty into the game. Because today's winners may be tomorrow's losers, they insulate agencies from all future political control by legislating counterproductive detailed rules, regulations, and requirements. The result is far from the bureaucratic ideal, where technical experts are given broad discretion to do what they do best.

As this thumbnail sketch suggests, new institutionalist arguments make a number of propositions about the creation and evolution of domestic policy agencies. For our purposes, three are critical. First, *both lines of new institutionalism contend that interest groups drive agency design and development.* As Moe writes, when it comes to agency origins, "structural politics is interest group politics" (Moe 1989, 269).[3] Average voters may not care about the gory details of bureaucratic structure, but interest groups do—and they have the political resources to induce Congress to cooperate. As one Senate aide commented, "We're very careful about groups back home. We know who got the senator into office."[4] Interest groups also play a central role in ongoing agency development, fueling congressional efforts to keep the bureaucracy in line and out of the president's hands.[5] In this political system, bureaucracy emerges willy-nilly. Built vote by vote, interest by interest, government agencies are designed with minimal regard for the overall picture.

Second, and equally important, these arguments suggest that it is not necessary to consider links between government agencies. Or, put another way, *new institutionalists implicitly claim that today's bureaucrats have no interest in the creation and development of tomorrow's agencies.* Moe offers the vague possibility that "agency bureaucrats [become] political actors in their own right" (Moe 1989, 282), but he has little more to say about this claim. In the end, he dismisses bureaucracies as primary actors in structural politics: "In our attempt to understand the structure and politics of bureaucracy, we turn to bureaucrats last rather than first" (284).[6] Barry Weingast and Mark Moran (1983) downplay the role of bureaucracies even further, assuming that bureaucrats respond in virtual lockstep to congressional desires. Other new institutionalists find congressional control more problematic but still view agencies as separate, unconnected islands, each unconcerned about the design, operation, and evolution of others.

Finally, these arguments make specific claims about how domestic policy agencies actually look and behave. We are told that *bureaucracy is not destined for success; the very hallmarks of American democracy—regular elections, separation of powers, majority rule —preclude effective agency design.* In Martha Derthick's words, "the most cherished structural features of American government pose obstacles to good administration" (Derthick 1990, 4). As for agency evolution, new institutionalists differ about the extent of congressional control, but agree that agencies cannot escape the parochial clutches of Congress. Understanding agency development requires understanding how and how much Congress oversees the bureaucracy.

Thus, using the basic notions of rational self-interested actors, transaction cost economics, and standard conceptions of American political institutions, new institutionalism offers a way to learn why domestic policy agencies arise and look the way they do. Working through the theory's logic, students of American politics have developed ideas about which actors most influence agency design and development, about how this influence works, and about what this means for public administration.

A WORD ABOUT BUREAUCRATIC POLITICS

Some critics of new institutionalism have charged the theory with providing little more than a bureaucratic politics approach in fancy clothes. It is worth spending a moment to address this criticism head-on, to clarify both the commonalties of these two schools of thought and the differences between them.

Graham Allison's writing on the Cuban missile crisis stands as the seminal piece in bureaucratic politics. At its core, Allison's work argues that foreign policy cannot be understood without looking inside the black box of the state. Process matters. The key to understanding this process is to realize that no one, not even the president, has a monopoly on power. "Government" consists of a tangled web of bureaucratic agencies, each with its own interests, capabilities, perspectives, and leaders. How international situations are perceived, what information gets relayed to top decision makers, how policies are implemented—all of these things are determined by a process of conflict and coalition building, by the "pulling and hauling" among political players situated in different governmental organizations. In reality, Allison argues, policies are rarely optimal and usually do not emerge from anything resembling a rational unitary state. Decisions are "collages" from different bargaining games (Allison 1971, 206).

A first glance reveals some major similarities between the old bureaucratic politics model and the new institutionalism. Both challenge realism's state-as-unitary-actor approach and look inside the black box of the state. Both focus on politics, on the pulling and hauling between political players who pursue interests of their own. And both models conclude that the foreign policies that emerge from this process are rarely optimal.

That said, the differences between the two theories are significant. For starters, new institutionalism is a deductive approach, whereas bureaucratic politics is inductive. Drawing heavily on microeconomics, new institutionalism makes some key assumptions about individual behavior in specified contexts. It is from these assumptions that we derive general theories of institutional design and testable hypotheses across a range of research areas. Bureaucratic politics, for its part, starts with the details and works backward. It draws conclusions about the policy process through careful reconstruction of historical events. Unfortunately, without testable hypotheses up front, any outcome can be explained.

Second, new institutionalism is fundamentally concerned with explaining government organizations, whereas bureaucratic politics seeks to explain how government organizations create different policies or results. One model's dependent variable is the other's independent variable.

This difference gives new institutionalism a serious edge over bureaucratic politics when it comes to developing a truly general theory of governmental organization. Make no mistake: such a general theory is still a long way off. Yet as the two models currently stand, new institutionalism seems better equipped and holds greater promise of reaching that goal than the bureaucratic politics model.

After all, how can we hope to develop systematic explanations of agency behavior without systematic explanations of agency origins and development? Bureaucratic politics implies that choices are always up for grabs. The players are always changing. Pulling and hauling begin anew with each issue. Certainly the model tells us nothing about the general ways in which politics can be expected to emerge and influence international outcomes, or about which action channels, agencies, or actors are more likely to be powerful than others across different events. How John F. Kennedy approached the Cuban missile crisis sheds little light on how Jimmy Carter handled the Iranian hostage crisis. The old aphorism "Where you stand depends on where you sit" captures something about bureaucratic behavior. But the far more important questions are "How did you come to sit there in the first place?" and "What power will you bring to the table tomorrow?"

These are precisely the kinds of questions new institutionalism can address. Starting with the structure of the American political system, new institutionalism focuses on the stickiness of organizational arrangements. This approach gets us closer to the truth. In reality, we know, choices are not always up for grabs and actors do not just emerge, full-blown, on the scene with each new crisis or event. Decision making is rarely a one-shot game. Rather, foreign policy choices are constrained by many things—by past actions, by institutional arrangements, by embedded norms and national values, to name a few. Without a better understanding of these constraints, bureaucratic politics will be relegated to producing snapshots of the policy process at particular points in time. New institutionalism has at least the potential to help us construct a moving picture of agency behavior.

Square Pegs, Round Holes: Crucial Differences Between National Security and Domestic Policy Agencies

New institutionalism may be well and good for understanding domestic policy agencies such as the Environmental Protection Agency and the Occupational Safety and Health Administration. But national security agencies look very different from such domestic policy organizations, and they act differently. The CIA is certainly not the same as the DMV—and with good reason. Here I focus on four fundamental factors that set national security agencies apart and suggest some implications for new institutionalist explanations.

THE INTEREST GROUP ENVIRONMENT

Domestic policy agencies live in a world littered with scores of powerful, long-standing, and varied interest groups.[7] From farm lobbies to labor unions to women's groups to business corporations, organized interests have played a central role in determining which agencies arise, what they look like, and how they develop. In Aaron Wildavsky's words, the interest group environment for domestic matters is strong, stable, and dense (Wildavsky 1991, 35).

Not so with national security agencies. For one thing, the general foreign policy interest group environment is relatively new. Whereas many of today's major domestic policy groups date back to the late nineteenth and early twentieth centuries, foreign policy-related interest groups are almost entirely a post–World War II phenomenon.[8] Consider these few examples: the largest education lobby, the National Education Association, began in 1857; the American Farm Bureau Federation started in 1920; business interests organized under the National Association of Manufacturers in 1895; even the environmental movement traces one of its leading organizations— the Sierra Club—back to 1892 (Ornstein and Elder 1978, 23–68).

By contrast, the vast majority of foreign policy lobbying groups accompanied the rise of U.S power, involvement, and conflict in international affairs after World War II. Polish, Israeli, Chinese, Cuban, Greek, and other ethnic lobbies arose in response to issues and events of the day. Defense contractors, for their part, did not even try to influence the awarding of government contracts until the late 1950s, and even then did little to lobby for overall military budgets or policies (Hill 1979; Wildavsky 1991).[9] Human rights and other international public interest organizations emerged even later. Amnesty International started in 1961 and Human Rights Watch opened its doors in 1978. Even the term "think tank" did not become part of the popular lexicon until the Kennedy administration. Nearly two-thirds of today's 100 policy research groups operating in Washington, D.C., were established after 1970 (J. Smith 1991, 130, 214). Arriving on the scene relatively late, responding to the ebb and flow of international events and issues, these foreign policy–related interest groups have provided a newer, more fluid interest group context.

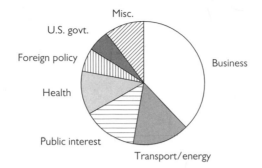

FIGURE 4. *Proportion of Interest Groups in Eight Issue Areas*

SOURCE: Arthur C. Close, Gregory L. Bologna, and Curtis W. McCormick, *Washington Representatives,* 14th ed. (Washington: Columbia Books, 1990).

Second, and perhaps more important, even with the rise of ethnic, defense, economic, and public interest lobbies, today's overall foreign policy interest group environment is still rather thin. In 1990, foreign policy lobbying organizations accounted for just 10 percent of the interest group universe (see Figure 4).[10] In terms of sheer numbers of organizations, health care–related groups alone outnumbered foreign relations lobbies.

Of course, it is possible that less may be more—that the foreign policy groups that do exist actually wield tremendous influence over policy outputs and agency operations. Yet evidence suggests this is not the case. For one thing, interest groups have trouble concentrating their efforts on foreign policy because decision makers are far more diffuse.[11] Whereas domestic policy agencies tend to have discrete jurisdictions, foreign policy agencies intersect, overlap, and interact. The Federal Aviation Administration may have sole jurisdiction over airline regulations, but the same sort of claim cannot be made for the State Department and U.S. policy toward Israel. As a result, foreign policy interest groups cannot just work through their favorite representative to target a particular agency. Instead, they must lobby all sorts of executive branch actors themselves—from the president to his White House staff to officials in the State Department, the Defense Department, and other executive agencies. Compared to members of Congress, moreover, many of these actors are not easy to reach. As Mark Peterson writes, while Capitol Hill "remains a highly permeable institution, the White House complex is open to groups largely by presidential invitation only" (Peterson 1992a, 224).

In addition, foreign policy groups have fewer and weaker levers at their disposal. Generally speaking, interest group membership is smaller, access to policy information is restricted, and money is in shorter supply. Indeed, foreign policy–related organizations accounted for only 6 of the top 100 contributors to the 1992 congressional and presidential campaigns. The top contributor among foreign policy–related lobbying organizations ranked just 43d—behind the Plumbers/Pipefitters Union, the National Beer Wholesalers Association, and the Federation of Teachers, to name a few. Even more telling, the number one campaign donor, the American Medical Association, outspent all 6 top-100 foreign policy–related contributors *combined* (Makinson and Goldstein 1994).

Foreign policy interests do no better in targeted congressional committees. In 1992, the typical member of the House Armed Services Committee received just 11 percent of his large campaign contributions from defense-related organizations and industries. Colleagues on the Agriculture and Banking committees fared much better, receiving more than 24 percent of their large donations from committee-related organizations and interests. The same pattern holds in the Senate. All things being equal, members of the House and Senate Armed Services committees would have filled twice as much of their 1992 war chests through committee work if they had switched to Agriculture or Banking (see Table 1).

Finally, while domestic policy groups appear to care a great deal about the structure of particular bureaucracies, foreign policy interest groups do not. In Terry Moe's case studies of the Environmental Protection Agency, the Occupational Safety and Health Administration, and the Consumer Product Safety Commission, interest groups of all stripes clearly saw the connection between agency design and policy outcome. "The policies . . . were never explicitly fought over," Moe writes. Instead, it seems that everyone knew "the struggles of genuine consequence were about bureaucratic arrangements, about powers and procedures and criteria" (Moe 1989, 323).

But personal interviews with former NSC staffers, members of Congress, Cabinet officials, and bureaucrats paint quite a different picture of foreign policy interest groups.[12] "Interest groups don't care

TABLE I.   Median Percentage of Large Campaign Contributions Made
to Congressional Committee Members by Committee-Related
Interests, 1992

Committee	*Contributions by Committee-Related Interests*
Senate	
Banking	29.0%
Agriculture	24.5
Armed Services	11.0
House	
Banking	19.5
Agriculture	13.0
Armed Services	6.0

SOURCE: Data from Larry Makinson and Joshua Goldstein, *Open Secrets: The
Encyclopedia of Congressional Money and Politics* (Washington:
Congressional Quarterly Press, 1994).

what the State Department looks like," remarked one veteran foreign policy official. "They want policy results and don't see those
results as tied to structural and procedural issues."[13] Commenting
on Senator Jesse Helms's effort to reorganize the State Department
in 1995, one Bush NSC staff member noted, "Now . . . you've got a
major effort to restructure the foreign aid apparatus—you know,
AID and ACDA—and I don't see interest groups rising up. I see the
administration going at it with the Hill and vice versa. . . . But I
don't see interest groups with a major interest in restructuring the
operations. Mostly, it's issue oriented."[14] This view was hardly confined to Republicans. In fact, out of 48 interviews, only 2 respondents noted any real interest group concern about agency design.
Douglas Paal, senior director for Asian affairs on George Bush's NSC
staff, commented that business groups "care a lot more about the
structure of the [NSC] staff these days than they used to." But he
emphasized that even in this case, attention had not turned to
action. Rather than pushing for structural changes, these groups
"write their congressman" in the hope of "finding the most efficient
way to their outcome."[15] A Democratic congressional staffer also

found interest groups to be more interested in NSC design, but noted that such attention was quite recent and limited in scope.[16]

I do not mean to suggest that defense contractors or other foreign policy interest groups are never powerful. In some areas, at some times, they can be.[17] But compared to domestic policy interests, the foreign policy interest group environment is strikingly weak. Organized interests are much newer, fewer, far less interested in agency design and less able to get what they want. For national security agencies, interest groups are not a large part of the political game.

What does all this mean? Two conclusions stand out. First, the relatively weak interest group environment substantially reduces Congress's interest and role in creating new national security agencies. With interest groups largely out of the picture, the average member has little incentive to expend significant time and political capital in designing foreign policy agencies.[18] Casework, district visits, pork barrel projects, and even public position taking on foreign policy issues all provide more cost-effective ways for legislators to bolster their reelection prospects.

Second, and closely related, Congress has little reason to oversee these agencies once they arise. In addition to the incentive issue, legislators face substantial information problems. In domestic policy, members can turn to any number of interest groups for vital information about ongoing agency activities, policies, and abuses; groups and information are both in abundant supply. But in foreign policy issues, the number of groups in a given area is sparse and information is often classified, so that it is difficult for interest groups to serve as low-cost information providers. As one Senate staffer who handles both domestic and foreign policy issues commented:

> On domestic policy, interest groups feed me unsolicited information on certain bills or amendments coming before the Senate all the time. They fax me even if I don't ask them to. I know if there's an abortion bill coming up, I can just call NARAL [the National Abortion and Reproductive Rights Action League]. They're on top of it. They know exactly what's going on. Within an hour, they'll fax me a fact sheet and talking points which I can use to brief the senator. But when it comes to foreign policy issues, with a few exceptions—like foreign aid and some ethnic lobbies— there are no groups who can do that. Nobody's feeding me.[19]

In order to challenge bureaucrats' claims and monitor their activities, then, Congress must develop its own expertise and information channels. All things being equal, these costs make oversight an unattractive activity.

TYPE OF WORK

A more obvious distinction between national security and domestic policy agencies lies in the nature of the work they do. Whereas domestic policy is fairly out in the open, much of national security agency activity is conducted in secret. From trade negotiations to arms control talks to state visits, the internal workings and policies of national security agencies are normally kept out of the public eye. Moreover, security clearances provide legal barriers to information sharing within individual agencies, across agencies, and between the executive and legislative branches. Even the first lady receives a separate declassified set of briefing materials for presidential trips abroad.

Secrecy has some important consequences for the conduct of foreign policy. Two are relevant here. First, secrecy grants the executive branch—and national security agencies in particular—wide latitude in carrying out foreign policy decisions and actions. To put it bluntly, the president and his national security agencies can forge policy without Congress's knowledge or consent. This is not necessarily a bad thing, as Kissinger's secret trip to China and the Cuban missile crisis suggest.[20] But it does indicate that national security agencies may not have to worry too much about servicing congressional interests. These "agents" may find themselves contending with far fewer "principals" than their domestic policy counterparts.

Second, secrecy compounds congressional information problems, making oversight of national security agencies even more difficult. Congress quite literally has a hard time getting its hands on information about what these agencies do and how they do it. The vast majority of members and staffers have no security clearance, so they are unable to gain access to even "confidential"-level information. Though reforms of the 1970s strengthened executive branch reporting requirements and expanded the number of members entitled to high-level clearance, there is still no way for these legislators to know whether foreign policy agencies are reporting the full range of their information and activities. Indeed, we know that they often do not.[21] As Amos Jordan, William Taylor, and Lawrence Korb (1993) note, "Members of Congress may, and many still do, complain that they are inadequately informed about national security matters [by the executive branch]. . . . The difficulty is essentially one of 'outsiders' in a policy process feeling that they are inadequately abreast of situations" (Jordan, Taylor, and Korb 1993, 134). Thus, with interest groups out of the information business, and with direct information channels that are at best dubious and hard to come by, the cost of overseeing foreign policy agencies seems high indeed.

FOREIGN AFFAIRS: THE EXECUTIVE DOMAIN

Although domestic issues routinely involve the legislative branch, foreign policy lies much more exclusively in the president's domain. As John Marshall declared before Congress in 1800, "The President is sole organ of the nation in its external relations, and its sole representative with foreign nations" (quoted in Henkin 1972, 45). From today's vantage point, it seems strange—and not a little unsettling—to imagine Senator X or Representative Y going out on her own and establishing diplomatic relations with China, conducting bilateral trade negotiations with Japan, negotiating German reunification or nuclear arms reduction accords with Russia. Such action would be more than just unusual; it would be considered inappropriate. Though certainly no president can afford to ignore Congress on foreign policy issues, and though Congress has some levers to influence foreign policy outcomes, the president bears unique responsibility and wields unique powers in pursuing U.S. interests abroad.

The roots of this expansive presidential authority lie more in history and the basic structure of government than they do in the explicit provisions of the Constitution. The Constitution leaves much unclear and unsaid (Rakove 1984). The Framers mention no general foreign policy authority, no power to recognize or break diplomatic relations, no power to declare policy doctrines or call an end to military hostilities. Moreover, the powers that are specified seem to fall somewhere between the executive and the legislature. Though the Senate must ratify treaties, the president alone bears the responsibility for negotiating them and can forge executive agreements without congressional consent. Similarly, though the power to declare war is lodged in the Congress, the president's powers as commander in chief suggest an executive responsibility and authority to direct U.S. military defenses (Henkin 1972; Haass 1982). In sum, as Edward Corwin writes, the Constitution provides little more than "an invitation to struggle for the privilege of directing American foreign policy" (Corwin 1957, 171).

Two factors have placed foreign affairs in the executive domain. First, generally speaking, the Constitution implicitly gives presidents the institutional upper hand. The chief executive is a single individual. He can act unilaterally, secretly, and quickly in foreign affairs.[22] Congress, by contrast, must contend with 535 equal members, all with disparate views and unique constituencies. As Louis Henkin suggests, "Diplomacy by Congress was ineffectual even under the Articles of Confederation when international relations were few and limited, and Congress was unicameral and small" (Henkin 1972, 37).[23] If anything, twentieth-century political developments—U.S. engagement in world affairs, the vastly increasing complexity and danger of international relations, the rise of the personal vote,[24] and decentralization of congressional power—have only increased the president's institutional advantage.

Moreover, the Constitution affords presidents overwhelming informational advantages. Charged with appointing and receiving ambassadors, presidents have unique access to information and bear sole responsibility for articulating U.S. policy. Thomas Jefferson wrote: "The [president] being the only channel of communication between this country and foreign nations, it is from him alone that foreign nations or their agents are to learn what is or has been the will of the nation; and whatever he communicates as such, they have a right, and are bound to consider as the expression of the nation, and no foreign agents can be allowed to question it" (quoted in Henkin 1972, 300).

Additionally, the Constitution's vagueness provides the executive some room to maneuver. Article II offers presidents general commander-in-chief and executive powers while making little, if anything, in foreign affairs explicitly off limits. As a U.S. appeals court put it in 1979, "We note . . . that the powers conferred upon Congress in Article I of the Constitution are specific, detailed, and limited, while the powers conferred upon the President by Article II are generalized in a manner that bespeaks no such limitation upon foreign affairs power" (*Goldwater v. Carter*, 617 F. 2d 197, 704–5). In short, the Constitution gives presidents the unified office, information, and potential to develop a broad foreign affairs role.

Second, foreign policy has come to lie in the president's purview through a process of historical accretion. If the Constitution made the enlargement of presidential prerogatives possible, the early presidents made it happen. George Washington became the first president to withhold information from Congress for national security reasons, as well as the first to unilaterally issue foreign policy statements that could lead to war. Notably, both the House and Senate knew of these acts and voiced no objection (Sofaer 1976). In 1789, Congress placed foreign affairs more squarely in the executive branch, making Foreign Affairs the first executive department and granting the president exclusive control over its operations and personnel (Casper 1989). Washington's successor, John Adams, prosecuted the first undeclared national war against a foreign power in 1798–99. Even Thomas Jefferson's anti-Federalist revolution managed to maintain, if not expand, executive foreign policy prerogatives. Jefferson institutionalized executive secrecy, used emergency powers to justify extraconstitutional action,[25] and solicited congressional authorization for an undeclared war against the Barbary pirates—an authorization he later used to justify the first American attempt to overthrow a foreign government (Sofaer 1976; Milkis and Nelson 1990).[26]

Powers gained are not easily removed. At the very least, history suggests that modern uses and abuses of presidential authority have early analogs. From Washington's 1793 Neutrality Proclamation to the 1947 Truman Doctrine, from Jefferson's efforts to oust the bashaw of Tripoli in 1801–5 to the CIA's efforts to subvert communist governments in the 1950s and 1960s, from John Adams's undeclared war against France to Lyndon Johnson's semideclared war against Vietnam, presidents have brought foreign policy into the executive branch in similar ways for similar reasons (Sofaer 1976; Spitzer 1993). Held responsible for U.S. policy abroad, chief executives have strong incentives to do what they can to control events and manage policy decisions. Incentive, of course, does not guarantee success. But it does suggest that presidents will fight hard to retain expanded authority once they acquire it—a fight they usually win.[27]

All of this suggests that presidents play a larger role in the design and development of national security agencies than they normally do with respect to domestic policy agencies. Though the Framers may not have intended it, foreign policy has become the president's turf. It is the executive who bears chief responsibility for U.S. decisions in the international arena, and who has developed the capacity to exercise that responsibility within the American political system. In some basic sense, this historical accretion of presidential authority has carried with it the idea that foreign policy properly belongs where it is usually found. As one Senate staff report put it in 1961, "By law and practice, the President has the prime role in guarding the Nation's safety. He is responsible for the conduct of foreign relations. . . . He, and he alone, must finally weigh all the factors— domestic, foreign, military—which affect our position in the world and by which we seek to influence the world environment" (U.S. Senate 1961).

Certainly Vietnam provoked some serious challenges to presidential prerogatives in the decades since the 1970s. Yet the striking thing is how little these challenges have actually changed the balance of foreign policy power or the idea of where it rightly belongs. Even during the Iran-Contra investigation, amid revelations that White House officials conducted illegal covert activities, lied to Congress, shredded classified documents, and violated official government policy on terrorism and aid to the Nicaraguan Contras, the president's bipartisan special review board underscored executive primacy in foreign affairs. The board's final report, written by former senator John Tower, former senator and secretary of state Edmund S. Muskie, and former national security adviser Brent Scowcroft, noted, "Whereas the ultimate power to formulate domestic policy resides in the Congress, the primary responsibility for the formulation and implementation of national security policy falls on the president" (*Tower Commission Report* 1987, 87). Indeed, by placing foreign policy squarely in the executive domain, the report offered a devastating indictment of President Reagan, his staff, and his national security policy-making process. As the Tower Commission suggests, legislators do not and should not take the lead role in formulating American foreign policy any time soon.

The president's gain is the legislature's loss; the growth of presidential preeminence in foreign affairs has helped to ensure that congressional oversight of foreign policy agencies and their outputs remains sporadic and relatively weak.[28] For one thing, executive primacy tends to let legislators off the electoral hook. Voters hold the president, not their local representative, accountable for the successes and failures of American foreign policy. It was Truman who lost China, it was Johnson's war in Vietnam, and it was Bush who presided over the end of the Cold War. As Richard Brody (1991) finds in his seminal study, presidential approval ratings can surge or fall precipitously during moments of international crisis.[29] Knowing all this, members of Congress have good reason to focus on issues closer to home. Moreover, it is easy for them to do so. On foreign policy matters, legislators can engage in activities that appeal to constituents without expending much effort, political capital, or time. They can take stands without taking action, and they can make pronouncements, hold hearings, and run investigations without having to produce results. Though rural Kentucky representatives may have to deliver farm subsidies to tobacco growers back home, they need not fear getting thrown out of office because of their stand on the Nuclear Nonproliferation Treaty. The incentives to pay attention to foreign policy organizational issues are even lower. Questions of JCS design do not make or break congressional elections.

Of course, not all members of Congress behave this way. In every Congress, there are always a few who develop considerable expertise and devote serious attention to foreign policy issues and agencies. These "national security intellectuals" hail from both sides of the aisle and come from diverse regions of the nation. All of these legislators share a normative concern for the public good in foreign affairs. Their intentions are not purely altruistic, however. National security intellectuals on the order of Senators Sam Nunn (D-Ga.) and John McCain (R-Ariz.) usually have presidential aspirations. And they almost always reap rewards from their role—amassing clout in Congress, gaining access to the president, and developing a national reputation. These benefits not only serve longer-term presidential ambition but for some curry immediate favor among voters who like having their representative in the center of action (Fenno 1978). Regardless of their specific motives, one thing is clear: national security intellectuals stand apart from the congressional herd.

Even these legislators, however, give presidents a good deal of latitude in running foreign policy. Ironically, their genuine concern for nationally minded foreign policy breeds a genuine belief in presidential authority. These legislators believe that deferring to the president is the right thing to do—precisely because presidents are better able to serve national interests than the vast majority of their reelection-seeking, pork-barreling congressional colleagues. Provided they are consulted by the president on major matters, the Fulbrights, Hamiltons, and Lugars of the world are content to leave Congress out of the foreign policy business. More important, national security intellectuals would have a difficult time taking on executive primacy even if they wanted to. Mustering the multiple majorities necessary to pass foreign affairs legislation is never a simple task. In unusual moments, legislative leaders can rally the rest of Congress behind them, but doing so requires precious political capital and produces uncertain results.[30] Indeed, rallying the Congress and controlling it are two very different things. Once average members are thrown into the legislative game, there is nothing to prevent them from undercutting a national interest bill by grandstanding on the issues or by tacking on all sorts of parochial provisions.[31] Eyeing his next election, that Kentucky representative may very well add self-interested and unrelated tobacco subsidies to the legislation. All this being the case, national security intellectuals almost never get their way. At the outset, they must choose their battles with care. And then they must fight the parochial interests of their colleagues at every step. It is fair to say that barriers to congressional activism in foreign affairs are high.

In addition to lowering congressional oversight incentives, executive primacy in foreign affairs helps to weaken Congress's capacity to oversee national security agencies. Within the American politics literature, much has been made of Congress's oversight power. Congress, we are told, "holds the power of life or death in the most elemental terms throughout the existence of any agency" (McCubbins 1985, 728).[32] House and Senate committees can induce agency compliance because they hold all the cards. They determine which agencies live, which ones do not, and how much money they get.[33]

But how real is this "power of life or death" when it comes to national security agencies? How credible can these congressional threats be? It seems hard to imagine that Congress poses an ever-present, looming danger to the existence of American national security organizations. Evidence suggests that, like the national security intellectuals, most average legislators feel strongly that national security agencies fall within the president's purview. We can see this, for example, by juxtaposing Congress's oversight initiatives in the 1946 Reorganization Act with its creation of major foreign policy agencies in the 1947 National Security Act. After the Reorganization Act of 1946 streamlined congressional committees and charged them with exercising "continuous watchfulness" over administrative agencies, the 1947 National Security Act gave the president rather broad authority to use and shape his new foreign policy agencies as he saw fit. Perhaps most telling, even on the heels of its oversight push, Congress did not establish a separate oversight committee for the Central Intelligence Agency (Congressional Quarterly 1971, 89). Even with oversight on the brain, members of Congress deliberately chose to set up national security agencies without substantial congressional ties.

Moreover, although Congress has tried to exert more control over intelligence activities in the post-Vietnam era, evidence indicates that members still see presidential authority over national security agencies as legitimate and paramount. As Senator Birch Bayh (D-Ind.) remarked in 1978, when President Carter signed a key executive order setting out specific restrictions on the intelligence community, "This is the first time in history that the Congress has had this kind of cooperation with the Executive Branch . . . the first time in history [when the president was] *willing to waive* [his] *inherent authority* to get involved in electronic surveillance" (quoted in Jordan, Taylor, and Korb 1993, 154; emphasis mine). Bayh's comment suggests that in intelligence, as in other foreign policy matters, legitimate authority is the president's to use or dispose.

But let us suppose for a moment that legislators, for whatever reason, actually want to use their formal authorization or their statutory or budgetary powers to change the organization or behavior of a particular national security agency. What happens then?

The short answer is that even under such circumstances, members would be unlikely to use these levers to bring national security agencies into line. Legislators know that presidents take their foreign policy agencies seriously; any move to eliminate, reform, or significantly reduce the funding of these organizations without presidential approval is bound to incur executive wrath and invite interbranch conflict—a fight that presidents almost always win. Why? Because the political system naturally favors any political actor who defends the status quo. And it grants presidents the ultimate weapon: the veto. The fact is that Congress has rarely sought to overhaul national security agencies without presidential consent, and when it has, the fight has not been easy or successful. The 1995 campaign by Senator Jesse Helms (R-N.C.) to reorganize the State Department is perhaps the most vivid recent example. Speaking from the Senate floor, Helms made no bones about the ferocity of executive branch opposition. Castigating the Clinton administration for "stonewalling to the nth degree," he noted: "The administration has refused cooperation at every juncture—every juncture, without exception. It has refused even to talk about a consolidation. It has refused to provide the Congressional Budget Office with the information that the Congressional Budget Office has to have in order to compute the billions of dollars the taxpayers will be saving by passing the legislation" (*Congressional Record* 1995, S10931).

Even Secretary of State Warren Christopher, who first devised the plan, opposed it once Helms made the issue a contest over executive authority. By insisting that State Department reorganization come through formal legislation, Helms and his colleagues shifted the central focus from bureaucratic efficiency to presidential prerogatives in foreign affairs. It proved a serious miscalculation. In a letter to Senator Claiborne Pell (D-R.I.), Christopher explained that although "S908 contains a number of management authorities sought by the Department of State, the cumulative weight of its restrictions, requirements and prohibitions would obstruct the President's ability to conduct America's foreign policy and cripple America's ability to lead. . . . In its current form," he stated flatly, "I will have no choice but to recommend a veto. This bill's attack on Presidential authority is unprecedented in scope and severity" (*Congressional Record* 1995, S10931–33). The bill went down to defeat.

In addition to inviting powerful presidential opposition, congressional attempts to change national security agencies leave legislators vulnerable to the vagaries of future events and public opinion. They create the possibility that Congress might be blamed for unintended, unforeseen, and even unconnected foreign policy fiascoes down the line. This is exactly the kind of uncertainty that members desperately try to avoid (Fiorina 1982a, 1982b; Moe 1989; Kiewiet and McCubbins 1991). We need only ask: What member would be willing to risk the charge that his oversight efforts ended up weakening U.S. defense capabilities or jeopardizing American national security interests? Moreover, congressional action requires information about agency operations, problems, and performance. Committees cannot impose rewards and sanctions if they do not know what agencies are doing. But in foreign policy, even more than in domestic policy, information is hard to come by.[34]

Finally, any major reorganization of the executive branch cannot occur without altering the corresponding organization of Congress—which invariably means redrawing committee jurisdictions, changing the way committees do business, and upsetting the seniority-centered distribution of power. One senior Senate committee staffer explained the situation this way:

> What a lot of people do not understand is that the organization of Congress is a very important factor in determining what gets looked at and what doesn't. And the organization of Congress obviously follows the organization of the executive branch to a large extent. So you really can't make major reorganizations of the executive branch without at the same time proposing major reorganizations of Congress. That's a very difficult thing to do, because . . . it means a realignment of who gets to do what in Congress and that means you are getting at the heart of where people's power comes from up here. And once you've got some power up here you ain't willing to give it up so easily.[35]

As we shall see, it was precisely these fears of congressional reorganization that blocked the creation of permanent intelligence oversight committees for over 25 years.

In sum, Congress's oversight threat is not nearly so strong in reality as it is in theory. Most legislators lack the electoral incentives to make oversight of national security agencies a top priority. Those that do—the national security intellectuals—are few and far between, and rarely choose to expend the capital and effort to rally their parochial colleagues to their cause. Moreover, Congress's formidable formal powers are unlikely to be used; at some basic level, members believe that presidents ought to take the lead in foreign affairs, and thus ought to be given the freedom and flexibility to design their foreign policy apparatus as they see fit. Legislators also know that in reality all presidents are inclined to fight hard to retain control over their national security agencies. In addition, legislators have good reason to leave well enough alone. They wish to avoid taking the fall for major foreign policy failures. They realize that Congress as an institution lacks the information channels to monitor agency activities in the first place. And they recognize that any major overhaul of the national security machinery requires corresponding changes in congressional organization that may upset the distribution of power within the legislature.

In the end, it seems that Congress's foreign policy tools are rather blunt instruments. The "power of life or death," when used on foreign policy agencies, threatens to impose significant costs on everyone, not just the targeted bureaucracy or program. When it comes to oversight of foreign policy agencies, legislators may not be lame ducks, but they are weak birds.

BUREAUCRATIC INTERCONNECTEDNESS

Finally, national security agencies live in a much more tightly knit, stable bureaucratic world than their domestic policy counterparts. In national security affairs, organizations cannot and do not operate in isolation. Their activities inherently overlap and intersect. Diplomatic negotiations have serious consequences for military action and vice versa. Intelligence is intimately connected to grand strategy, military power, and diplomacy. To do their jobs, national security officials must concern themselves with other agencies. The same cannot be said for most domestic policy bureaucrats. It is hard to imagine the Federal Communications Commission taking an interest in the activities of the Social Security Administration. As Leslie Gelb noted, "In domestic policy, it's a much more diverse world. You have your health care crowd, your tax reform crowd, and they live in separate universes. In foreign policy, anyone would play in Latin America if it's hot."[36] To use a geographic analogy, if regulatory agencies operate as a series of islands, national security agencies more closely resemble the European Community.

In economic terms, foreign policy bureaucracies have a high degree of "asset cospecialization": the value of one agency's work hinges, at least in part, on the work of another. Although this arrangement can be mutually beneficial, it can also lead to "holdup problems"—situations in which one selfish party imposes demands that adversely affect the performance of another. In the private sector, companies minimize holdup problems by limiting their cospecialized assets through vertical integration, by trying to get more complete contracts with partners, and by using noncontractual mechanisms such as reputation to signal commitment and trust (Milgrom and Roberts 1992, 134–65).

For foreign policy bureaucracies, however, options are not so plentiful. Competition in the public sector is inherently more limited. General Motors may be able to buy out its auto body contractor, but the State Department is not free to take over the CIA if it becomes unhappy with the agency's intelligence. Government agencies can try to build reputations and working relationships, but the political appointments system makes this difficult to do. Presidential appointees "bear the burden of being transients in office," writes G. Calvin Mackenzie. "Their lease runs for only four years, and that is rarely enough time to allow them to learn all they need to know about the federal personnel system. . . . It takes time for the permanent and the transient governments to get comfortable with one another, if they ever do at all" (Mackenzie 1981, 114). The increasing politicization and decreasing tenure of political appointments have only exacerbated the trust dilemma in recent years. This is not to say that agencies are completely helpless. But national security organizations do face a more serious holdup threat than the average firm does. In foreign policy, government agencies must constantly contend with the possibility that another agency may be working against them.

The upshot is that national security agencies have powerful incentives to worry about the design and operation of organizations other than their own. Most domestic policy agencies have clearly delineated spheres of influence, but national security agencies do not. Instead, bureaucratic interconnectedness guarantees that changes to any one organization will affect others. New agencies arise, then, in an environment filled with preexisting bureaucratic actors, all with a large stake in the outcome. There are always bureaucrats out there who have something—quite a lot, actually—to gain or lose by new organizational arrangements. Bureaucratic actors figure as major players in the politics of national security agency structure.

SUMMARY

National security and domestic policy agencies operate in two vastly different worlds. In domestic policy, interest groups are plentiful, powerful, and varied, providing representatives with information and incentives to play a part in agency design. On top of this, widely available information about agency activities lowers the cost of congressional action—both in designing agencies and in overseeing them. Congressional participation in policy issues is not only rational but right; when it comes to such things as taxes, health care, and education, legislators are expected to weigh in. At times, presidents can and do enter the fray. But bureaucrats do not—given the breadth and variable nature of domestic policy issues, agencies naturally have little reason to care about any organization but their own. Thus, in domestic policy, it seems reasonable to conclude, as new institutionalists do, that interest groups drive the politics of bureaucratic structure, that bureaucrats don't matter much, and that the end result is a poorly designed bureaucracy that is kept under Congress's "watchful eyes" (Aberbach 1990).

National security agencies are another story. In foreign affairs, interest groups are relatively new, fluid, and weak. Information is not widely available. Policy issues are seen to lie predominantly in the president's domain. And the same basic issues involve a relatively small set of interacting foreign policy organizations. Taken together, these factors suggest that Congress has little reason to participate much in the creation and oversight of national security agencies. With information at a premium, with interest groups essentially out of the picture, and with a sense that foreign policy is the president's responsibility, legislators do better to turn their attention elsewhere. Presidents and bureaucrats then appear much larger. National security policy is presidential policy. And bureaucrats—from soldiers to diplomats to spies—have a stake in how the overall national security apparatus is designed. In short, using the same set of new institutionalist assumptions—about the importance of institutions, about rationality, about transaction costs and the nature of political actors—we come to some very different conclusions about national security agencies. These can be formulated in four specific hypotheses or propositions.

PROPOSITION 1: The executive branch drives the creation of national security agencies. Congress plays, at best, only a secondary role.

PROPOSITION 2: This does not mean an absence of conflict. Although presidents have the national interest at heart, they are not the sole players in the executive branch. In national security affairs, existing bureaucratic actors have much to gain or lose by the creation of a new agency, and will fight to preserve their own institutional interests. Such conflict within the executive branch gives rise to national security agencies that, by design, cannot do their jobs well.

PROPOSITION 3: The evolution of national security agencies, like their creation, is driven by forces within the executive branch—by the president, by the agency itself, and by its supporters and opponents in other bureaucratic offices.

PROPOSITION 4: National security agencies develop with sporadic, largely ineffectual oversight by Congress. Members have neither the incentives nor the capabilities to keep constant watch over agency activities.

These propositions spell good news for new institutionalist theory. Rather than having to do away with the approach, we can transform it. We can adjust it to work in a policy realm that its original adherents never imagined or anticipated. Juxtaposing domestic agencies with their national security counterparts allows us to see just how far new institutionalism can travel (see Figure 5).

Relaxing the Foreign/Domestic Dichotomy

Up to this point, I have painted a picture of sharp distinctions between national security and domestic policy agencies. By this account, the CIA and the DMV have little in common. Interest groups, information, interbranch norms, and patterns of bureaucratic activity change in significant ways once we move from domestic issues to national security ones. While such bold distinctions help clarify little-known differences between these two agency types, they tend to obscure real and important distinctions *among* national security agencies. Reality is not nearly so neat. National security agencies vary. They do not look alike at birth. Nor do they develop along the same path or go through similar developmental stages.

Even a quick glance at history makes this point clear. Birth dates mean very little where national security agencies are concerned. The National Security Council system, the CIA, and the Department of Defense were all created by the same act at the same time to respond to the same Cold War threat. But they hardly look alike. Agencies also develop at different speeds. Whereas some institutions, such as the Joint Chiefs of Staff, go for decades without major structural or operational change, others, such as the National Security Council staff, rapidly develop into organizations their creators never intended or envisioned. Even within a single functional area, agencies develop at unequal rates. In the intelligence community, the Central Intelligence Agency has greatly expanded its jurisdiction, whereas the National Security Agency has essentially been involved in the same kinds of activities since 1952, when it was first established (Lowenthal 1992). Perhaps more important, agencies develop in different ways—from informal executive branch reforms and secret directives to major, public acts of Congress. Even here, some agencies appear to be more immune than others to particular reform strategies. Scandal may have triggered congressional intervention and over-

Summary of Key Differences

Domestic Regulatory Agencies	National Security Agencies
1. Interest group environment is strong, stable, and dense.	1. Interest group environment is fluid, thin, and weak.
2. Work is conducted in the open; information is widespread, easy to obtain.	2. Work is conducted in secret; information is difficult, costly to obtain.
3. Legislative domain	3. Executive domain
4. Bureaucracies are loosely connected.	4. Bureaucracies are tightly connected.

Summary of Propositions

Domestic Regulatory Agencies	National Security Agencies
1. Congress drives initial agency design.	1. Executive branch drives initial agency design.
2. Agencies reflect conflict between contending interest groups and their legislative champions.	2. Agencies reflect conflict between contending bureaucrats and the president.
3. Congress drives agency evolution.	3. Executive branch drives agency evolution.
4. Congress oversees the bureaucracy; members have strong incentives and tools to keep a close watch.	4. Congress exercises sporadic, largely ineffectual oversight; members have weak incentives, blunt tools.

FIGURE 5. *Transforming New Institutionalism into a National Security Agency Model*

sight of the CIA in the 1970s, but it did nothing to prompt congressional oversight or reform of the NSC staff after Iran-Contra. Aside from holding some hearings, Congress left the NSC staff alone.

As these examples suggest, a compelling explanation of national security agency evolution needs to take diversity into account. It must offer an explanation for the different developmental paths that national security agencies take. In other words, such an argument must begin by pinpointing the sources of agency variance.

Of course, the obvious explanation focuses on agency function. This argument basically contends that agencies that perform different tasks must be differently designed. It makes little sense to think an intelligence agency would resemble a military one. By this account, function and function alone determines the initial design and subsequent development of national security organizations.

But we know this is not true. National security agency design is much more than a matter of function; it is a matter of politics. Presidents, bureaucrats, and, to a lesser degree, legislators continually fight for agency structures that serve their own interests. Though the demands of an agency's task must play some role, it is hardly a paramount one. If new institutionalist arguments about domestic policy agencies do anything, they lay this functionalist hypothesis to rest. For if function were the sole or even primary determinant of agency design, then bureaucracies would be destined for success. They would perform their jobs well.

Instead, looking more broadly, we can identify three sources of agency variance, three major factors that cause national security agencies to evolve in different ways. In order of descending importance, they are: (1) the structural choices made at an agency's birth; (2) the ongoing interests of major political players; and (3) exogenous events.

Founding moments loom large in national security agency evolution. As we shall see more clearly in the case studies to follow, national security agencies emerge as reflections of their political environment. Their initial design stems from compromises and conflicts between political institutions that are bent on protecting their own power. These design choices are sticky. In the American system of separated powers, legislation is difficult to enact; the congressional committee system, bicameralism, and presidential veto authority provide multiple veto points along the legislative path. Theoretically, acts of Congress can always be amended or even rescinded. Realistically, separation-of-powers ensures that agency mandates, procedures, and structures that manage to get written into law tend to endure (Moe 1987b, 240). Once an agency is created, then, its future is no longer completely up for grabs. Enacting legislation makes some developmental paths more likely than others.

The preferences of presidents, legislators, and bureaucrats constitute a second set of shifting pressures on agency evolution. National security agencies are not just out there, twisting in the wind. They are caught in a web of competing, crosscutting, and often conflicting interests among legislative and executive branch actors. How these interests align and change over time has important consequences for agency development. The American separation-of-powers system may make agencies difficult to change, but it does not make change impossible. We know that legislators, bureaucrats, and presidents have a variety of tools they can use to shape agency design and behavior. The question is, When do they? When do the incentives become high enough for one or more of these actors to jump in and change the way national security agencies do their business?

Third, and finally, real-world events must be thrown into the mix. Agencies and other political actors are not immune to events. Rather, domestic and international political developments serve as external shocks that can entrench an agency in its current developmental path or, in rare instances, shift it to a new one. Budget deficits, military confrontation, domestic political scandals, economic recession, partisan electoral sweeps, international trade agreements, to name a few—these things can, at times, affect agency development. They can move the focus of public debate, change the political context in which these agencies operate, and alter the interests and capabilities of relevant political players. It does not take much expertise to realize how much or how quickly a well-timed major development can move the battleground, empower some, or spell trouble for others.

Thus, while national security agencies vary, they do so for certain reasons. Initial structural choices produce institutional "birthmarks" that are difficult to change. Basic features of agency design—such things as explicit provisions for congressional oversight, organizational location within the executive branch, staffing arrangements—provide the roadways for future agency development. But not everything is preordained. Presidents, legislators, and bureaucrats all have interests and capabilities of their own. It is these interests and capabilities that determine the particular course an agency will follow. Finally, domestic and international events have the potential to reinforce an agency's trajectory or to spark turns from it. There is no mystery here. Whether an agency flourishes of flounders hinges on its available evolutionary options, on actors' rational calculations of costs and benefits, and on the timing of key events.

Domestic Policy Agencies	National Security Agencies
An individual agency's evolution can be explained by changes in the interest group environment, the composition of congressional committees, or congressional interests.	An individual agency's evolution can be explained principally by its initial design, and to a lesser extent by the ongoing interests of relevant political actors and events.

FIGURE 6.   *Transforming New Institutionalism into a National Security Agency Model: Explaining a Specific Agency's Developmental Trajectory*

These arguments suggest a fifth proposition about the development of national security agencies:

PROPOSITION 5: Although the executive branch drives the creation and development of all national security agencies, those agencies evolve along different trajectories. Explaining agency evolution requires first and foremost understanding agency institutional birthmarks. In addition, the analyst must consider the ongoing interests of key political actors and the influence of world events.

When we compare domestic policy agencies with national security organizations, as in Figure 6, we can see how different this proposition becomes in the two policy realms.

Politics, Presidents, and Bureaucrats Revisited

Before proceeding any further, we need to bring politics more centrally into the equation. Foreign and domestic policy may be different, but this does not mean that politics is absent.

Two issues need to be clarified. First, it is important to distinguish what presidents want from what they actually get. Although presidents may have strong incentives to think in terms of the national interest, and although they may wield some powerful levers when it comes to designing national security agencies, they almost never get the kind of responsive, effective agencies they desire. Why not? If Congress has little reason to intervene in national security agency design or development, then why can't presidents create or change agencies to suit their needs and effectively promote U.S. national security interests?

Second, although I contend that bureaucratic agencies are powerful actors, it is not clear why anyone should allow them to play such a role. After all, bureaucracies are subordinate to the legislators and presidents who create them. Congress and the chief executive can theoretically ignore, thwart, or even punish agencies that go against them or step out of line. What is it about bureaucratic organizations that makes them independent, forceful actors on the political scene?

We turn to each of these issues below.

1. If Congress has little reason to play a major role in the creation or development of national security agencies, then why can't presidents get exactly the kind of agencies they want?

At first glance, the factors examined above appear to suggest that presidents should have a relatively easy time designing and altering national security agencies to suit their needs. Given what we know about presidents, such agencies should be shaped to serve the national interest. They should be optimally designed to protect and further American national security interests abroad.

Yet, with the exception of the National Security Council staff, this has not been the case. President Eisenhower became so disaffected by JCS disloyalty and opposition to his policies that he commented to Defense Secretary Charles Wilson, "[I am] inclined to think that the Chiefs of Staff system . . . has failed" (quoted in Kinnard 1977, 205). Eisenhower's sentiments have been echoed by virtually every one of his successors. In perhaps the most colorful assessment, Kennedy remarked that the Joint Chiefs "advise you the way a man advises another one about whether he should marry a girl. He doesn't have to live with her" (quoted in Sorensen 1965, 391).

Chief executives have expressed similar frustrations with almost every other major national security agency. Kennedy's feelings toward the State Department are well known. Special Counsel Theodore Sorensen writes, "The President was discouraged with the State Department almost as soon as he took office. He felt that it too often seemed to have a built-in inertia which deadened initiative and that its tendency toward excessive delay obscured determination. It spoke with too many voices and too little vigor" (Sorensen 1965,

287). Nixon agreed but carried his dislike of foreign policy agencies even further, distrusting most organizations outside of his own staff. As Henry Kissinger recalls, the president-elect was extremely concerned with circumventing the self-interested, slow, and ineffective national security machinery. At their first meeting during the presidential transition, Kissinger writes, Nixon's "subject was the task of setting up his new government. He had a massive organization problem, he said. He had very little confidence in the State Department. Its personnel had no loyalty to him. . . . He felt it imperative to exclude the CIA from the formulation of policy; it was staffed by Ivy League liberals who behind the facade of analytical objectivity were usually pushing their own preferences" (Kissinger 1979, 11).

Jimmy Carter became so dissatisfied with the State Department during the fall of the shah that he sent his own military representative to Iran to provide intelligence and analysis. Carter writes in his memoirs, "As I compared what . . . [General Robert Huyser] told me with what our Ambassador in Iran had done and said, I became even more disturbed at the apparent reluctance in the State Department to carry out my directives fully and with enthusiasm." Shortly thereafter, the president took the unusual step of summoning the Iranian desk officers to the White House. "I laid down the law to them as strongly as I knew how. . . . I told them that if they could not support what I decided, their only alternative was to resign—and if there was another outbreak of misinformation, distortions, or self-serving news leaks, I would direct the Secretary of State to discharge the officials responsible for that particular desk, even if some innocent people might be punished" (Carter 1995, 458). It seems Carter's bigger diplomatic problem was not with Iran but with his own Department of State.

As these comments suggest, no modern president has been fully satisfied with his institutional resources in national security policy. Whether in gathering information, analyzing and presenting policy options, or implementing particular programs, national security agencies appear to frustrate chief executives more than they please. Although presidents play a large role in the creation and development of American national security agencies, they often do not obtain the kind of bureaucratic responsiveness they seek.

How can this be?

We can find the answer by looking more closely at delegated authority, at what happens when one person must rely on others to get things done. It seems fairly evident that no president can single-handedly make foreign policy. Instead, presidents are forced to rely on a network of others—on intelligence officers, on diplomats, on military strategists, on policy advisers—to handle the everyday affairs of state. But reliance is a double-edged sword; presidents cannot always know, much less control, what bureaucrats do. They cannot guarantee that agencies will work in their own best interests. The reality is that most agencies do not serve the president's interests. They have other obligations, other aims, and other constituencies that conflict with his. As Richard Neustadt wrote, presidents must wage a constant battle to get bureaucratic compliance because "no one else sits where [the president] sits or sees quite as he sees; no one else feels the full weight of his obligations . . . the obligations of all other men are different from his own" (Neustadt 1960, 8).

In organization theory terms, this is the classic principal-agent problem.[37] Presidents (principals) have no choice but to rely on bureaucrats (agents) who do not completely share their interests; this necessity, coupled with the president's inability to monitor agency activity fully, provides fertile ground for bureaucratic non-compliance. Agencies can ignore presidential directives, delay implementation of presidential programs, and limit presidential options when it suits their needs to do so because presidents do not have the time or resources to watch them. The following account by a Roosevelt aide brings this principal-agent problem to life: "Half of a president's suggestions, which theoretically carry the weight of orders, can be safely forgotten by a Cabinet member. And if the President asks about a suggestion a second time, he can be told that it is being investigated. If he asks a third time, a wise Cabinet officer will give him at least part of what he suggests. But only occasionally, except about the most important matters, do Presidents ever get around to asking three times" (quoted in Neustadt 1960, 32). The question is not whether but how much agencies shirk their responsibilities in favor of more parochial self-interests.

Presidents are not completely helpless in the face of bureaucratic shirking. As we shall see, much of the story about agency evolution centers on how presidents use low-cost measures to get around agency problems—to compel agencies to heed presidential interests or to transfer agency responsibilities to those who do. Theoretically, presidents have an array of tools to reform willful bureaucracies, ranging from executive orders and political appointments to reorganization plans to legislative reform. But whether and when presidents actually employ these measures is another story. As McGeorge Bundy, Kennedy's national security adviser, put it, "Presidents are not public administrators. They do not look at the United States government as something they should tune. They look at it as something that they've got to get the help of, however they can."[38] In reality, presidents are constrained by two major factors.

First, the chief executive faces severe time constraints. Presidents have at most only eight years to achieve their major domestic and international policy goals and secure their place in history. While bureaucratic reform may be important, even instrumental, in achieving those goals, it is not something for which great leaders are likely to be remembered. For instance, if we think of President Reagan's administration, we are far more likely to recall the Strategic Defense Initiative (SDI), the invasion of Grenada, and U.S.-Soviet nuclear arms reduction talks than the reorganization of the Joint Chiefs of Staff.

Second, presidents are embedded in a broad network of political institutions that limit what they can do. To legislate major, long-lasting changes in national security agencies, presidents must get the consent of a congressional majority. But members of Congress have their own interests that make such reform efforts difficult to achieve. In addition, presidents cannot afford simply to ignore bureaucrats' wishes. The chief executive needs bureaucratic support and expertise for his policy initiatives. Given these circumstances, presidents may find it better to use their limited political capital on other pursuits.[39] As Brent Scowcroft put it, "You know, the president can change the Defense Department if he wants to. But you don't take on those things lightly."[40]

Two conclusions can be drawn. The first is that presidents often will not get what they want from their national security apparatus. If we accept the standard view of presidents and their motivations, this is bad news: for as long as presidents cannot get their way, national security agencies will tend to serve the interests of the particular at the expense of the whole.

Second, all presidents will seek to overcome the principal-agent problem in ways that minimize their political costs. Consequently, major reform efforts should be rare. Instead, informal strategies such as centralizing decision making in the White House staff, reconstituting agency responsibilities and capabilities through executive orders, and granting different players more or less access to the president are likely to be common.

2. *What are the sources of bureaucratic power? Why do bureaucrats, who are subordinate to legislators and presidents, play such a prominent role in the design and development of national security agencies?*

Strangely, new institutionalists talk a lot about bureaucracy but fail to treat bureaucratic agencies as important actors in their own right. For Barry Weingast, Mark Moran, Mathew McCubbins, and others, legislators are the principal players. Coming from a research program geared toward understanding Congress, they find, not surprisingly, that Congress plays the lead role in shaping government agencies. Terry Moe finds such congressional control of the bureaucracy inherently problematic, but he, too, fails to give bureaucrats much credit when he seeks to explain the development of other agencies. As I have argued, this omission is a serious one. In the creation and evolution of national security agencies, bureaucrats turn out to be a major piece of the puzzle.

It is worth taking a minute to consider how this would be possible and ask: Where does bureaucratic power come from? How do bureaucrats get legislators and presidents to grant them a seat at the table?

The classic explanation begins with Max Weber and focuses on expertise. Bureaucrats wield influence among politicians because they are known to have a detailed, specialized, and sophisticated knowledge of a given policy area. This is precisely why they are hired in the first place. Delegating the details to the bureaucrats frees politicians to consider a broader range of issues. The downside, of course, is that on any single issue, legislators and presidents must face experts who know more than they do. As Weber writes, "The 'political master' finds himself in the position of the 'dilettante' who stands opposite the 'expert,' facing the trained official who stands within the management of administration" (Weber 1946, 232). In the real world of politics, this makes it tough for politicians to force their will on unwilling agencies; who is to debate the Navy about what it needs to provide an effective fleet? Knowledge, indeed, is power.

The bureaucrats' advantage in expertise becomes especially pronounced in foreign policy matters. It is one thing for presidents to ignore the EPA's position on water quality standards. It is quite another for presidents to ignore the CIA's analysis of Iraq's military capabilities. National security agencies, by definition, deal with vital defense issues, so elected officials ignore, oppose, and reform those agencies at their peril. When being wrong could lead to biological or nuclear warfare, presidents and members of Congress are likely to trust the opinions and desires of experts. It is this reliance that gives national security bureaucrats power.

Though expertise is by far the bureaucrats' most potent weapon, three other sources of their power are worth mentioning. The first is asymmetrical incentives. We already know that presidents care much more about national security agencies than most legislators do. But bureaucrats care most of all. While presidents fight hard to design agencies in certain ways, bureaucrats fight for their lives. Agencies are more willing than other political players to stick to their guns, to battle until the bitter end over questions of agency capabilities and jurisdiction. With this willingness comes power. Presidents, after all, have full agendas and limited time. If faced with intense bureaucratic opposition, they will almost always settle for something rather than nothing, for partial reforms and compromises instead of their ideal agency design. Bureaucrats know this. They know that holding out forces presidents to make concessions. And they are right. Within the executive branch, asymmetrical incentives can give national security agencies de facto veto rights over reform initiatives.

Second, as I noted earlier, bureaucrats shirk. They can resist, ignore, and circumvent orders, even those that come directly from the president. During the Cuban missile crisis, for example, John F. Kennedy was stunned to learn that an arsenal of obsolete Jupiter missiles had not been removed from Turkey, even though he had issued direct orders to that effect in early 1961 and again in August 1962 (Allison 1971, 141–43). It seems that State Department officials were more concerned about maintaining good bilateral relations with Turkey than with carrying out the president's wishes.[41] Kennedy was not alone. Harry Truman best captured the essence of the bureaucratic shirking problem back in 1952. Anticipating Eisenhower's management troubles, Truman remarked, "He'll sit here and he'll say 'Do this! Do that!' *And nothing will happen.* Poor Ike—it won't be a bit like the Army. He'll find it very frustrating" (quoted in Neustadt 1960, 9; emphasis his).

The point to be made is this: shirking does not actually have to occur to be effective. The *anticipated threat* of bureaucratic resistance gives government agencies a strong hand against elected officials, particularly presidents. Why bother to force reform down the throat of an unwilling agency? Why run the risk that agencies will resist directives they oppose behind the scenes? Especially in national security affairs, the possibility of insidious bureaucratic rebellion makes agency reform or reorganization a chancy proposition. Combined with expertise and asymmetrical incentives, the shirking threat makes bureaucrats a force to be reckoned with.

Third, bureaucrats can gain political leverage over elected officials by appealing directly to the public. Press leaks, high-level resignations, public congressional hearings, and targeted publicity campaigns all hit presidents and legislators where it hurts—in the electorate. By leveling charges that reform proposals would cripple American defense or undermine U.S. intelligence operations, national security bureaucrats can erode public support for the president or Congress. This outcome, in turn, can undermine policy goals and diminish prospects for reelection. All else being equal, presidents and legislators will hesitate to tamper with national security agencies that are willing to go public with their demands.

All these things give government agencies room to maneuver. Presidents and members of Congress listen to bureaucrats because they cannot afford to do otherwise. Armed with expertise, extraordinary incentives, shirking mechanisms, and public appeals, government agencies do not have to remain the servile subjects of their political masters.

Thus, to say the executive branch drives the creation and evolution of national security agencies is not to say the process is easy, agreeable, or even successful. While institutional incentives push presidents toward action, institutional constraints work to hold them back. Although it is possible in theory to ignore the bureaucrats' interests and concerns, it is impossible to do so in practice. Agency officials hold more cards than the statutes suggest.

Conclusions

This chapter makes two central claims. First, national security agencies are very different animals from the domestic policy bureaucracies traditionally studied in political science. With a relatively weak interest group environment, with high levels of secrecy, with a deeply embedded norm of executive primacy in foreign affairs, and with strong bureaucratic interconnectedness, national security agencies arise and evolve in ways fundamentally different from those of their regulatory counterparts. In foreign affairs, the "politics of bureaucratic structure" (Moe 1989) is played out largely within the executive branch—between the president and existing foreign policy agencies. Once formed, agencies do not develop according to the shifting interests of congressional committees. Instead, evolution of national security agencies is driven by institutional birthmarks, by the constellation of political interests and capabilities, and by events.

Second, and relatedly, national security agencies are not designed to serve the national interest. New agencies are literally created by actors who are out for themselves, who put their own interests above national ones. Presidents do have broad concerns, but usually they cannot get the kind of national security agencies they want. Existing bureaucratic actors have an enormous stake in the creation of new national security organizations, and are well armed to hobble them at birth. Today's bureaucrats have reputation, expertise, incentives, shirking capabilities, and public outlets on their side. Unfortunately, they use these weapons to enhance their own power, resources, and interests at the expense of the overall policy-making apparatus. That is how politics works. As for Congress, the average member has little reason to play a major role in designing new foreign policy agencies. With its district-based representation, internal committee system, and majority rule requirements, Congress is structurally unsuited to take an activist role in most foreign policy issues, much less the nitty-gritty structural battles over national security agency design. Some legislators undoubtedly enter the political fray out of ideological or national concerns. These national security intellectuals, however, usually defer to the executive branch; they know how hard it is to rally their colleagues, and they rightly fear that including them in the debate may debilitate national security agencies even more.

A second sense in which national security agencies are not designed to serve the national interest has to do with agency performance over time. Poorly designed to begin with, national security agencies must fight an uphill battle from day one. As we shall see, presidents and even legislators are able to improve agency performance only somewhat, in some cases, at some times. The price of initial structural choices appears to be high. In an absolute sense, American national security agencies are not created to serve American interests in a truly effective or efficient way. They do not do their jobs as they should, or at least as well as they could. Ironically, some of the very hallmarks of American democracy— separation of powers, regular elections, majority rule—inhibit good agency design and provide incentives for political actors to keep it that way. American national security agencies are not created by international relations realists who think in terms of organizational optimality. They are created by political actors who must operate in a reality suffused with conflict, contention, and compromise at the domestic level.

Origins of the National Security Council System: A "Brass-Knuckle Fight to the Finish"

Ask any student of U.S. foreign policy about the rise of the National Security Council system[1] and you will likely hear the following story:

In the beginning, Congress imposed the NSC system on an unhappy and reluctant Harry Truman. Concerned about Franklin Roosevelt's freewheeling, ad hoc leadership during World War II and worried about the impending challenges of the postwar world, Congress in 1947 set out to embed all presidents in a broader foreign policy decision-making system. The National Security Act of 1947 did this, among other things, by creating a formal, statutory National Security Council comprising the president and his highest-ranking foreign and military policy officials. The idea was both to help and to restrain the chief executive at the same time. Foreign policy had become too important to leave in one person's hands.[2] Once the National Security Council system became a reality, however, each president recreated and reinvented the system in his own image. Whereas Eisenhower's military training made him obsessive about hierarchy, staffwork, and formalized committees, Kennedy favored a looser, more flexible decision-making system of task forces and informal debate. Whereas Nixon monopolized decision making in the White House basement—conducting international negotiations and formulating major foreign policy initiatives with Henry Kissinger and few others—Reagan pushed it outward, to the State Department and the self-appointed foreign policy "vicar," Secretary of State Alexander Haig. In short, what began as a creature of Congress has evolved into a series of unique institutional creations reflecting each president's distinctive personality, demands, and leadership style.[3] Or so goes the conventional wisdom.

I take issue with this account. The conventional wisdom gets the NSC story wrong because it has no theory to guide it—no clearly developed conception of which variables matter. At best, the NSC system literature grafts broad trends onto the particulars: the National Security Act is portrayed as part of a larger effort by Congress to restrain the growing institutional presidency, and the NSC system's evolution is viewed as a prime example of the personal nature of presidential power. At worst, these accounts pass off description for explanation. "It depends on the president" arguments may help us understand the day-to-day workings of the NSC system, but they cannot tell us much about the underlying forces that have created and shaped the system's development over time.

Even a quick glance should raise some questions about how wise the conventional wisdom actually is. How could Congress have foisted the NSC system on a reluctant Harry Truman when Truman proposed the idea himself? How can we reconcile the apparent hostility of this legislative act with the traditional view of foreign policy bipartisanship and executive-congressional harmony in the immediate postwar period? As for evolution, if each National Security Council system reflects the chief executive's personality, policies, and proclivities, then why have all presidents since Eisenhower ended up controlling foreign policy making from the White House instead of the State Department? Why do we see such continuity across administrations?

In this chapter and the next I present a different story—one that is rooted in the National Security Agency Model developed in Chapter 1. I start by asking: Who are the relevant political players? What positions would further their rational, self-interested goals? And what kind of power do they have? Focusing on institutional interests and capabilities, we find that the NSC system was never a major bone of contention. It was more of an accident—a by-product of a protracted, contentious battle between the president, the War Department, and the Navy Department to unify the military services under a single Department of Defense. Legislators and interest groups were bit players in this drama. They were never pushing for the national interest, anyway. Only the president was. And in the face of intense interservice military conflict, he did not succeed. Indeed, the origins story reveals that the NSC system did not originally emerge out of any ideal vision of foreign policy making or executive restraint. It was a ploy by the Navy to retain its preeminent position among the military services. Truman may not have welcomed the NSC system at first, but he ultimately championed it as a way to get the Navy on board his unification plan. National interest was not a paramount concern.

Similarly, the evolution of the National Security Council system appears markedly different from the popular picture when we look at it through new institutionalist lenses. Continuity, more than change, is what we find. In relatively short order—between 1947 and 1963—Presidents Truman, Eisenhower, and Kennedy laid the foundations for a White House–centered, modern NSC system. Gone was State Department dominance in foreign policy making. Gone was the preeminence of the formal National Security Council. Instead, the system that emerged was one in which the president's own appointed NSC staff—led by the special assistant to the president for national security affairs—managed the policy process, analyzed policy options, and offered policy advice with only the president's interests in mind. Though subsequent presidents altered the system in various ways, none of them changed these basic elements. A long view of the NSC system finds an evolutionary pattern of rapid development followed by a prolonged period of stasis.

Why and how this happened fits with what we know about legislators, presidents, and bureaucrats. With weak electoral incentives and collective action problems, Congress had little reason to take an active role in the NSC system's development. Although presidents are normally constrained from getting their way, in this case they had powerful incentives and capabilities to mold the National Security Council system to their needs. In the wake of America's newfound internationalism and in the shadow of potential nuclear war, chief executives had more reason than ever to gain maximum control and power over their own foreign policy–making apparatus: the margin for error had become razor-thin. More important, the NSC system was ripe for takeover. Presidents could change the NSC system immediately, unilaterally, and easily—without congressional approval, confirmation, or legislation. Bureaucrats resisted the trend toward White House domination, but they did not win. In this rare case, the president acted as the 500-pound gorilla.

The NSC system was born out of conflict. When Harry Truman signed the National Security Act on July 26, 1947, he capped off four years of some of the most intensive, protracted public military debate in U.S. history.[4] In public speeches, in congressional testimony, in private correspondence, and in press conferences, members of the Army, Navy, Air Force, and White House accused each other of lobbying, of pandering to public fears, and of destroying U.S. military capabilities. At one point President Truman publicly assailed a naval commandant, and at another Navy Secretary James Forrestal threatened to resign. The *New York Times* called it a gloves-off, "brass-knuckle fight to the finish" (Oct. 20, 1945).

The NSC system itself was never the central concern. Instead, from day one, the critical issue involved military unification—whether, how much, and how to merge the Army, Navy, and their air forces under a central Defense Department and military chief of staff. This represented no small change; since 1798, the departments of War and the Navy had exercised virtual free reign over their respective realms.[5] To them, unification unavoidably threatened some and benefited others. It meant changes in the relative power, prestige, resources, and influence among the military services. The National Security Council system became a weapon in this contest, designed by the Navy for its own protection. Initially, the Navy proposed the NSC system as part of a broad substitute for a unified Defense Department. More than anything else, the proposal was a way to protect the Navy's power, autonomy, and resources in the postwar era. In the end, however, the council and its staff became little more than a throwaway provision—a conciliatory presidential gesture to get the Navy's acceptance of a unification compromise plan. Not even Congress paid much attention to the National Security Council system in its final floor debates.

The Players

THE DEPARTMENT OF WAR

The battle lines were clear and sharp. On one side, the Department of War—which included the Army ground and air forces—championed the notion of comprehensive military unification. Army Chief of Staff George C. Marshall first proposed the idea even before the end of World War II, claiming it would save money and strengthen

American defenses. Public claims aside, three underlying motivations lay behind the War Department's position.

First, the Army believed that unification would give it a greater share of the postwar national defense budget. In the Army's view, its lack of glamour, along with the existing two-department structure, had deprived the War Department of its share of national defense appropriations during the prewar years. General Dwight Eisenhower made this point clear during the unification debates:

> Now, can you conceive, with the glamour that attaches to the Navy and to the Air Forces, that the ground forces, the boys who finally have to wade in and fight and take the losses, and win the battle, are going to get anything out of this? Not for an instant. The tendency is going to be to give appropriations and great concern to these more glamorous people, those who would win wars by pushing buttons. And the poor doughboy who finally has to trudge in and take his losses and win his battle, is the one who will suffer. (U.S. Senate 1947, 114) [6]

Evidence suggests that the Army's claims were not far off the mark. In the 1930s, congressional funds built the Navy into one of the three strongest in the world, while the U.S. Army ranked about 17th. In 1939, appropriations for a single battleship exceeded the budget for all Army weapons. Ground forces were left to make do with outdated World War I rifles (Caraley 1966, 62). Postwar conditions only exacerbated these concerns. Faced with expected budget cuts and the creation of an autonomous Air Force Department, the Army saw unification as its best defense against budgetary discrimination.

Second, traditional Army philosophy favored unified command. In his review of National Security Act testimony, Demetrios Caraley notes, "Implicit in the testimony of the Army leaders was the belief that in any decision-making situation, there was an optimum solution . . . [which] could never be reached through bargaining and compromise" (Caraley 1966, 64). Within the War Department, this preference for central, hierarchical command and clear lines of authority had long taken hold. In 1903, the War Department integrated its own command under a chief of staff. And for decades, the department favored organizing U.S. defenses on the basis of weapons: ground-based weapons belonged in the Army's domain, sea-based weapons in the Navy's, and aerial weapons in the Army's air arm, the Army Air Forces.

Finally, the War Department, like other military players in this battle, saw unification ultimately as a contest for service supremacy.

World War II marked the transition to a new era of warfare—one in which air power became decisive. Between 1939 and 1944, the Army Air Forces skyrocketed from 22,000 men to 2.4 million. Introduction of the atomic bomb and the jet engine, moreover, guaranteed an unprecedented role for air forces after the war (Congressional Quarterly 1965, 20). Indeed, the establishment of an Air Force Department separate from the Army was considered a foregone conclusion by most. Such changes could not help but threaten the traditional roles of both ground and sea forces. As Robert J. Donovan writes, unification "aroused passion in Washington because it affected careers, pride, tradition, the roles of air, sea and land power, political influence, and allocation of funds among the military services" (Donovan 1977, 138). The stakes were high. As one Army Air Force general starkly put it, "The Navy had the transport to make the invasion of Japan possible; the Ground Forces had the power to make it successful; and the B-29 made it unnecessary" (U.S. Senate 1945, 290, 308). In this context, the War Department saw unification as much more than a policy conflict; it was a fight for the future of the Army.

THE DEPARTMENT OF THE NAVY

On the other side, vociferously opposing unification, stood the Navy. As the preeminent service, the Navy had much to lose and little to gain by changing the existing dual department military system. Caraley notes that "the navy during and immediately after World War II was a satisfied service. It wanted nothing more than to be left undisturbed, with its own secretary dealing with its own committees and appropriations subcommittees in Congress and presenting its case to the President" (Caraley 1966, 90). During the war, the Navy had become the strongest seagoing force in the world, with a Marine Corps amphibious landing force second to none and an aviation arm that accounted for nearly 40 percent of its budget (U.S. Senate 1946, 278). The Navy had prospered from its favored treatment by Congress and President Roosevelt. Unification threatened its position by placing a civilian "supersecretary" of defense and military chief of staff above the service heads and chiefs on all military matters—from budget appropriations to training to strategy.

In addition, unification violated core Navy decision-making principles and values. Unlike the Army, the Navy traditionally favored a looser, horizontal, collective decision-making system (Hammond

1961, 901). To the Navy, unified commands were appropriate only for theaters of war. Otherwise, the complexity of problems facing military strategists required broad-based discussion, bargaining, and input from all the services. Complementing this idea, naval civilian and military leaders had long believed that rigid lines between services impaired rather than improved defense capabilities. Whereas the Army sought strict service distinctions based on weapon type, the Navy believed that American forces should be organized by function: each service should be assigned a basic mission and given whatever weapons were needed to achieve it—regardless of whether they operated on the ground, in the water, or in the air. As Assistant Secretary of the Navy Artemus Gates argued before one congressional committee, "Determine the functions and missions of the services, but leave to them the final voice as to what type of weapons they must have in order to carry out best those functions and missions. In other words, tell them what to do but not how to do it" (U.S. House 1944a, 124). Paradoxically, the Navy saw integration as a product of service autonomy; placing the services on independent footings best guaranteed their success in combat and their cooperation in planning.

Perhaps even more than the Army, the Navy viewed the postwar world of airplanes and atomic weapons as a zero-sum survival game between the services. Three related concerns pervaded senior naval ranks. First, the Navy believed it would be left out of new air-based weapons development. In the words of Admiral Thomas C. Kincaid, commander of the Sixteenth Fleet, "It has been clearly indicated that the Army Air Force intends to monopolize the research and development" of guided missiles, rockets, and "all such new weapons" (U.S. Senate 1946, 262). Second, Navy officials believed service merger would inherently favor ground and air services at their expense. They worried that the Army and Air Force would gang up against them in budget votes, and that a unified system would invariably undervalue the role of sea power—concentrating instead on ground troops out of the "sheer weight of numbers" (Zacharias 1947).[7]

Third, and most important, many believed unification would strip the Navy of its integrated ground and aviation arms—forces critical to its Pacific war successes. According to Marine Corps Commandant Alexander Vandegrift, the Marine Corps's amphibious landing operations proved so successful that they quickly became the model for Army forces and U.S. allies. Other officers testified that Navy planes sank almost a quarter of all Japanese ships, providing key air support in campaigns where the Army's planes could not or would not assist (U.S. Senate 1946, 106–8, 305–22, 346). In spite of, or perhaps because of, these successes, the Army and its air division openly advocated a scaling down of both non-sea-based naval units. Vandegrift made no bones about his view: "The War Department is determined to reduce the Marine Corps to a position of studied military ineffectiveness" (U.S. Senate 1946, 106). Admiral John H. Towers delivered a similar message about naval air power. "I fear—and I have good reason to fear—that the Army Air Forces . . . have well established in mind the plan . . . to absorb naval aviation" (U.S. Senate 1946, 278). Navy leaders believed that diluting or absorbing the Marines and naval aviation would decimate the service, leaving American shores without a first line of defense. Rear Admiral A. S. Merrill, a former Pacific combat commander, warned, "When the next war comes we will need the finest army and air force in the world because, with a greatly weakened navy, submerged under army control, the fighting will be on our shores" (quoted in Caraley 1966, 130).[8]

THE PRESIDENT

President Truman was the third and most important player in this political struggle. Solidly backing calls for unification as a vice presidential candidate, Truman became more flexible as president. In a campaign article for *Collier's* called "Our Armed Forces Must Be United" (Truman 1945), Truman staked out a strong position—even stronger than the Army's—calling for a new secretary of defense and a new General Staff system to replace the Joint Chiefs of Staff. Yet, once in the White House, he retreated substantially from this proposal. Though partial to the Army from his World War I service and his days on the Senate Military Affairs Subcommittee on War Department Appropriations, Truman became driven by distinctly presidential incentives. Facing a barrage of Cold War crises, severe time constraints, and the pressing need to exercise effective leadership, Truman came to desire, above all, *some* form of unification. As his White House aide George Elsey remarked, "As a matter of fact, while Truman felt that unification was a practical necessity, he did not feel so strongly about the particular form it took" (quoted in Donovan 1977, 140). Driven by his own institutional demands,

Truman worked consistently only for some kind of unified military; the specifics of his proposals shifted a great deal between 1945 and 1947.

All three sets of actors lined up to serve their own institutional interests. To the War Department, the postwar world offered a chance to gain some of the prestige, resources, and input long denied in the previous two-department system. Unification meant a step up for the Army. But for the Navy, unification spelled disaster for all the same reasons. The Navy stood to lose its special treatment by congressional Naval Affairs committees, its relatively generous budget allocations, its institutional autonomy (including control over the Marine Corps and naval aviation forces), and its influence in military policy making. Truman backed the basic idea of unification, but ultimately modified his stand when faced with the Navy's opposition. He did so to enhance the powers and effectiveness of his own office; by shifting military coordination to a supersecretary and a chief of staff, Truman hoped to free himself for more immediate concerns. At the same time, unification promised in some measure to integrate the strategy, supply, and operations of the military services at a time when national security appeared more important than ever before.

TWO MISSING PIECES: INTEREST GROUPS AND CONGRESS

Two other actors were conspicuously missing from the unification debate: interest groups and Congress. In the most comprehensive study of interest group participation in the unification debate, Demetrios Caraley concludes that "interest group activity did not play a major role either in the creation or the resolution" of the issue (Caraley 1966, 234). The *New York Times* and the *Congressional Record* mention just nineteen such organizations. These fell into two broad categories: veterans' groups and smaller, service-specific associations. But veterans' groups, by virtue of their multiservice membership, could not take sides in the debate, while service-related groups (such as the Air Power League) did not have the membership or clout to wield influence in Congress or the administration (Caraley 1966, 234–35). Moreover, business organizations, including defense contractors, made no real effort to influence events in Washington. If anything, World War II contractors opposed large peacetime military budgets, fearing such government spending would take valuable resources away from the private sector and cripple the postwar economic recovery (Hill 1979, 70). Although in general, interest groups were alive and well in the 1940s, they focused on other issues. Even V. O. Key's seminal 1948 work identifies strong pressure groups in agriculture, business, and even religious and women's issues, but makes no mention of any military-related interests.

Congress also played a relatively passive role. The absence of strong interest group pressures removed one major set of incentives for legislative leadership. More important, Army-Navy sparring ensured that most legislators would stay on the sidelines. While each service certainly had its key allies in the House and Senate, most were unwilling to decide the unification issue without some kind of military consensus (Caraley 1966). Congressional deference to military expertise was both militarily and politically prudent. Unification involved making critical judgments about military organization, force requirements, service roles and missions, and longer-term defense needs in the Cold War—judgments that senior Army and Navy officers were in a far better position to make. Understandably, few members were willing to risk challenges by cither Army or Navy World War II heroes about their votes on the future of American defense. Indeed, even hard-core Navy supporters recognized the vital importance of expert military opinion. As Senator Harry Byrd (D-Va.) advised his colleagues on the Naval Affairs Committee, "The only way we can make a fight . . . is to show that the Secretary of the Navy did not agree with what is in this bill. We may as well be frank about it. That is the only way that those of use who are opposed to unification can make a fight on the floor of Congress" (U.S. Senate 1946, 227).

Thus Congress served less as an active player in the unification conflict than as the stage on which it was played out. Divisions between the Military Affairs and Naval Affairs committees mirrored Army-Navy cleavages within the executive branch. Committee hearings served as forums in which Army and Navy officials fought their case. Key committee members—such as Senator David Walsh (D-Mass.), Senator Lister Hill (D-Ala.), and Representative James Wadsworth (R-N.Y.)—worked at the behest of their military allies, holding hearings, drafting legislation, and erecting legislative roadblocks when necessary. Yet without high-level agreement between the services, these actions got unification nowhere. Without the blessing of both services, unification debates raged in Congress for three years. Once Truman engineered an Army-Navy compromise plan, legislation sailed through Congress in five months.

Overview: Unification and the NSC System

The National Security Council and its staff were the Navy's brain-child, and arrived none too early. For almost two years—from the fall of 1943 to the fall of 1945—the Navy had been on the defensive, objecting to War Department calls for unification but offering no alternative of its own. During that time, pro-unification forces had seized the initiative. A special committee of the Joint Chiefs of Staff had come out in favor of full service merger. The departments of War and the Navy would be abolished and placed under the authority of a secretary of the armed forces and a single armed forces military commander.[9] Representative James Wadsworth, a War Department ally, had successfully created a Select Committee on Post-War Military Policy (the Woodrum Committee) to investigate postwar military requirements. Though the Woodrum Committee ultimately decided to postpone consideration of "detailed legislation" until after the war, its hearings in the spring of 1944 gave momentum to the idea of unification. On April 12, 1945, Franklin Roosevelt died, leaving the Navy without its key supporter in the White House. Roosevelt's successor, Harry Truman, was known to be a pro-unification Army partisan. Given these developments, the Navy needed a constructive alternative, one that could integrate military policy making without subordinating the Navy to an overarching Department of Defense or military chief of staff.

The Navy's solution was a 250-page study written by Ferdinand Eberstadt, one of Navy Secretary Forrestal's closest friends. It was presented to the Senate Military Affairs Committee on October 22, 1945. Instead of backing a merger of the military services under a single department, the Eberstadt Report recommended coordinating them through a committee system.[10] At the apex of this system stood the National Security Council. Eberstadt's NSC was designed to be a strong, independent, collaborative institution. Rather than merely advising the president, the council would be a "policy-forming" body. It would have statutory responsibility for (1) "formulating and coordinating overall policies in political and military fields"; (2) "assessing and appraising our foreign objectives, commitments and risks" in light of U.S. military capabilities; and (3) advising the president on the combined military budget. This was no small charge. In short, the council was given primary jurisdiction over integrating all U.S. military and foreign policies and influence over Army, Navy, and Air Force Department purse strings. It was, in Eberstadt's words, the "keystone of our organizational structure for national security" (Eberstadt 1945, 7, 35–46).

To ensure action on NSC decisions and recommendations, Eberstadt suggested NSC membership be "at the highest level." The president would serve as the council's chairman. Other members would be the secretaries of state, Army, and Navy and the holders of two new positions—the secretary of the Air Force and the chairman of the National Security Resources Board. In addition, the NSC would be given a nonpartisan, permanent staff of unspecified size, headed by a full-time executive, to prepare agendas, provide data, and distribute the council's conclusions to relevant departments and agencies. To Eberstadt, the staff was critical. It was to be a permanent professional secretariat—*not* appointed by the president—to ensure that the right information reached the right people for the right problem. The nonpartisan staff would provide institutional strength and continuity in an NSC whose membership would naturally change over time (Eberstadt 1945, 37, 50–56).

It should come as no surprise that Eberstadt (and the Navy) publicly championed the looser, coordinate NSC system on the grounds of efficiency and effectiveness. In a section headed "Coordination Versus Unification," Eberstadt argued that a coordinate system would better conform to American democratic ideals, would protect civilian control of the military, and would prevent domination by one military service—all that while improving cooperation between the services and integrating U.S. military and foreign policies (Eberstadt 1945, 35–46).

While Navy officials may have supported Eberstadt's plan in part for these reasons, the report all too conveniently protected naval interests. It preserved direct high-level contact between the Navy secretary and the president. It ensured the Navy's participation in budget decisions. It expanded the Navy's purview to more general foreign policy issues. In fact, Eberstadt's NSC system avoided the one thing we know the Navy—by its own admission—feared most: a unified defense apparatus controlled by a secretary of defense and a chief of staff. It seems evident that whatever its claims and rationales, the Eberstadt Report sought to protect the Navy. The

National Security Council system was the linchpin of Eberstadt's anti-unification scheme.

Despite the Navy's efforts, Truman publicly rejected the NSC system in a special address to Congress on December 19, 1945. He called explicitly for "legislation combining the War and Navy Departments into one single Department of National Defense" to protect American interests and reinforce American leadership in the postwar world. Though he listed nine specific provisions for this proposed legislation, nowhere did the president mention a National Security Council or any such coordinating committee (Truman 1961–66, 1: 546–60).

Truman's address precipitated a period of fierce lobbying by both War and Navy departments. Caraley (1966) notes that "hardly a week went by that a speech by [Secretary of War Robert] Patterson, [Senator Stuart] Symington, or one of the high Army and Army Air Forces generals did not, whatever its nominal subject, also manage to promulgate the War Department 'doctrine' on unification." On February 16, 1946, while a House subcommittee began drafting its version of the president's unification bill, General Lauris Norstad wrote the Army Public Information head that "an extensive press and radio program should now be organized to be touched off at the moment the text of the bill is announced." He even suggested specific editorial "lines" that could be taken (Caraley 1966, 220). The Navy, meanwhile, set up an unofficial Secretary's Committee on Research and Reorganization (SCORER) to push its own point of view through the press, official speeches, and tours of key naval installations. Moreover, in April 1946, Forrestal got the friendly Senate Naval Affairs Committee to hold hearings publicizing the Navy's objections to the president's bill. The Navy's counterproposal, though modified, still centered on a National Security Council system. Forrestal offered instead of a Defense Department a "Director of Common Defense," who would coordinate the military departments in his role as NSC chairman (Caraley 1966, 132).

By mid-May, the Navy's multifaceted publicity campaign had raised the unification debate to a feverish pitch. With his public support faltering, Truman decided he'd had enough.[11] On May 13 he called together Forrestal and Secretary of War Patterson and suggested they work out a compromise unification plan. Within two weeks, Patterson and Forrestal reported agreement on some major issues, including the need for a National Security Council system, the continuation of three autonomous military departments rather than a single Defense Department, and the need for an overall defense coordinator or secretary. The secretary's role, however, remained a major bone of contention (Congressional Quarterly 1965, 245).[12]

Until this point, the NSC and its staff had been a central component of the Navy plan. They had been presented as a replacement for, not a complement to, a unified Defense Department. But on June 15, 1946, Truman changed the game. In his second unification plan presented to Congress, the president recommended *both* a single Defense Department and a National Security Council system (Truman 1961–66, 2: 306–8). It was a clever move, intended to placate the Navy while steering clear of its antimerger proposal.

The Navy's response is telling: rather than welcome Truman's acceptance of the NSC, Forrestal and his colleagues stepped up their opposition to the president's unification plan. Four days after Truman's announcement, Forrestal called on the president and threatened to resign if his proposal went forward (Donovan 1977, 201). It seems the Navy was far less interested in the NSC system for its own sake than in what it could do for the Navy.

Forrestal now shifted his attention away from the NSC system to the two provisions that most threatened the Navy's power and integrity: the establishment of a new Defense Department and the future status of the Marine Corps and naval aviation. Exchanging letters with the president over the summer of 1946, Forrestal succeeded in wresting major concessions on these points.[13]

By February 1947, Forrestal and the Navy had all but forgotten about the National Security Council system. Indeed, when the Budget Bureau jumped into the unification fray at the eleventh hour, suggesting major changes to the president's NSC provisions, the Navy did nothing.[14] The Budget Bureau managed to strip the National Security Council of its policy-making authority, reducing it to a purely advisory body. More important, it removed all authoritative NSC functions from the statute. The council was now limited to "making recommendations to the President" and performing even basic activities (such as coordinating overall policies) at his direction. Budget officials even removed statutory reference to the president's right to meet with the council, making it far easier for the president to ignore NSC decisions and recommendations. Yet Forrestal and Admiral Forrest Sherman, deputy chief of naval operations, both summarily approved these new provisions. As George Elsey noted, "Sherman and Forrestal O.K. . . . This is a great concession by them" (quoted in Sander 1972, 378–80). With the Navy's approval, Truman made the changes and submitted his fourth and final unification proposal to Congress on February 26, 1947.[15]

In the next five months, the National Security Act made its way through Congress with relatively few changes. In the Senate, the Armed Services Committee reported a more detailed unification bill (S. 758) by a unanimous vote. Senate floor debate, described by Caraley as "not very exciting," lasted two days and resulted in only one amendment, a minor change in wording accepted without debate. The bill passed easily by voice vote. In the House, the Expenditures Committee hearings opened a torrent of rank-and-file Navy objections, but the committee, determined to report its unification bill, essentially passed a Senate counterpart with some additional provisions protecting the Marines and naval aviation. After two days of floor debate, the House passed H.R. 4214 with seven amendments, the most significant of which defined the functions of the Navy in greater detail and eliminated the requirement for individual services to show their annual budget requests. After three days of Conference Committee discussion, both chambers approved the National Security Act by voice vote with little debate (Congressional Quarterly 1965, 249; Caraley 1966, 168–80; Hartmann 1971, 68–69). The final National Security Council system was identical to Truman's proposal in every respect but one: the Senate Armed Services Committee formalized presidential involvement by making the president a statutory member who, when present, would preside over council meetings. Still, nothing in the legislation mandated that the president ever attend or even call such meetings.

What began as the heart of the Navy's anti-unification offensive became, in the end, a largely ignored presidential concession.

Conclusions

Two major conclusions can be drawn from this overview. First, *the executive branch played a principal role in the NSC system's creation* (proposition 1). Between 1943 and 1947, the most heated, protracted, and substantive debates occurred not in congressional committees or even on the House and Senate floors. They took place in the White House, between the War Department, the Navy Department, and the president. The military services and their commander in chief slugged it out—in the press, in congressional hearings, in private negotiating sessions—for four years, going through four presidential unification proposals, while Congress played a far less active role. Though congressional committees drafted and amended legislative proposals, these proposals always came at the president's urging and closely followed his own plans. At one point, the Senate Military Affairs Committee simply added Truman's recommendations to its working draft of the unification bill, marking at the top, "Printed with the amendments of the Senate carrying out the recommendations of the president in his letter to Senator Thomas of Utah of June 15" (U.S. Senate 1946, 214). Even congressional hearings were held at the behest, or at least the approval, of the War and Navy departments.[16]

Substantively, Congress did not shape the National Security Act nearly as much as other political players did. *Congressional Quarterly* notes that the House and Senate bills, "while differing in nomenclature and containing far more detail than proposed, followed the essentials of the Administration request" (Congressional Quarterly 1965, 249). The Senate Armed Services Committee reported its bill, S. 758, with a unanimous vote, and the Senate passed it by voice vote with only one minor amendment. The House passed a similar measure with a few additional provisions by voice vote after minimal debate (Congressional Quarterly 1965, 249; Caraley 1966, 168–80).[17] As for the National Security Council system, Congress gave the administration everything it wanted, with only one modification.

Second, *the formation of the NSC system illustrates how national interest took a back seat to self-interest* (proposition 2). Certainly, broad national concerns were not absent from the debate. Truman, from his presidential vantage point, saw unification as a way to improve the efficiency and effectiveness of the military services at a time of decreasing postwar budgets and increasing international tension (Truman 1956, 46–52; 1961–66, 1: 546–60). In his view, a secretary of defense would be able to devote greater time and resources to keeping interservice competition in check, to eliminating wasteful duplication among the services, and to making the military establishment more receptive to the president's concerns and needs. Under a unified system, the secretary would set standard policies and budgets for all the services. The Army and Navy would no longer be able to run to their congressional allies on the Military and Naval Affairs committees in search of separate budgets, favors, and influence (Caraley 1966, 83–84). Truman also foresaw vast improvements in joint operations from integration, citing the tragic attack on Pearl Harbor as a classic case of poor Army-Navy coordination and collaboration (Truman 1961–66, 1: 547). Finally, he saw a single Defense Department as a valuable means to free himself for other pressing issues. Truman writes: "The President, as Commander in Chief, should not personally have to coordinate the Army and Navy and Air Force. With all the other problems before him, the President cannot be expected to balance either the organization, the training or the practice of the several branches of national defense. He should be able to rely for that coordination upon civilian hands at the cabinet level" (U.S. House 1945, 7). These ideas did not arise uniquely from Harry Truman's personality or outlook. Rather, they stemmed from the demands of the presidency itself. Truman, like anyone else in his shoes, sought ways to make his military more potent, more cost-effective, and more responsive to the needs of the commander in chief.

The president's position, in short, closely approximated what we would expect to find in an ideal realist model of the unification debate. Responding to a new and ever-threatening international environment, the president tried to build a national security apparatus that would centralize foreign policy decision making, rationalize military budgets, and maximize military readiness and responsiveness. Viewed along a simple continuum (see Figure 7), Truman's preference for a wholesale military service merger can be seen at one extreme end of the spectrum. Note that even the War Department favored less service integration than the president did.

The problem was that domestic politics intervened. For the military services, unification meant a zero-sum game of budgets, power, and prestige. Though both the Navy and War departments publicly defended their positions in the name of improved military effectiveness and foreign policy making, the reality was far more selfish. The Navy's NSC system proposal was intended to protect the Navy's preeminence among the services. As Admiral Chester Nimitz confessed in a moment of candor, "I have come to the conclusion that the yardstick by which we should measure any proposal to change our military organization should be, how does it affect our sea

Navy   War   Truman

|--|------------------------|

Status quo: Merger
service autonomy

FIGURE 7.   *Ideal Preference Points in the Unification Debate*

power?" (U.S. Senate 1945, 386). The Navy stood to win only if it could prevent the creation of a central Defense Department. Its NSC-centered, loose committee framework promised to do just that.

If the Navy cared about the NSC system for its own sake, we would have expected two developments during the unification conflict: (1) an end to the Navy's opposition in June 1946, when Truman submitted a new plan that included both an NSC system and a central Department of Defense; (2) a resumption of intense opposition in January 1947, when the Budget Bureau stripped away much of the proposed council's statutory powers. In fact, we find the opposite. In June, the Navy escalated attacks on the president's plan, even though it included a National Security Council and staff. And in January, when confronted with drastic changes to the council, Forrestal and his naval officers did not utter a peep. Once it became clear that the NSC proposal could not forestall unification altogether, the Navy focused on ways of limiting the new defense secretary. It worked for other measures to guard its interest. The NSC system was never the issue.

The War Department, in its support for Truman's unification plan, was no more public-spirited than the Navy. Unification was the Army's best shot at bigger budgets, at fighting the rising dominance of air power, and at preserving its own doctrine of centralized military command. Recognizing the Navy's NSC-centered proposal for what it was—namely, a substitute for unification—the War Department sought ways to get around its more damaging provisions. During compromise negotiations, War Secretary Patterson cleverly decoupled the Navy's proposal for a National Security Council system from its broader anti-unification framework. After quickly assenting to every NSC-related provision, Army representatives dug in their heels on the role of the secretary of defense, the status of naval aviation and the Marines, and the relative autonomy of the three coordinate service branches (Truman 1956, 46–52).

In the end, Truman could not get everything he wanted. The structural realities of American politics made it all but impossible. The president could not simply call upon his formal powers as chief executive, head of state, or commander in chief to integrate and improve the services. Indeed, as Neustadt (1960) argues, cases of unilateral presidential action are rare. In the American system of "separated institutions sharing power," presidents must elicit the cooperation of other political actors to get things done.

In Truman's case, this principal-agent problem was compounded by three specific factors. First, there was no congressional majority early on to dampen military infighting. While vocal minorities gathered on both sides of the unification issue, most legislators preferred to stay uncommitted and undecided until after the executive branch had reached accommodation (Caraley 1966). This should not be surprising. The average member had little to gain by taking a stand before knowing which service would emerge victorious. Especially in the Cold War climate, standing on the losing side posed huge political risks. Losing legislators would be exposed to attacks that they were "soft" on defense or, even worse, communist sympathizers.

Second, the Navy proved a particularly strong political opponent. Navy leaders used every weapon in their bureaucratic arsenal. They capitalized on their expertise advantage by couching their arguments and demands in terms of military effectiveness. They made it clear to Truman and his War Department allies that they would go the distance, that they would resist complete service integration in every way possible. In essence, such obstinacy forced Truman and the War Department to settle for much less than they originally wanted. As Figure 8 illustrates, Forrestal and his sailors succeeded in moving the National Security Act away from the president's ideal point and much closer to their own.

The implicit threat of shirking only added fuel to the Navy's fire. Unification was just one of many important items on Truman's agenda; the president needed Secretary Forrestal's support on a range of questions, from universal military training to Cold War military doctrine. Domestic political problems exacerbated the situation. With threats of massive railroad, coal, and steel strikes, with plummeting approval ratings, and with reelection looming, the president needed all the help he could get.[18] As Robert Donovan writes, "In the midst of the angry controversies that were already swirling over labor troubles in the coal mines and the railroads, as well as over the

Navy   National Security Act   War   Truman

|----------------------X--------------------------------|---------------|

Status quo: Merger
service autonomy

FIGURE 8. *A Picture of Navy Influence: Locating the National Security Act Among Actors' Ideal Preference Points*

extension of OPA [Office of Price Administration], the exit of the man who had led the navy through its greatest days would have strained the Truman administration" (Donovan 1977, 201). Truman could not fire Forrestal, and he certainly could not afford to let his antagonism against the naval secretary fester over the unification issue. Seen in this context, the price of forcing unification on an unwilling Navy seemed high indeed.

The Navy Department also benefited from a massive and multifaceted publicity campaign. Using congressional hearings, newspaper editorials, public speeches, and other overt lobbying tools, the department voiced its opposition to anyone who would listen. In one important episode, Secretary Forrestal managed to stall Senate consideration of a key unification bill by getting it referred to a friendly Naval Affairs Committee for additional hearings. During the April 1946 hearings, every one of the nineteen Navy witnesses testified that unification would severely injure the Navy's military strength.[19] Such strident, public objections of naval officers and civilian officials carried great weight in Congress and in public opinion; these officials were, after all, the most credible sources to assess the effects of unification on sea-based fighting capabilities. The hearings and the negative press they created did the trick. Growing concerned about Truman's weakening support among the public and the Congress, White House officials made their first major move toward a compromise plan (Congressional Quarterly 1965, 245; Truman 1956, 46–52; Donovan 1977, 201).

Third and relatedly, Harry Truman was particularly constrained by public opinion because he was known to harbor strong Army sympathies. As George Elsey, assistant naval aide in the White House, wrote to White House Counsel Clark Clifford, "It is being assumed publicly that the President has become a partisan of the Army against the navy, that he has developed prejudices against the navy which cause him to disregard naval wishes and that he will force the navy into a single Department of Defense which will be dominated by the Army and Air Forces" (Elsey Papers, Box 82, Unification folder, quoted in Caraley 1966, 140).

By the summer of 1946, public perceptions that he was siding with the Army and muzzling the Navy had greatly eroded the president's public support. After a series of press conferences in which Truman blasted the Navy for "lobbying" and demanded its acceptance of his unification policy, a majority of U.S. newspapers came out against the president. Notably, most of them had originally supported Truman's unification plan (Caraley 1966, 145).[20]

For Truman, victory required much more than just issuing an executive order or persuading a few bureaucrats to change their ways. It demanded nothing short of legislation for an issue that drew no natural congressional majority, that gave military expertise great influence, that elicited staunch naval opposition from the outset, and that attracted unusual public interest.

Consequently, Truman—and the Navy—settled for partial success. The president and his War Department allies got their secretary of defense but no corresponding Defense Department. They succeeded in creating a permanent Joint Chiefs of Staff but failed to get a single military commander to exercise decisive leadership over the other chiefs. They established a system that appeared unified in name but was decentralized in substance; the Army, Navy, and Air Force would each be administered primarily by its own service secretary, who had full Cabinet status and a great deal of administrative autonomy.

The Navy retained considerable independence, but still had to contend with a new defense secretary who had enough power to make life difficult. At a minimum, establishing this "principal assistant to the President in all matters relating to the national security" placed an adviser between the individual service secretaries and the president on a number of key issues, including budget appropriations. Forrestal also got a National Security Council, but a far different one than he had envisioned. Instead of a central policy-making body to institutionalize the Navy's power, the National Security Council became a purely advisory council that pitted the Navy against two powerful new players: the defense secretary and the glamorous new Department of the Air Force. Without policy-making authority, without express statutory powers, without a congressionally confirmed executive secretary, and without clear service independence, the NSC came nowhere close to Eberstadt's original vision.

In sum, new institutionalism goes a long way toward explaining why the various political actors behaved in the ways they did, and why the National Security Council system emerged as a result. Contrary to the conventional wisdom, the NSC system was not foisted on a reluctant Harry Truman by a public-spirited Congress. Instead, it was, as Anna Kasten Nelson notes, a "creature of compromise" (Nelson 1981, 231). What began as a self-interested ploy by the Navy to stave off unification ultimately became a forgotten concession by the president. Interest groups and legislators did not play big parts in this process. They did not have to. In the face of unification, the military services had plenty of reasons to jump into the political battle.

Evolution of the National Security Council System: "From King's Ministers to Palace Guard"

The NSC system did not stay on the sidelines for long. Between 1947 and 1963, Presidents Truman, Eisenhower, and Kennedy each took steps that ultimately produced a national security apparatus that differed radically from the one set out in the National Security Act. By the time of Kennedy's assassination, the locus of foreign policy making had moved from the Cabinet to the White House—in Leslie Gelb's words, from the "king's ministers" to his "palace guard" (Gelb 1980, 26). The president, his national security adviser, and the NSC staff had taken the lead in formulating policy, in negotiating with foreign governments, and in managing the daily affairs of state. This rise of the informal NSC staff paralleled the decline of the formal, statutory National Security Council. As the NSC staff grew from a purely administrative, coordinating secretariat to a powerful presidential policy staff, the council itself fell into relative disuse. By 1963, the organization that held what Eisenhower had called "the most important weekly meeting of the government" had become a shadow body, legitimating decisions that were debated and decided elsewhere. An altogether different national security system had emerged—one whose essential features have remained unchanged to the present day.

Though few scholars dispute this transformation, most discount it, focusing instead on how each president remakes the national

In short, the original statutory provisions laid out a foreign policy–making system designed to ensure active participation by the Cabinet. It was to be centered on the statutory National Security Council and administered by a secretarial NSC staff. While Cabinet officers and the president would discuss policy options and issues within the council, the executive secretary and his NSC staff would make sure that the right papers got to the right people at the right time.

When Truman took charge of the NSC system in the summer of 1947, however, much was still unclear, unsaid, and unsettled. How active would the council—and hence the Cabinet—be in deciding foreign policy issues? Would council meetings be decision-making forums or merely discussion sessions between the president and his key foreign policy Cabinet officers? Would the executive secretary serve the council or the president? Would policy advice and formulation be dominated by the new secretary of defense or by the State Department? Would the NSC focus on long-term or more day-to-day national security needs?

In deciding these and other questions, President Truman took the first, critical steps toward personalizing and presidentializing the NSC system. Viewing the council as a potential threat to his own foreign policy prerogatives, Truman seized the recommendations of a Budget Bureau memo that discussed how to prevent the council from gaining "power over" the president (James E. Webb to Truman, Aug. 8, 1947, Webb Papers). In memos and meetings, the president made clear that the NSC was *"his* Council" (Forrestal 1951, 320; emphasis his), that it possessed no policy-making or supervisory authority, and that its executive secretary reported to him (Sander 1972, 336). To emphasize the advisory nature of the council, Truman stayed away from its formal sessions, attending only 12 of the first 57 meetings. Finally, as an added safeguard against military domination of the NSC system, Truman declined the offer of Forrestal, now defense secretary, to house the NSC staff in the Pentagon, placing it instead in the Executive Office Building—just across the street from the White House.

Prompted by the outbreak of the Korean war and an internal investigation of the NSC process, Truman initiated a second round of changes in 1949–50. These changes bolstered both the formal National Security Council and the informal NSC staff. On one hand, Truman strengthened the council by directing it to hold regular weekly meetings and to consider all major matters of national security. To enhance discussion, he limited NSC attendance to a manageable size. And to signal his support for the council, Truman frequently presided over its sessions (Nelson 1981, 241–42; Falk 1964, 412–17).[2]

On the other hand, the president made some significant changes to the NSC staff. In August 1949 he insulated the staff from Congress and enhanced its status by officially placing it in the Executive Office of the President (EOP).[3] Soon thereafter, Truman reorganized the staff system entirely, replacing the inattentive, department-based "staff consultants" with a more active "senior staff" composed of representatives formally nominated from each of the NSC member departments, as well as from the Joint Chiefs of Staff, the Treasury Department, and the CIA. He also eliminated the old position of "staff coordinator"—a post that had previously been filled by a State Department official—transferring its responsibilities to the NSC executive secretary. This was a major move. As Stanley Falk notes, the executive secretary now had "an intimate view of the President's opinions and desires that he could bring to bear quite early in the planning process" (Falk 1964, 415).

To be sure, Truman's executive secretary, Admiral Sidney Souers, was no Henry Kissinger. And the Truman NSC system was still a far cry from the presidential, personal, White-House centered system that took shape during the Kennedy years. It is certainly true that Truman's various secretaries of state—James Byrnes, George Marshall, and Dean Acheson—played the commanding foreign policy role in his administration. It is also true that the president turned toward the entire NSC system with great reluctance and hesitation, and that Souers saw his own role as that of honest broker, transmitting presidential and department views rather than working to influence them (Souers 1949). At the same time, however, the president made choices about his NSC and NSC staff that set valuable precedents.

If Truman set up the NSC system, Dwight Eisenhower is best known for institutionalizing it. According to traditional accounts, Eisenhower moved quickly to increase the council's role and to make it the centerpiece of an elaborate, highly structured committee network. The revamped NSC met far more regularly and for longer periods of time than its predecessor.[4] Sitting on top of "policy hill,"[5] the Eisenhower National Security Council considered policy papers only after they had been thoroughly prepared by an interdepartmental Planning Board of assistant secretary–level officials. On the implementation side, presidentially approved policies flowed down from the NSC to the Operations Coordinating Board (OCB) of undersecretary-level officials and then to the relevant departments and agencies. The OCB was clearly the operational linchpin. Charged with translating policy recommendations into specific guidance, the OCB coordinated a multitude of interdepartmental working groups—typically, 35 to 40 at any given time—and often took as long as six months to determine an operational plan (Cutler 1956; Nelson 1981, 248; Destler, Gelb, and Lake 1984). With so many layers, committees, and council meetings, little wonder the Eisenhower NSC came to be seen as a highly formalized, Cabinet-driven process.

However, this is only part of the story. At the same time that he set up "policy hill," Eisenhower took deliberate steps to control foreign policy making from the White House. Chief among them was the March 1953 creation of a new position, special assistant to the president for national security affairs.[6] Charged with running the council's operations and infusing the policy process with a presidential perspective, the special assistant—or national security adviser, as he later came to be called—was appointed at the president's pleasure, without Senate confirmation. Eisenhower signaled his intention to have "his" man in the job early on;[7] rather than choose a Cabinet official, professional bureaucrat, or policy expert as the first national security adviser, he selected Robert Cutler, an energetic banker and former campaign adviser who had already served on his White House staff (Stevens 1989, 57). The president put Cutler in charge of the NSC Planning Board, ensuring that presidential views would be brought to bear in the earliest phases of the NSC process.[8] Although Cutler was not expected to advocate particular policies or positions, he was expected to ensure that the board presented the president and the NSC with clear, viable policy options.[9] As John Hart writes, by creating the position of national security adviser, "Eisenhower signaled as clearly as any president has done that the NSC system was there to serve the president's purpose" (Hart 1995, 73).

Less known but equally important, Eisenhower created a second position—staff secretary—to handle his day-to-day national security affairs. While the national security adviser oversaw development of longer-term policy in the NSC system, the staff secretary managed the president's paper flow, attended most of his meetings, oversaw sensitive intelligence activities, briefed the president on current developments, and ensured effective policy coordination among the departments and agencies. Tellingly, no report recommended this role, and no directive established it. Fed up with snafus in the policy process, Eisenhower declared one day in 1953 that he did not wish to be his own sergeant major and asked Brigadier General Paul "Pete" Carroll to serve as staff secretary on the spot (Destler 1986, 233). Carroll and his successor, Brigadier General Andrew J. Goodpaster, were more than glorified doormen. Keith Clark and Laurence Legere write in their now-classic history of the NSC system: "Through his daily information and intelligence briefing to the President and his attendance at most of the President's meetings . . . Goodpaster was thoroughly familiar with the President's views and interests, and he served as an active channel for conveying them to the departments and agencies through formal points of contact" (Clark and Legere 1969, 61). With an office in the West Wing of the White House and with the job of running the president's daily national security affairs, Goodpaster essentially played the role later assumed by McGeorge Bundy and his successors (Destler 1986, 234).

Under Eisenhower's direction, the National Security Council staff also developed an autonomous analytical capability for the first time. Noting that "the NSC staff should be strengthened," the president's guiding NSC system directive established "a small Special Staff" with broad jurisdiction and substantial authority. Staff responsibilities included analyzing and amending Planning Board reports before submission to the council, examining "the totality of national security policies with a view to determining if gaps exist," and evaluating "the capabilities of the free world versus the capabilities of the Soviet [bloc]" (Lay 1953). Though Eisenhower made little mention of this superstaff, at least one special assistant found it "indispensable." At the very least, Clark and Legere conclude, the existence of the Special Staff provided the president with an "independent source of analysis of departmental recommendations" (Clark and Legere 1969, 64–65).

Finally, more recently released archival material suggests that Eisenhower supplemented formal National Security Council meetings with a host of informal mechanisms. Studies reveal that on major foreign policy issues—such as Indochina in 1954, the Suez crisis in 1956, and Lebanon in 1958—the president made key decisions after informal Oval Office meetings with trusted advisers (Neustadt 1970, 103–6; Nelson 1983, 315–18; Destler, Gelb, and Lake 1984, 176; Burke and Greenstein 1989, 57, 59; Prados 1991, 81–85). Moreover, throughout his administration, the president spoke regularly with his secretary of state by telephone, and met often with defense and intelligence officials in the Oval Office, with his staff secretary taking notes (Nelson 1983, 324). As Destler concludes, "the findings of scholars on most specific issues suggest overwhelmingly that Eisenhower made his major policy choices as all other Presidents have made them—after informally organized, Oval Office consultations with those members of his administration whom he trusted personally and/or whose involvement was critical to these specific issues" (Destler 1986, 232). Eisenhower relied on the formal National Security Council far less than he claimed.

All of this suggests that Eisenhower's institutionalization of the NSC system masks important developments in the opposite direction. While the president held an unprecedented number of NSC meetings, he frequently made critical policy decisions outside of the council. While he established an extensive network of interdepartmental committees, he placed his special assistant for national security affairs in charge of the two most important ones and authorized a special NSC staff to stand watch over the system, pointing out gaps, analyzing papers, and amending policy recommendations. Like Truman before him, Eisenhower made organizational choices that gave public preeminence to Cabinet-centered policy making but that also worked behind the scenes to presidentialize, personalize, and centralize the system.

John F. Kennedy accelerated these trends in three respects. First and foremost, he vastly expanded the role of the national security adviser. He did so by merging the Eisenhower-era jobs of national security adviser and staff secretary—in essence, placing overall responsibility for *both* long-term foreign policy formulation and daily foreign policy management with a single individual. As Destler notes, the job "now had enormous potential for engagement and influence" (Destler 1981c, 267),[10] because it combined the formerly separate roles of coordinating interagency decision making and providing personal staff assistance to the president. Kennedy's appointment of McGeorge Bundy to the post was telling. As a Harvard junior fellow at age 22 and dean of the Harvard Arts and Sciences faculty at 34, Bundy was known for his towering intellect and boundless self-confidence. In the words of one Harvard observer at the time, "Bundy is a take-over guy. They say [Harvard President Nathan] Pusey was glad to see him go. He'll take over in Washington, too" (Wise 1961).[11]

A second change stemmed directly from the first. Under Bundy, the NSC staff became a truly presidential foreign policy staff for the first time. Whereas previous staffs had concentrated on the technical aspects of managing the NSC process, Bundy's team was concerned almost exclusively with developing policies and providing advice for the president. Rather than serve as the executive branch's professional bureaucrats, they served as Kennedy's personal advisers. As the senior NSC staff aide Roy Komer recalled in 1964, "Kennedy made it very clear we were his men, we operated for him, we had direct contact with him. This gave us the power to command the kind of results that he wanted" (quoted in Destler 1980b, 579). The staff now reached far beyond simply transmitting departmental views, amending interdepartmental committee reports, and filling in gaps. They provided independent analysis, recommended specific courses of action, generated policy ideas, and acted as the president's eyes and ears in the foreign policy bureaucracy.[12] Eisenhower's staff provided a small stream of independent analysis; Kennedy's let open the floodgates.

Third, accompanying the rise of the NSC staff came a sharp downgrading of the formal council. Although Truman and Eisenhower both used extra-NSC meetings and conversations to make policy decisions, Kennedy used such ad hoc, informal mechanisms to an unprecedented degree. In a 1961 interim report about the NSC system to Senator Henry Jackson, Bundy remarked rather euphemistically, "The NSC meets less often than it did. . . . Much that used to flow routinely to the weekly meetings of the Council is now settled in other ways" (Bundy to Jackson, Sept. 4, 1961, in Inderfurth and Johnson 1988, 106). Whereas Truman averaged an NSC meeting every two weeks and Eisenhower averaged one every ten days, Kennedy's council typically met just once a month.[13] Moreover, the meetings themselves were seldom significant forums of policy debate or decision. As Theodore Sorensen writes, "At times [Kennedy] made minor decisions in full NSC meetings or *pretended* to make major ones actually settled earlier. . . . He strongly preferred to make all major decisions with far fewer people present, often only with the officer to whom he was communicating the decision" (Sorensen 1965, 284; emphasis his).

It is worth noting that in May 1961, immediately after the Bay of Pigs disaster, two additional changes were instituted that had lasting effects on the NSC system: Bundy's office was moved from the Old Executive Office Building to the West Wing of the White House, and a new communications center, the Situation Room, was constructed in the White House basement. Both of these changes increased the president's control of foreign policy making considerably, allowing him more direct contact with his closest foreign policy adviser and enabling him to monitor for the first time the outgoing cable traffic of the departments and agencies.

In any case, by the time Kennedy was assassinated in 1963, a new, modern NSC system had been put in place—a system that hardly resembled the one originally created by the National Security Act.

Hallmarks of the Modern NSC System

Three major hallmarks distinguish the modern NSC system from the old one. First, the national security adviser has evolved from a purely administrative executive secretary servicing the council's needs to a powerful political presidential adviser. Whereas Truman's executive secretary faithfully transmitted departmental issues and analyses to the president and Eisenhower's special assistant occasionally offered his own opinion, McGeorge Bundy and his successors have clearly seen themselves as the president's men; they have engaged in policy debates, offered policy advice, and managed the NSC process in ways that serve the particular political interests of the president and no one else. Beginning with the Kennedy administration, all national security advisers have had offices in the White House, close to the Oval Office. All have enjoyed frequent informal contact with the chief executive.[14] And all have played a central role in designing and articulating the administration's foreign policy. Today's national security advisers certainly view themselves differently than their pre-Kennedy predecessors did. Whereas Sidney Souers, the first executive secretary, saw himself as an "anonymous servant of the *Council*" (Souers 1949, 537; emphasis mine), Clinton's first-term national security adviser, Anthony Lake, described his job as making sure "that the *president* is getting all points of view" (emphasis mine). Lake confessed that such views typically included his own. "If you don't have views, you shouldn't be doing the job," he told an interviewer (Jason DeParle, *New York Times Magazine*, Aug. 20, 1995).[15]

A second feature of the modern National Security Council system follows from the first. The rise of the national security adviser has increased the power, jurisdiction, and capabilities of the NSC staff. As Bert Rockman describes, the NSC staff has moved from "a once-anonymous role . . . to a prominent contender for policy-making power in foreign affairs" (Rockman 1981, 914). Whereas early staffs consisted almost entirely of apolitical career bureaucrats on loan from other departments and agencies, modern NSC staffs feature a mix of bureaucrats and fast-track, independent academics. All are appointed at the pleasure of the president and are expected to view foreign policy from his perspective.[16] Dependent on the president for their positions, power, and policy successes, NSC staffers have more than lived up to the job. As Henry Kissinger observes, "every president since Kennedy seems to have trusted his White House aides more than his Cabinet" (Kissinger 1979, 47).

Moreover, Kennedy and his successors have allowed and even encouraged the NSC staff's dominance by expanding its jurisdiction and bolstering its capabilities. Under Truman and Eisenhower, the NSC staff was limited to overseeing long-term policy planning; day-to-day national security affairs were not in its domain. Since 1961, however, this distinction has become blurred. NSC staffs now routinely handle long-term planning as well as the more immediate business of national security—managing crises, clearing cables, and preparing state visits. Part of the reason NSC staffs now do these things is that they can. Kennedy's creation of the Situation Room after the Bay of Pigs gave the president and his aides complete access to CIA, State Department, and Defense Department cables for the first time.[17] This proved critical in controlling the bureaucracy. NSC staffers could find out exactly how, and how much, department officials were implementing the president's directives. The Situation Room also enabled the president to communicate with U.S. embassies without the State Department's knowledge and to conduct negotiations with foreign diplomats in secret. By enabling the president to bypass regular channels, this new communications center allowed the president to be his own secretary of state. Not surprisingly, every president since Kennedy has kept the Situation Room in good working order.[18]

Third, the modern NSC system is marked by a pronounced decline in the role of the formal National Security Council. As Destler wrote in 1977, "The council itself has increasingly been treated as a bore, if not an encumbrance" (159). The NSC has not met on a prolonged, regular weekly basis since the Eisenhower administration. Presidents have instead turned to the NSC staff and to a host of informal meetings with relevant Cabinet members to solicit information, analysis, and advice. Kennedy is perhaps best known for his persistent use of ad hoc working groups, task forces, and other arrangements. As he declared, "We have averaged three or four meetings a week with the Secretaries of Defense and State, McGeorge Bundy, the head of the CIA and the Vice President, but formal meetings of the National Security Council which include a much wider group are not as effective" (quoted in Sorensen 1965, 284). Though no president since him has relied so extensively on informal arrangements, each has used some key informal mechanisms to work outside the formal National Security Council. Lyndon Johnson's Tuesday lunches, the Kissinger-Nixon channel, Jimmy Carter's Friday breakfasts, Ronald Reagan's National Security Planning Group—each of these has served as a prime foreign policy channel: the president invited whomever he wished, written records were sparse, leaks were low, and discussions and decisions did not have the formal stamp of a regular NSC meeting.

Changes made in the essential features of the NSC system are outlined in Figure 9. Taken together, these hallmarks reveal a modern NSC system that has steadily drawn foreign policy–making power away from the Cabinet departments and into the White House. It is the president and his national security adviser, not the secretary of state, who serve as the principal architects of U.S. foreign policy. Indeed, the names of most secretaries of state since 1961 are difficult to recall. Dean Rusk, William Rogers, Cyrus Vance—each of them was overshadowed by the more domineering personality of his national security adviser counterpart. Reagan's two secretaries of state—Alexander Haig and George Shultz—are better known for their complaints about being shut out of foreign policy decisions than for their influence over them. Although James Baker, Bush's secretary of state, stands as the exception to this rule, Warren Christopher's role in the Clinton administration should quell any speculation that the secretary of state has achieved anything resembling a comeback. The palace guard has, indeed, eclipsed the king's ministers.

Hallmark	Pre-Kennedy System	Modern System
NSC staff head	• Administrative, professional; executive secretary	• Political, policy-oriented; national security adviser
	• Neutral coordinator between council and president; responsible for faithfully transmitting ideas, policies	• President's personal staff assistant; responsible for transmitting, assessing, and advocating ideas, policies
NSC staff	• Department detailees who view national security from home agency perspective	• Mix of detailees and outside experts, all of whom are appointed at the president's pleasure and view national security from his perspective
	• Limited power; jurisdiction restricted to long-range affairs, planning; no independent monitoring capability of other agencies; president must use official channels for negotiations	• Substantial power; broad jurisdiction encompassing the full range of near, immediate, and long-term affairs; Situation Room enables staff to monitor other agencies and implement policy from White House
National Security Council	• Central forum for policy discussion	• Marginal forum; infrequent meetings; used mostly to ratify decisions made elsewhere

FIGURE 9. *Pre-Kennedy and Modern Security Council Systems*

Explaining Evolution the Conventional Way

For students of national security, the steady refrain has long been that the council and its staff vary according to the person they serve; the system responds to and reflects each president's personality, policy preferences, and operating style. As I. M. Destler writes, the NSC system is "at the mercy of particular Presidents, to be used, reshaped, or ignored as they prefer" (Destler 1977, 160). This is a story of variance. Since different presidents can design the system in different ways, its structure, operation, and power are always up for grabs.

If this explanation is correct, then we would expect to see two things when we look at the NSC system's development. First, the essential features of the system should vary across presidential administrations. Jimmy Carter, after all, was no Richard Nixon. Second, barring any major crisis or scandal, we should find little variation in the NSC system *within* a presidential administration. Presidents may tinker here and there, fine-tuning the foreign policy process, but that is about all. Presumably the system's basic determinants—the president's personality, operating style, habits, and views—do not radically change in four to eight years.

But this is not what we find. A look across administrations reveals a pattern of continuity, not change. Although each post-Kennedy president has modified the foreign policy process, none has successfully altered the system's three essential features. Instead, presidents with very different personalities, proclivities, and policies have handled national security affairs in the same manner.

Consider Richard Nixon and Jimmy Carter. By all measures, these two presidents stood worlds apart. Nixon, a Republican, approached foreign policy with hard-nosed realism. Carter, a Democrat, elevated human rights—the "search for justice and peace"—as the cornerstone of U.S. foreign policy (Carter 1995, 22). Nixon was a grand strategist. Carter was a micromanager, insisting on approving every government-to-government arms sale reported to Congress (Gelb 1980, 33). Whereas Nixon's operating style favored secrecy, Carter's favored openness. Nixon freely engaged in illegal activities, from wiretapping his own staff to obstructing the Watergate investigation. Carter's openly proclaimed religiosity and moral conviction pervaded all aspects of his presidency.[19]

Yet both presidents ended up employing remarkably similar national security policy–making systems. Both chose strong-willed, outspoken academics to be their national security advisers. To an unprecedented degree, Henry Kissinger and Zbigniew Brzezinski served as powerful policy advocates and administrative spokesmen. They drafted broad strategic policies, recommended specific courses of action on issues ranging from China to the Iranian hostage crisis, directly participated in international negotiations, and defended the administration's policy before the press. With over 1,700 appearances in the *New York Times* between them—more than all other national security advisers combined—Brzezinski and Kissinger stand as the most public, most recognized national security advisers in history.[20] The Kissinger and Brzezinski systems were not identical, but they had much in common: these two national security advisers and their staffs dominated the foreign policy process to a degree unmatched by any NSC staff before or since. In both administrations, major issues were decided far away from the State Department, the Defense Department, and the National Security Council.[21]

Moreover, when we look within administrations, we find far more change than we would expect. All presidents since Kennedy may have ended up using the modern National Security Council system, but not all of them started out that way. In particular, Presidents Carter and Reagan entered office with a deep-seated and well-publicized commitment to Cabinet government—to the notion that foreign policy should be run out of the Department of State instead of the White House and the NSC staff. Yet both presidents soon jettisoned these experiments.

Carter expressed his desire to renew the Cabinet-centered foreign policy system from the outset. During the 1976 presidential campaign, he made a point of castigating Kissinger's Lone Ranger style of foreign policy–making and pledged to end the excessive centralization and secrecy that characterized the Nixon years (Brzezinski 1985, 58). There was no mistaking the president's intentions. The president selected Secretary of State Cyrus Vance and the rest of his Cabinet before naming his White House team. During the transition, the president, Secretary Vance, and National Security Adviser Brzezinski agreed that Vance would serve as the principal foreign policy adviser, with Brzezinski and the NSC staff playing less prominent, coordinating roles.[22] On Inauguration Day, Carter issued a presidential directive that dismantled the Nixon NSC system, established a new one, and explicitly declared, "The reorganization is intended to place more authority in the departments and agencies while insuring that the NSC, with my Assistant for National Security Affairs, continues to integrate and facilitate foreign and defense policy decisions" (Carter 1977b, 1).[23]

Yet within a matter of months, this Cabinet government experiment had failed and faded to a distant memory. Vance's reluctance to articulate the administration's policy left the door open for

Brzezinski to play a more active, public role—a move that Carter encouraged and Brzezinski readily accepted.[24] It was Brzezinski who appeared on television, gave interviews, and served as the administration's major spokesman. Internally, too, Brzezinski and the NSC staff increasingly controlled the foreign policy–making process. In the rush of events and in the face of the State Department's reluctance to offer political solutions with the president's interests at heart, Carter turned more and more to his NSC staff for ideas and policy options (Gelb 1980; *Washington Quarterly* 1982). On issues ranging from U.S.-Soviet relations to the Iranian hostage crisis to China, Vance and the State Department found themselves routinely outvoted and outmaneuvered by the NSC staff.[25] The NSC staff, not the State Department seventh floor, had the president's ear and spoke with his voice. As Kevin Mulcahy writes, "The irony is that although Carter entered office pledged to oppose the Kissinger model of foreign policymaking, the actual result was the concentration of nearly as much power in the White House as had been the case in the Nixon administration" (Mulcahy 1986, 286).

Like Carter, Ronald Reagan came to Washington with a Cabinet government model in mind.[26] In appointing Alexander Haig as secretary of state, Reagan got a secretary who was exceedingly well versed in foreign affairs, well schooled in White House politics, and well known for taking charge. National Security Adviser Richard V. Allen was no match for Haig, and was not expected to be; in both public speeches and private conversations, Reagan made it clear that "the Secretary of State will be the President's principal spokesman and adviser" (Haig 1984, 12). Judging from press interviews, congressional testimony, and personal memoirs, it seems that Haig and Allen agreed. Haig testified during confirmation hearings that the secretary of state should be the sole "general manager of American diplomacy" (Inderfurth and Johnson 1988, 100). And Allen repeatedly told the press that as national security adviser, he would offload most of the traditional NSC staff responsibilities to the Department of State (*New York Times*, Nov. 19, 1980). He would eschew running the day-to-day business of foreign policy or forging policy initiatives from the White House. Instead, Allen promised to serve as a staff coordinator and honest broker between the Cabinet and the president (Mulcahy 1986, 291; Inderfurth and Johnson 1988, 100; Lord 1988).

Organizational arrangements reflected and reinforced the down-graded role of the national security adviser and his staff. Allen stands as the only national security adviser in history who operated without direct access to the president. He officially reported to White House Counselor Edwin Meese, he worked out of an office in the White House basement, relatively far from the Oval Office, and he soon found that even his daily presidential national security briefings could not be conducted in private. In addition, though no official presidential directive outlining the Reagan NSC system was signed during Allen's tenure, a series of interdepartmental groups and senior interdepartmental groups was established to cover a range of functional and geographic areas. None of them was chaired by the national security adviser or his staff (Melbourne 1983; Haig 1984; Mulcahy 1986; Lord 1988; Meese 1992; Hart 1995).

This foreign policy system did not last long. As Brent Scowcroft notes, "After the first year, everyone realized it didn't work."[27] At the beginning of 1982, Allen resigned and the administration began restoring the White House–dominated, modern NSC system. Reagan replaced Allen with Judge William Clark, a close personal friend and former chief of staff from his gubernatorial days. The change was dramatic; Clark's relationship with Reagan gave him unlimited access to the president—access that enabled the national security adviser to assume control over long-range policy reviews previously controlled by the State Department, to handle the daily management of key foreign policy issues ranging from Nicaragua to technology transfers, and to bolster the influence and responsibility of the NSC staff. Geoffrey Kemp, a Reagan NSC staffer, described the change from Allen to Clark in these colorful terms:

> I can tell you, the day Richard Allen resigned, the power of the people like myself dramatically increased literally overnight, because of William Clark. Uncle Bill could walk in to see Ronald Reagan any time. . . . [Michael] Deaver [and] Meese used to defer to Uncle Bill. . . . Now that is what power is all about in this town. . . . Essentially, the power of the NSC staff is the capacity to use the president's name and be taken seriously. Now if your opposite numbers in the Pentagon and the State Department and the CIA—I think those are the three examples that I know most about—knew, as they did during the first year of the Reagan administration, that your boss had been downgraded, they treated you in a very different way in terms of answering phone calls and going to meetings, which is what it's all about, right? The moment the Washington press started the stories about "Clark is different," our life was different.[28]

To be sure, the Reagan administration's NSC system never fully recovered from its first year. In fact, Kissinger (1986), Scowcroft,[29] and others argue that the Iran-Contra imbroglio stemmed partly from the continued weakness of the NSC staff.[30] But the point here is that after only one year of operation, the system had already lurched back significantly from the Cabinet government model.

The Carter and Reagan experiments suggest that divergence from the modern NSC system has been short-lived and unsuccessful. Though both presidents entered office with a strong philosophical and political dedication to Cabinet government, both rapidly retreated from the model. More generally, these failed forays into Cabinet government, when coupled with the overall resilience of the modern NSC system across administrations, call conventional explanations into question. In the end, "It depends on the president" does not appear to explain very much. It predicts variance where we find continuity and continuity where we find change. Though individual presidents no doubt matter, coloring particular aspects of the foreign policy–making process, the broad outlines of the system have been remarkably impervious to change. To explain the evolution of the NSC system, then, we must turn not to what makes presidents different but to what makes them alike. We must take a closer look at the options they face, the political opposition they confront, and the benefits they receive in bringing national security policy making into the NSC staff. In short, we need to ask why all presidents since Kennedy have been compelled to use their NSC systems in similar ways.

A New Institutionalist Alternative

As originally set out in Chapter 1, the National Security Agency Model explains agency evolution in terms of three related factors: (1) the agency's original setup; (2) the ongoing interests and capabilities of key political players; and (3) exogenous events. Design choices made at an agency's birth condition its development from that moment forward. Change is not impossible, but evolution is constrained at the outset; initial structural choices make some evolutionary paths more likely while ruling others out. Within these constraints, agencies are shaped by conflict between political actors—presidents, other bureaucrats, and legislators. Whether and how these actors jump into the fray hinges on their relative interests, incentives, and capabilities. Finally, events can at times shift the balance of power between political actors—by raising the stakes, by weakening some or empowering others. We turn to each of these factors in turn.

INITIAL DESIGN: THE NATIONAL SECURITY ACT OF 1947

The NSC-related provisions of the 1947 National Security Act are more remarkable for what they omitted than for what they included. First and foremost, the act did precious little to tie the fortunes of the NSC system to Congress. No members of Congress were included as statutory members of the council or were privy to its discussions. No mechanisms required the National Security Council to report to, consult with, or even notify Congress of its activities and deliberations. No NSC staff member was subject to Senate confirmation or was required to testify before any congressional body. Under the law, presidents did not even have to use the NSC system. They were not required to hold or attend council meetings. In short, the National Security Act provided Congress with few levers, short of freezing funds or passing new legislation, to shape the National Security Council or its staff. As Kennedy's national security adviser, McGeorge Bundy, described the NSC system, "Congress can't get into it. That's the most interesting thing about it."[31]

In addition, the act granted statutory legitimacy to the idea of a National Security Council staff. No matter that the staff was originally intended to serve as a purely administrative secretariat. The actual legislation only vaguely provided for an NSC staff to "perform such duties as may be prescribed by the Council in connection with the performance of its functions." Given that the council's functions were themselves subject to presidential discretion and authority, this was hardly a ringing mandate for a council-controlled administrative unit. More important, the act called for the staff "to be headed by a civilian executive secretary who shall be appointed by the President" (*U.S. Statutes at Large* 1948, 497). No Senate confirmation was required. Taken together, the positive provisions created statutory grounds for the president to appoint an NSC staff of his choosing, while the ambiguities and gaps left much room for him to use the NSC staff as he wished.

Finally, the act implicitly recognized and reaffirmed presidential prerogatives in foreign affairs. The council could advise on national security matters and issue assessments of them, but it could not decide them. The act made clear that the president and the president alone bore responsibility for forging U.S. foreign policy (*U.S. Statutes at Large* 1948, 496–97).

No doubt, part of the reason for these provisions—or lack thereof—was constitutional. The president's powers as commander in chief and chief executive grant him extensive prerogatives in foreign affairs and wide latitude to choose his own counselors and personal assistants. It is also true that more restrictive provisions might not have made much difference; presidents still might have been able to use, transform, or discard the NSC system as they saw fit. At the very least, however, the National Security Act threw up few roadblocks for presidents to overcome. The legislation gave presidents substantial room to maneuver, permitting them to appoint their own foreign policy staffs without much fear of congressional scrutiny or punishment.

ONGOING INTERESTS AND CAPABILITIES OF POLITICAL ACTORS

The National Security Act provided an opening for presidents to transform the foreign policy system. The constellation of interests and capabilities among presidents, bureaucrats, and the Congress made it possible—indeed, likely—that such change would take place. Presidents had both the motivation and the capabilities to command the changes they desired. Though the departments of Defense and State certainly tried to block these efforts, they ultimately could not succeed for two reasons. First, presidents would not let them; on this issue, presidents were willing to go to the mat because the price of failure—of maintaining an unresponsive, inertial foreign policy system—far exceeded the cost of success. Second, because presidents could act unilaterally through executive orders and decision memoranda, bureaucratic opposition was more easily surmounted. Congress, for its part, lacked both the drive and the weapons to combat these changes. Once the National Security Act was passed, legislators had little to gain by getting involved in the intricacies of national security decision-making operations. Perhaps more important, the National Security Act tied their own hands in key respects. Short of passing new legislation, there was not much legislators could do to prevent presidents from getting what they wanted.

Presidents. Two basic forces have compelled all postwar presidents to pull the locus of foreign policy making into the White

House and the hands of the NSC staff. First, presidents of all stripes have been held responsible for things they cannot possibly control. In Terry Moe's words, "The expectations surrounding presidential performance far outstrip the institutional capacity of presidents to perform" (Moe 1985, 269). Nowhere has this fact of life been more evident than in postwar foreign affairs. When it comes to domestic issues such as tax cuts and environmental policy, presidents can point fingers and shift the blame to other actors—Congress, interest groups, and the press, to name a few. But in foreign affairs, success or failure often clings to the president alone.[32]

Postwar developments have exacerbated the situation. The Cold War's onset raised both the stakes and the complexity of foreign policy issues to new heights. Suddenly American presidents had to contend with the specter of nuclear confrontation over regions as remote as Israel and Vietnam. In addition, revolutionary developments in communications and transportation demanded real-time responses to international crises. No longer could American presidents rest content in geographic and philosophical isolation. To do their jobs well, chief executives needed more information, more analysis, more advice than ever before. Ideally, they needed a bureaucracy that could see the world as they did, that possessed sophisticated knowledge across the foreign policy spectrum but kept presidential interests at heart.

The National Security Act of 1947 solved only part of the president's problem. The act expanded the foreign policy apparatus without granting the president sufficient means to control it. While new departments and agencies such as the Central Intelligence Agency, the Department of Defense, and the National Security Resources Board vastly increased the amount of information and advice coming to the president, these organizations filtered such information through self-interested prisms. It is no secret that bureaucracies have their own agendas, missions, cultures, routines, and ways of viewing the world. As one Bush NSC staffer put it, "There is not an institution in this town that does not ride its own ax and transmit messages as it perceives . . . its interests."[33] One need not impute sinister motives here. The simple fact is that the resources, goals, and incentives of various agencies all differ from the president's. Thus enlargement of the foreign policy apparatus proved to be a mixed blessing. Creating so many new agencies only intensified the cacophony of voices in the president's ear. Although the National Security Council provided a forum where these bureaucratic players could come together, it did not provide a way to coordinate, prioritize, or adjudicate between their views. At the end of the day, there was still no agency or body that could view foreign policy events and decisions from the president's perspective. As Theodore Sorensen suggests in his vivid account of the Kennedy administration, asking the various bureaucracies to step outside their own interests and perspectives was simply asking too much: President Kennedy "knew that, in his administration, Cabinet members could make recommendations on major matters, but only the President could make decisions; and that he could not afford to accept, without seeking an independent judgment, the products and proposals of departmental advisers whose responsibilities did not require them to look, as he and his staff looked, at the government and its programs as a whole (Sorensen 1965, 258).

Little wonder presidents almost immediately began changing the national security system. Charged with leading the United States in an ever more uncertain and dangerous world, held solely responsible for the successes and failures of foreign policy, and assisted by a foreign policy bureaucracy with its own interests and views, presidents had overwhelming incentives to act.

There is a second factor that has prompted presidents to reshape the NSC system and that explains why the system has evolved along its particular path. Shifting the locus of foreign policy making to the NSC staff promised high returns at low cost. Though a modern NSC system did not offer a perfect solution, it did vastly improve policy making from the president's point of view.[34] Because staff members were appointed at the president's pleasure and were dependent on him for their pay, promotions, prestige, and power, they tended to be far more loyal to presidential needs and interests than their bureaucratic counterparts.[35] To a striking degree, NSC staffs from Kennedy to Clinton have viewed themselves as the *president's* staff. As McGeorge Bundy put it, "We were not in the business of having an NSC corporate view. We were in the business of . . . helping the president do his business."[36] In addition, the staff's small size and access to the Oval Office made monitoring relatively easy; a president could discover rather quickly when staffers were not doing their jobs or not acting on his behalf. Armed with rewards, sanctions, and a direct monitoring ability, presidents could trust the NSC staff to weigh and assess the conflicting policy recommendations coming from the foreign policy bureaucracies.

Equally important, transforming the NSC system has been relatively easy to do. The National Security Act made it possible for presidents to institute major changes without new legislation. This is exactly what they did—using executive orders, presidential directives, and other self-executing commands to create the national security adviser's position; to alter fundamentally the NSC staff's role, power, and jurisdiction; and to downgrade the operation of the formal National Security Council. The NSC system's history is striking in this respect: with one exception, every major developmental milestone, every single innovation to the system, has been the product of unilateral presidential action.[37] Though certainly the departments of State and Defense did not welcome such developments, they could do little about them. In this rare case, presidents have possessed the overpowering incentives and sufficient capabilities to overcome bureaucratic opposition single-handedly.

Bureaucrats.   Bureaucrats did not lose the battle without a fight. Officials in the State Department and the newly created Department of Defense had every reason to oppose the transformation of the NSC system. For them, a prominent council meant a prominent Cabinet, which would guarantee each department a roughly equal chance of influencing administration policy. A White House–centered system, by contrast, left both departments on the sidelines. An active, powerful NSC staff not only added another competing source of foreign policy advice but quite literally posed a buffer between the departments and the president, making it more difficult for Cabinet secretaries to air their views or influence the president's decisions.

For bureaucrats, the problem was not incentives but capabilities. In the end, the departments of Defense and State both lacked the institutional power to mount a strong defense, as we can see by viewing the two major phases of bureaucratic opposition to the NSC system. During phase 1—from the act's passage on July 26, 1947, to the first NSC meeting on September 26—the new Department of Defense tried to take command of the council and the foreign policy process. At this point, the NSC staff was not an issue. These critical weeks were a time for determining the operational details of the new foreign policy apparatus. For Defense Secretary James Forrestal, it seemed a golden opportunity to wrest foreign policy power away from the president and Department of State. Forrestal moved quickly to strengthen the council and control its staff—entrenching military influence in the process. He offered to house the NSC staff in the Pentagon and staff it with military officers (Clifford 1991, 163; Sander 1972, 87). He argued that NSC meetings should be chaired by him in the president's absence (Nelson 1981, 234). And he tried to order the NSC executive secretary to take policy action on the council's behalf (Truman 1956, 60). The idea, as Clark Clifford writes, was "to [use] the new NSC system . . . to circumvent the State Department . . . [and] diminish the President's role" (Clifford 1991, 163).[38]

The second phase of bureaucratic opposition has lasted from September 1947 until the present, and has pitted the State Department against the president and his NSC staff. From William Rogers's fight against the Nixon-Kissinger back channels to Cyrus Vance's ill-fated effort to block the attempted rescue of American hostages in Iran, most postwar secretaries of state have waged an uphill battle for foreign policy preeminence. As Rockman writes, "A common perception is that, since the Kennedy administration, policy power has drifted steadily from the State Department to the president's team of foreign policy advisers" (Rockman 1981, 911). Since John F. Kennedy's presidency, State Department–NSC staff competition has provoked the resignations of three secretaries. Even with the relative resurgence of Cabinet government during the Reagan years, Secretary of State George Shultz found it difficult to gain a seat at the foreign policy table, much less an upper hand. "I would have to struggle incessantly to do my job," he noted in his memoirs (Shultz 1993, 313).

Both of these bureaucratic efforts failed—and for the same reason: in this case, the departments of Defense and State lacked the institutional capabilities to win. The military establishment of 1947 was institutionally weak on two counts. First, it did not possess the unity, strength, or authority to compete with the State Department (Nelson 1981). A creature of compromise in the National Security Act, the military emerged with fragmented and confused authority. The act charged the secretary of defense with "general direction, authority, and control" over the individual military services, but at the same time insisted that the departments of the Army, Navy, and Air Force "be administered as individual executive departments by their respective Secretaries" (*U.S. Statutes at Large* 1948, 500). The secretary of defense could not even speak for the military in the National Security Council, because the secretaries of the Army, Navy, and Air Force also sat as statutory members. Without a united front, Forrestal and the military were poorly positioned to take on either the State Department or the president.

Second, the defense secretary failed because in the end, Truman just said no. I have already mentioned the overwhelming incentives for presidents to risk bureaucratic opposition and centralize foreign policy making. Here it is worth noting that Truman did not make up his mind alone. In considering the issues, the president relied heavily on the counsel of the Budget Bureau. Why he did so speaks volumes about the power of bureaucratic location. While Forrestal could be expected to push for parochial interests, the Budget Bureau's position in the Executive Office of the President tied its fate to the institutional presidency. More prerogatives and power for the president meant more authority for the president's office. Truman knew this, and came to see the Budget Bureau as an organization he could trust. As Director James Webb noted, "[Truman] thought we really were there to serve him as the President" (quoted in Nelson 1981, 233).[39] Forrestal, by comparison, could not make a persuasive case that what was good for the Defense Department was good for Truman.

The natural inclination for presidents to trust their own staffs more than their Cabinet departments and agencies also explains why the State Department has been unable to restore much of its power in foreign affairs. The modern NSC staff has strong motivations to act on the president's behalf and to see policy issues from his point of view, but the State Department does not. Its mission is to worry about U.S. diplomatic relations with particular countries, not about how those relations affect domestic politics or the president's reelection prospects.[40] Its organizational structure—posting Foreign Service officers abroad—is designed to develop a wide-ranging knowledge base about foreign affairs. Yet this same structure fosters a tendency for Foreign Service officers to "go native," to identify more with the host country than with the United States. Moreover, the very nature of bureaucracy—its routines, its institutional memory—often makes it the enemy of innovation. Knowing what has been tried before, State Department officials are naturally reluctant to help the next president try again. No wonder presidents have come to view the State Department as an outsider. As Leslie Gelb writes, "Once a president comes to believe that Foggy Bottom is not attuned to politics, they are doomed to being ignored. Once he concludes that his staff has political savvy, that staff is on its way to dominating policymaking" (Gelb 1980, 28).

One final point bears mentioning. In this particular case, because presidents were able to change the NSC system without congressional involvement, the departments of Defense and State could not turn to Congress for support. Without legislation or other legislative action, the bureaucracy could not use congressional levers to push its cause.

Legislators. In the evolution of the NSC system, Congress has been the proverbial dog that did not bark. Members, staffers, and NSC officials all agree on this point: congressional oversight of the National Security Council system has been virtually nonexistent. As Richard Garon, chief of staff for the House International Relations Committee, put it, "We really haven't done that."[41]

A quick glance at history reveals that Congress has not done much either to obstruct or to shape the National Security Council system since 1947. The legislature has amended the NSC provisions of the National Security Act only once—in 1949, at President Truman's request. It has conducted five investigations of the national security policy–making process, none of which have produced any changes to the NSC system. If anything, the two best-known investigations—the Jackson Committee of 1959 and the Iran-Contra hearings of 1986–87—tell us more about Congress's weakness than about its strength. In 1959, President Eisenhower succeeded in pulling the teeth out of the Jackson Committee before it even began—preventing the committee from discussing any substantive national security policies, vetting testimony from past and present government officials, and reminding the committee that he could simply avoid using the National Security Council if it intruded on presidential foreign policy prerogatives.[42]

As for Iran-Contra, the House and Senate select committees produced more show than substance. Though the hearings made for good television, they proceeded slowly, produced little new information, and ultimately played a minor role in changing the Reagan administration's foreign policy system. Far more instrumental in revamping the Reagan NSC system was the president's own bipartisan special review board, the Tower Commission. Charged with clarifying events, pinpointing problems, and recommending improvements to the foreign policy–making process, the commission issued its report in February 1987, well before the House and Senate select committees got fully under way. The commission's speedy work and its attention to improving the system received prominent attention within the Reagan administration. Paul Stevens, the NSC executive secretary at the time, recalls: "The Tower Commission looked at the history of the NSC for insights into how this could happen or how it could be prevented. Congress didn't bother. So it was really the Tower Commission that had the executive branch/the Executive Office of the President institutional perspective on the NSC system, and those were the ones that we were paying closest attention to."[43]

Attention led quickly to action. On March 31, 1987—four months *before* Lieutenant Colonel Oliver North's televised testimony before Congress—Reagan issued a sweeping directive adopting all of the Tower Commission's recommendations and instituting additional changes to the NSC system (Powell 1989; Stevens 1990). By the time Congress weighed in, there was no more overhauling left to do; restructuring the NSC system had become a moot point. Even congressional committee leaders admitted they did not expect their findings to have a substantial impact on the administration (Congressional Quarterly 1990, 268–69).

As with presidents and the bureaucracy, Congress's actions can be explained in large part by its institutional interests and capabilities. On the incentives side, it seems clear that average legislators do not get rewarded for delving into the intricacies of the foreign policy–making system. In fact, most get little benefit from acting on foreign policy matters at all. As one House member put it, "My constituents back home don't care how I vote on Bosnia."[44] On the House side, at least, appointment to the Foreign Affairs Committee is not highly prized. Ranking the committee's popularity somewhere in the middle, one veteran congressional staffer observed, "Members have gotten much more assertive on getting their first committee choice . . . [and] not a lot of members come out and say 'I want Foreign Affairs.'"[45] For these members, overseeing the foreign policy apparatus demands a lot of guts for little glory. At least policy issues such as Bosnia afford an opportunity to grandstand, to appear statesmanlike. But the details of agency design appeal to few interest groups and even fewer voters. Members are not likely to get much political support by vaunting their expertise about the bureaucratic predilections of Foreign Service officers.

On the capabilities side, Congress is woefully ill suited to oversee or change the NSC system. For one thing, oversight jurisdiction in foreign affairs is splintered among a host of committees, from intelligence, to armed services, to foreign affairs, to appropriations.[46] In addition, oversight weapons are poorly matched for the job. Thanks to the 1947 National Security Act, Congress can hold hearings about NSC staff activities but it cannot compel staff members to testify. Nor does it enjoy the right to confirm appointments to the NSC staff. Moreover, although no law prevents Congress from using the power of the purse to influence the NSC system's development, norms and self-interest certainly do. When it comes to personal staffing arrangements, especially in foreign affairs, congressional deference to the executive runs deep. As one senior congressional staffer said, "People of both parties tend to feel that the president ought to have as his advisers the people he wants. . . . They don't like George Bush or whoever it may be, but they step back."[47] Perhaps more to the point, the president's roughly $5 million NSC staff budget pales in comparison with congressional staff allocations.[48] Members know this, and they realize that any showdown over the NSC staff budget is sure to invite closer public scrutiny of their own personal staffs. In any such executive-legislative budget contest, the Congress is bound to lose.

Taken together, the electoral interests of individual members, the initial setup of the National Security Council system, and the collective capabilities of Congress have made it costly and difficult for Congress to influence the development of the NSC system.

Summary. When we survey the constellation of institutional interests and capabilities, we find that presidents have enjoyed a natural advantage over other political actors in shaping the NSC system. They are the only ones who possess both the motives and the means to act unilaterally. The dangers and responsibilities of foreign policy leadership provide strong incentives for presidents to seek control of the foreign policy apparatus—to forge a system that serves their interests, promotes their policies, and sees the world from their political vantage point. What's more, the formal powers of office have enabled them to make these changes alone, even in the face of bureaucratic opposition. Although transformation of the NSC system spelled bad news for bureaucrats, they could do little about it without the president's trust or Congress's support. Bureaucratic expertise and information proved no match for a president bent on creating his own foreign policy staff. Congress, finally, could never get into the game. The National Security Act, the electoral connection, and the institution's own design made discretion the better part of valor.

EVENTS

Though an agency's initial structure may rule some developmental paths out, and though the interests and capabilities of political actors may lead development in a certain direction, not everything is written in stone. In the rough-and-tumble world of politics, crises arise, things happen, interests shift, and possibilities change. It seems reasonable to believe that events in the real world can accelerate, delay, or change the course of agency development.

In this case, foreign policy crises and scandals appear to have reinforced, not reversed, transformation of the NSC system. On a general level, this should not be too surprising; crises, by definition, require fast action and involve high political stakes—they are the stuff of presidential staffs. Scandals, as well, often lead presidents to circle the wagons, to trust the White House staff far more than those on the outside.

But a closer look suggests that three particular events—the Korean war, the Bay of Pigs, and the Iran-Contra affair—have exerted more direct influence on the NSC system's development.

First, the Korean war prompted Harry Truman to initiate a series of changes to the nascent NSC system. Though the reforms worked in two directions—bolstering both the formal NSC process and the informal NSC staff—the greater significance lies in the fact that Truman acted at all. In some sense, the war provided political cover for the president to experiment with his foreign policy machinery. It made tampering with the system politically acceptable.

The Bay of Pigs accelerated the pace of change. Coming early in Kennedy's administration, the failed Cuban invasion highlighted with devastating clarity the need for better White House coordination, better communications, and better military advice. As Arthur M. Schlesinger, Jr., writes, "[Kennedy] took a new view of the White House staff. . . . In the future, he made sure that he had the unfettered and confidential advice of his own people. For our part, we resolved to be less acquiescent the next time. The Bay of Pigs gave us a license for the impolite inquiry and the rude comment" (Schlesinger 1965, 277–78). Kennedy had already taken several steps to centralize foreign policy making in the White House, and the Cuba fiasco prompted him to build a new communications center and to vest unprecedented power in his national security adviser, McGeorge Bundy. In the aftermath of the Bay of Pigs, Bundy quite literally moved from outside to inside, from his office in the Old Executive Office Building to the White House. In subsequent administrations, these two changes would become the pillars of the modern NSC system—enabling the president and his national security adviser to, in Schlesinger's words, "tighten [the president's] personal hold on the sprawling mystery of government" (Schlesinger 1965, 278).

Third and finally, the Iran-Contra imbroglio rang the death knell for Reagan's experiment in Cabinet government. To be sure, the system was already moving in the direction of recentralization. The rapid departures of National Security Adviser Richard Allen and Secretary of State Alexander Haig signaled a quick end to the State Department vicar days. Lingering vestiges of Cabinet government were laid to rest in the aftermath of Iran-Contra. Reagan cleaned out the staff and cleaned up the process, restoring management of day-to-day national security affairs to the national security adviser, revamping the interagency structure to give the NSC staff more coordinating authority, and removing operational responsibilities from the staff's portfolio.

In all three cases, major events triggered changes to the NSC system. Even more striking, however, is the fact that these changes worked in the same direction. In all three cases, presidents with very different ideas and challenges were driven by the force of events to seek greater control of the foreign policy–making system. The Korean war pushed Truman—who distrusted the entire NSC apparatus—to give it a go. The Bay of Pigs prompted Kennedy to go even further toward centralizing the foreign policy system than he ever envisioned. And Iran-Contra forced Reagan to let go of his deep-seated commitment to Cabinet government. For the NSC system, major events served as a reinforcing mechanism, reminding presidents of the imperatives of office and the price of failure.

Conclusions

Like the origins story, that of the evolution of the NSC system provides strong empirical support for a new institutionalist National Security Agency Model over its realist alternative.

A realist explanation would argue that the NSC system arose and evolved in response to changes in the international environment rather than to domestic political forces. In addition, a fair reading of realism suggests that though lags may occur between catalyzing international events and responses in agency design, these lags should not be terribly long or serious. At any given time, a state's national security apparatus should be well designed to meet its needs and protect its vital interests.

In reality, however, realism seems only partly to explain the NSC system case. Though the onset of the Cold War undoubtedly contributed to the birth of the National Security Council and its staff, it by no means determined their original statutory forms. As we saw in Chapter 2, none of the participants in the unification debate considered the national interest when they worked out the particulars of NSC system design. Instead, the National Security Council system emerged as an artifact, an all but forgotten remnant of larger battles between the War Department, the Navy Department, and the president. International factors may have prompted the unification issue to arise, but only domestic political wrangling explains how the issue was settled.

As for evolution, realism has a hard time explaining why the modern NSC system took shape during the Kennedy administration, and why it has not fundamentally changed since then. To explain the dramatic transformation from the pre-Kennedy to the modern system, realism would have to appeal to changes in the international system. But no such major changes occurred between 1947 and 1963. As we have seen, events—most notably the Bay of Pigs—did accelerate the pace of change. Yet all three hallmarks of the modern system—the policy-oriented political national security adviser, the increased power and independence of the NSC staff, and the downgrading of the formal National Security Council—were in place before the Cuban invasion. Accounting for the system's resilience since 1963 is even more problematic. One would expect some major shift in NSC system design and operation with the Cold War's end. But we don't find any such shift. Ironically, the modern NSC system arose during a time of minimal flux in the international system and has remained essentially unaltered despite the most momentous international systemic change since World War II. Even if we concede that the modern NSC system now serves the national interest, realism cannot tell us why or how.

Turning to the National Security Agency Model, we find a more satisfying account of the facts. Let's review the model's three evolution propositions:

PROPOSITION 3: Agency evolution is driven by forces within the executive branch.

PROPOSITION 4: Congressional oversight is sporadic and largely ineffectual.

PROPOSITION 5: Evolution of a particular national security agency can be explained primarily by its original design and to a lesser extent by the shifting interests of key political actors and world events.

All three appear to be borne out in this case. The executive branch has been the driving force behind the development of the modern NSC system. From Truman's first moves to place the NSC staff in the Executive Office of the President to Eisenhower's creation of the post of national security adviser to Kennedy's construction of the Situation Room, presidents have been the dominant players in transforming the National Security Council system. Bureaucrats have failed to resist the changes, but not for lack of effort. Even in Eisenhower's time, State Department officials—including John Foster Dulles—waged continuous battles to wrest power away from other departments and from the NSC staff. From the Kennedy years to the present day, secretaries of state have sought presidential guarantees, directives, and other measures to regain the mantle of power. Throughout, however, this has been an executive branch affair. It has been a contest between king's ministers and palace guard. Congress and interest groups have not played meaningful parts.

It also seems readily apparent that Congress has not exercised extensive oversight of the NSC staff. Five investigations and one amendment in more than 50 years hardly seem the stuff of a vigorous and vigilant legislature. Of course, it could be that members stay out of the NSC system's business because they like the way it works. Absent any major crises or "fire alarms" (McCubbins and

Schwartz 1984), legislators have little reason to get involved. Yet two things should give us pause. First, almost every major study of the national security apparatus, including several sponsored by Congress, has recommended moving policy-making authority back to the Department of State. From the first Brookings study of 1960 to the Institute for Defense Analyses study of 1969 to the Murphy Commission Report of 1975, the chorus has not exactly been singing the NSC system's praises. Second, Congress has not sprung into action even when the fire alarms have sounded. The Bay of Pigs fiasco, for example, prompted no congressional action. Aside from one set of friendly pro forma hearings (whose tone resembled a cocktail-party conversation more than a serious congressional investigation), Congress left the NSC system alone. Even Iran-Contra, arguably the most intensive and public scandal in the history of the NSC staff, produced much congressional public posturing with little effect. Committee hearings and investigations by and large did not unearth new facts, did not squarely address organizational issues, and did not proceed quickly enough to contribute to the Reagan administration's overhaul of the NSC system (Congressional Quarterly 1990). As one congressional staffer dejectedly concluded after serving on the Tower Commission staff, "Congress grandstands. They don't care. They just want the show."[49] It appears that philosophical objections and fire alarms have not been enough; congressional oversight of the NSC system has, indeed, been sporadic and weak.

Finally, my new account takes proposition 5 at its word and attempts to paint a picture of NSC system development in terms of three specific variables. Such a picture not only fits with the facts but calls conventional explanations into question. Since 1947, the national security decision-making apparatus has not developed according to the shifting styles of various presidents. It has developed along a path made possible by the original National Security Act, made likely by the constellation of interests and capabilities of political institutions, and made real by critical events of the day.

CHAPTER 4

Origins of the Joint Chiefs of Staff:
"Fighting for the Very Life of the Navy"

Like the National Security Council system, the Joint Chiefs of Staff traces its roots to the National Security Act of 1947. It, too, began as part of the postwar debate over military unification. And it, too, was crafted by conflict between the War and Navy departments, while Congress sat on the sidelines. The origins of the NSC system and the JCS differ in one key respect, however: whereas the NSC system arose as the Navy's negotiating tool, the Joint Chiefs of Staff was a major bone of contention from the start. The NSC system found its way into the final National Security Act almost by accident. It was an artifact of compromise. The Joint Chiefs of Staff took center stage from day one.

At issue was not whether a JCS would be created. An informal wartime Joint Chiefs of Staff had been operating since 1942. Originally cobbled together to meet the immediate demands of Allied war planning, this first JCS had no formally defined duties or functions. It had no basis in law, operating without any legislative charter or presidential directive. By the end of the war, however, the JCS had established relatively clear membership guidelines, responsibilities, and operating procedures. The Joint Chiefs of Staff officially consisted of four members: the chief of naval operations, the Army Ground Forces chief of staff, the Army Air Forces chief of staff, and a nonvoting chief of staff to the president—Admiral William Leahy—who served as Roosevelt's de facto military liaison.[1] According to its official history, the wartime Joint Chiefs of Staff soon "became the primary agency for coordination and strategic direction of the Army and Navy." This corporate body answered directly to the president, advising him about "war plans and strategy, military relations with allied nations, the munitions, shipping, and manpower needs of the armed forces, and matters of joint Army-Navy policy" (JCS 1980, 3). Notably, the chiefs played no role in determining military budgets. Procedurally, the wartime Joint Chiefs of Staff functioned as a collective body of equals, making all decisions by unanimous consent.

Beginning in 1944, the critical disputes involved how much to alter this organization for the postwar world. The War Department fervently supported measures to expand the JCS's jurisdiction, increase its power, and centralize its decision making under a single head.[2] Specifically, Army and Air Force officials within the War Department pressed for measures to (1) transfer authority over the military budget from the civilian departments of War and the Navy to the Joint Chiefs of Staff; (2) change wartime JCS decision rules from unanimous consent to majority vote; and (3) create a senior ranking military commander or chief of staff with operational authority over all the armed forces and with decisive influence within the JCS. The Navy opposed all of these efforts, preferring to keep the more limited and collegial wartime Joint Chiefs of Staff intact.

Ironically, the very importance of the Joint Chiefs of Staff guaranteed it would be poorly designed to serve the national interest. Everyone knew that questions of JCS budget authority, operations, and leadership had far-reaching implications for service autonomy and power. Lying at the heart of the unification debate, these issues drew heavy fire. From the start, War Department officials set out to transform the old wartime Joint Chiefs of Staff, while the Navy vehemently fought to maintain it. For Navy Secretary Forrestal and his colleagues, this was the Alamo, the last stand. Holding their ground on the JCS, these leaders gave Truman and his War Department allies a stark choice: concede on the Joint Chiefs of Staff or risk scuttling military unification entirely. In the end, the president realized he needed the Navy more than the Navy needed him. Firing Forrestal or ignoring Navy demands would have, in Clark Clifford's words, "enraged the Navy's powerful supporters in Congress, further entrenched the rest of the Navy, turned Forrestal into a martyr, and doomed hope for military unification on *any* basis." Realizing this, the president began "a slow, patient, and skillful strategy designed to move Forrestal as far as possible without losing him" (Clifford 1991, 151; emphasis his).

Unfortunately for Truman and the Joint Chiefs of Staff, Forrestal did not move far. In July 1947, the National Security Act created a JCS with no single head, no authoritative decision-making system, and no control over the individual service budgets. It was weak by design.

The Players

THE DEPARTMENT OF WAR

Battle lines over JCS design mirrored those of the broader unification conflict. The War Department, on one side, propelled the unification campaign. Even before the war's end, civilian and military officials proposed merging the departments of War and the Navy into a single Department of Defense. As we would expect, War Department plans included major changes to strengthen and centralize the Joint Chiefs of Staff. During the war, the Joint Chiefs of Staff had functioned as a collective military authority—determining military strategy, exercising operational authority, and advising the president by unanimous consent. The proposed postwar JCS, by contrast, would be headed by a senior military commander or chief of staff with supreme authority over all American sea, air, and ground forces. It would, for the first time, take the lead in formulating a coordinated military budget. And it would function by majority vote.[3]

Publicly, War Department officials took great pains to frame their proposals in terms of the national interest, emphasizing the twin themes of effectiveness and efficiency. In congressional hearings, department witnesses repeatedly attacked the wartime Joint Chiefs of Staff as unproductive and incapable of effectively managing joint military operations. They blasted the customary JCS practice of unanimous decision making, arguing it granted each service chief an effective veto over any and all proposals. They recounted numerous tales of how JCS disputes and delays imposed added hardships on combat units. And they questioned the wisdom of decentralized military management in general. Secretary of War Robert P. Patterson captured the essence of these arguments in his 1945 Senate testimony: "I will concede that coordination by committees is better than no coordination at all. But in military matters action by committee is not the equivalent of action by a single authority. There should be in our Military Establishment a final voice that takes the full responsibility and determines the policy to be pursued. Someone has said that one poor commander is better than two good commanders sharing a command" (U.S. Senate 1945, 21).[4]

Economic efficiency claims also pervaded War Department testimony and public statements. Department officials denounced the customary practice of funding the War and Navy departments separately. They argued that a single unified defense budget formulated chiefly by the JCS would produce more defense for the dollar. As Lieutenant General Lawton Collins remarked, "It is believed that this [new] procedure would have great advantages over the current method. . . . The Congress would know in advance that the budget submitted to it would have been based on the considered opinion of the country's leading military experts—that it had been reviewed as an integrated program by the executive branch" (U.S. Senate 1945, 158).[5] Secretary of War Patterson went so far as to suggest that this new budget system would have saved "billions of dollars" during the war (U.S. Senate 1945, 13).

This public posturing belied far more parochial concerns. The War Department had little doubt about who would benefit from its proposed changes to the Joint Chiefs of Staff. For one thing, chances were good that the new chief of staff would be partial to the Army. Senior Army officers vastly outnumbered their Navy counterparts, providing a more plentiful pool of potential candidates (Pratt 1947). Moreover, although the Army Air Forces would soon break from the Army to become a separate Department of the Air Force, its officers had been trained in Army thinking and had risen through Army ranks. Even if the position of chief of staff rotated among all three military services, the Army was guaranteed a pro-Army chief two-thirds of the time.

In addition, majority voting gave the Army a way to circumvent the Navy's opposition in the JCS. Under the old Joint Chiefs of Staff system, a single service chief could veto any proposal. But majority voting promised to change the game. With a postwar JCS composed of the chief of naval operations, the Air Force chief of staff, the Army chief of staff, and the military chief of staff, the Army/Air Force coalition would have an almost permanent majority. Even in the worst-case scenario—a naval military chief of staff—the Army could still generally count on a 2-to-2 split. For the Army and Air Force, majority voting stacked the deck.

Perhaps most important, the JCS's new budget responsibility promised to improve the Army's share of the postwar appropriations pie. As Caraley writes, Army leaders "felt that the [old] two-budget system discriminated against the unglamorous but highly important ground Army, which [General] Marshall specifically feared would be 'starved' in another period of peace" (Caraley 1966, 62). Glimpses of the War Department's underlying budget motives appear throughout the 1945 Senate hearings. Secretary Patterson declared, "We ought not to tolerate in our military budget overlarge sums for one purpose and insufficient sums for another which must inevitably result from a lack of a single direction over the planning of all the constituent service elements" (U.S. Senate 1945, 14). General Eisenhower intimated that preferential treatment of the Navy had hurt morale among the ground forces: "If you have a system that is so arranged that some one group feels that it is favorably treated and another one, correspondingly, that it is unfavorably treated, it is a very hard thing to keep up morale" (U.S. Senate 1945, 374). Though Patterson and Eisenhower did not name names, they left little doubt about which service suffered under the status quo.

Finally, and more generally, the War Department's vision of a postwar Joint Chiefs of Staff promoted its philosophy of unified command. All sides realized that abstract ideas about the nature of military command had concrete consequences for service power, prestige, and influence in the postwar world; already, under the principle of service autonomy, the Navy had developed its own mini-military, complete with sea, air, and ground forces.[6] Against this backdrop, the War Department had good reason to forge a Department of Defense and Joint Chiefs of Staff in its own image, with clear lines of authority, a hierarchical decision-making structure, and individual components that carried out narrow, clearly defined missions.

THE DEPARTMENT OF THE NAVY

The Navy Department stood on the opposite side, opposing military unification in general and the War Department's JCS proposals in particular. From the beginning, the Navy railed against the idea of a single military chief of staff, challenged the imposition of JCS majority voting, and adamantly resisted JCS control over an integrated military budget. Instead, it sought to freeze into law the existing Joint Chiefs of Staff with its unanimous consent rule and limited jurisdiction. Like their War Department counterparts, Navy officials presented these objections in terms of national interest. They, too, used the public good to justify self-interested positions and proposals.

Two strands of arguments permeated the Navy's public case. First, Navy officials darkly warned that the War Department's unification plans threatened civilian control of the military. Secretary James Forrestal raised the specter of militarism as early as 1944 (U.S. House 1944a, 233).[7] By the time of the Senate hearings in 1945, Forrestal and others had become more direct. The secretary testified that unification "in effect amounts to an isolation and derogation of the civil authority"; Assistant Secretary of the Navy Struve Hensel charged that "the main effect, if not the objective," of the War Department's JCS proposal "seems to be the reduction of civilian control over the armed services"; and Admiral Ernest J. King, chief of naval operations, went even further, declaring that "a single commander of all the armed forces . . . is, potentially, the 'man on horseback' " (U.S. Senate 1945, 101, 121, 245). Their message was unambiguous: only the existing weak JCS system would maintain the proper relationship between military and civilian branches of government.[8]

Military effectiveness was the Navy's second public line of defense. Navy officials argued that centralization itself ensured defeat on the battlefield: unified militaries were unsuccessful militaries. The reasoning was straightforward: any overall military commander would naturally favor the strategic thinking and combat weapons of his own training. As a result, other service components would be undervalued in strategic planning, underfunded in budget decisions, and underutilized in combat—a recipe for disaster. In making their case, Navy officials frequently invoked the vanquished unified militaries of the past, from the Romans to Napoleon's troops to Hitler's general staff. As Admiral Ellis Zacharias succinctly put it in the *Washington Post* (May 27, 1947), "History shows that every nation which has had a merger of its armed forces has gone down to defeat."[9]

As with the War Department, such public posturing masked more selfish interests. Arguments about civil-military relations and combat effectiveness may have been useful tactics, but they were not the driving force behind the Navy's objections. Instead, four chief concerns fueled Navy opposition to the War Department's JCS plan.

First, Navy officials were convinced that a chief of staff or supreme military commander threatened the power, prestige, and role of the Navy. Secretary Forrestal admitted he feared the chief of staff proposal more than any other, believing it to be "an Army plot" to weaken the Navy (Clifford 1991, 149). Publicly, Forrestal and others warned that a supreme commander would inevitably underappreciate and overlook some combat elements; privately they knew the slighted service would be their own. Hints of the Navy's underlying fears are not hard to find. The Navy's own Eberstadt Report notes: "The appointment of a single commander of all the armed forces, particularly in the light of the past education and training of our military men, might lead to domination by one branch of the military services over the others. In those countries where a single commander has existed, the needs and interests of one service have always predominated in the determination of a comprehensive strategic plan" (Eberstadt 1945, 38). One does not have to read much between the lines to realize which branch would dominate. Indeed, according to the Navy, every case of unified command told the same story: an overall commander who favored ground forces, ignored the Navy, and went down to defeat.[10]

Second, Navy leaders strenuously objected to the idea of majority voting in the Joint Chiefs of Staff. They knew full well that any JCS organization would likely leave them in the minority, at the mercy of an Army/Air Force coalition. Navy leaders had already missed one brush with this particular danger. In 1942, when a 3-to-1 JCS vote approved cutting battleship and cruiser building programs, the Navy representative objected and insisted on a policy of unanimous consent. He "replied coldly that so far as he was concerned, the Joint Chiefs were not a voting organization on any matter in which the interests of the Navy were involved" (Frye 1947, 325). Postwar conditions made the Navy's veto right even more valuable. With fluid strategic circumstances, rising air power, and declining military budgets, the Navy could not afford to be outnumbered.[11]

A JCS with majority rule was bad enough; a Joint Chiefs of Staff with budget authority appeared life-threatening. Under the old dual-department system, Navy leaders could determine their own budget priorities, present their program to the Budget Bureau without War Department competition or interference, and lobby Congress directly for their appropriations. For a host of reasons—the department's prestige, its lobbying skills, its big-ticket building projects— Navy programs had prospered. But this War Department proposal threatened to turn the tide in two ways. First, majority voting on the JCS naturally favored Army and Air Force budget priorities. As Fleet Admiral William Halsey colorfully put it, "If this would not give the Army control over the Navy's budget, then I've forgotten my arithmetic. With [the Air Force's and Army's] admitted prejudice toward the battleship and the carrier it seems clear what use they would make of their 2-to-1 vote" (U.S. Senate 1945, 543). Second, the plan made appeals all but impossible. Though the Navy could send a "minority report" to the president, it could not directly negotiate with the Budget Bureau or with Congress. Taken together, majority voting and budget authority spelled serious trouble for Navy appropriations.

Finally, the War Department's proposed Joint Chiefs of Staff challenged fundamental principles of Navy organization and decision making. For decades, the Navy's philosophy of collective decision making and service autonomy had worked to its own advantage: decision by committee guaranteed that the Navy's voice would be heard in joint planning. In addition, service autonomy helped justify the Navy's development of a complete sea/air/land fighting force. But the War Department's JCS struck at the core of these ideas. A single military commander, an integrated budget, a JCS with majority rule—all of these provisions concentrated authority and narrowed service missions. In doing so, they undermined the very rationale that justified Navy dominance.

In sum, the War and Navy departments took opposing sides on the Joint Chiefs of Staff for the same reasons. Both departments sought to gain advantage in the changing postwar world. For the War Department, advantage lay in pushing for an entirely new kind of Joint Chiefs of Staff organization. For the Navy, however, advantage came from resistance, from maintaining a wartime Joint Chiefs of Staff that used unanimous decision rules, answered to no senior military leader, and exercised no control over service budgets. Both sides knew the stakes of agency structure were high. As Forrestal confessed, "We are fighting for the very life of the Navy" (quoted in Clifford 1991, 149).

THE PRESIDENT

President Truman was a third and decisive actor in this contest. He supported the War Department's proposals, but on entirely different grounds. Truman's overriding aim was not the preeminence of any service but national survival. As president, he sought a new military apparatus that would provide superior strategy and advice, better performance, and a bigger bang for the buck. These goals, he thought, would be reached only with a Joint Chiefs of Staff that could not be held captive by any one of its members, that could forge a streamlined national defense budget, and that would be led by a senior military chief of staff. Above all else, the president sought a Joint Chiefs of Staff organization that worked well (Truman 1961–66, 1: 546–60).

Truman's stand reflected the unique incentives and imperatives of his office. As the only political actor with a national constituency, Truman had good reason to consider broad national interests and to resist narrow political pleas (Moe and Wilson 1994). As we would expect, general interests in economy, in military performance, and in presidential control of the military heavily influenced his thinking. "The basic question," Truman declared in 1945, "is what organization will provide the most effective employment of our military resources in time of war and the most effective means for maintaining peace" (Truman 1961–66, 1: 550). National, not parochial, concerns drove the president to support the War Department's plan.

TWO MISSING PIECES: INTEREST GROUPS AND CONGRESS

As in the NSC case, the Joint Chiefs of Staff arose with little input from either interest groups or Congress. Here, too, interest groups were simply too few, too weak, and too divided to have much impact. Caraley (1966) concludes as much from his survey of group appearances in the *New York Times* and the *Congressional Record*. A closer look at congressional hearings further underscores the point (see Table 2). Between 1945 and 1947, House and Senate committees heard 87 pieces of personal testimony. Of these, only 6 came from interest group representatives. Even more significant, almost all of the interest groups that did appear before Congress came late in the

TABLE 2.   Number of Interest Group Witnesses Appearing at
            Congressional Unification Hearings, 1945–1947

Committee	Year	Interest Group Witnesses	Total Witnesses
Senate Military Affairs	1945	0	29
Senate Naval Affairs	1946	1	23
House Expenditures	1947	5	26
Senate Armed Services	1947	0	9
TOTAL		6	87*

*Includes witnesses who testified before more than one committee.
SOURCE: Data from U.S. Senate, Committee on Military Affairs, *Department of the Armed Forces, Department of Military Security: Hearings on S. 84 and S. 1482* (79th Cong., 1st sess., 1945); U.S. Senate, Committee on Naval Affairs, *Unification of the Armed Forces: Hearings on S. 2044* (79th Cong., 2d sess., 1946); U.S. House, Committee on Expenditures in the Executive Departments, *National Security Act of 1947: Hearings on H.R. 2319* (80th Cong., 1st sess., 1947); U.S. Senate, Committee on Armed Services, *National Defense Establishment (Unification of the Armed Services): Hearings on S. 758* (80th Cong., 1st sess., 1947).

game, after War and Navy positions had hardened. In the critical period between 1945 and 1946, when all sides were most susceptible to influence, only one interest group leader offered his views.

Congress also played a small part in determining the Joint Chiefs of Staff design. As the following section discusses in more detail, legislators deferred to the executive branch on virtually every substantive and procedural issue. Congress did not fashion any of the major unification proposals and recommended few changes to the proposals it received. Indeed, when we compare the Truman administration's final compromise plan with the National Security Act, we find virtually identical JCS provisions. In over four months of hearings, debates, and conference committee negotiations, legislators insisted on just one substantive change: the chiefs were given the added duty of formulating coordinated educational policies for the military (*U.S. Statutes at Large* 1948, 505).

Why did Congress acquiesce so readily on the Joint Chiefs of Staff and on other aspects of the unification debate? For one thing, without interest groups calling the office, testifying before committees, or sending mail, the average legislator had relatively weak electoral incentives to delve into the details of military structure. In addition, most legislators tended to defer to military expertise, which was itself divided on this issue. As Senator Styles Bridges (R-N.H.) explained during the 1947 Armed Services Committee hearings, members of Congress normally approached military matters with far greater caution and hesitancy than other issues: "In many ways, it is more difficult for Congress to deal with problems of national defense. There is a certain hesitancy of a Senator, *even though he may have been on the Armed Services Committee, or the Appropriations Committee, and may have been dealing with these things over a long period of years*, in setting his judgment up against that of a man who is devoting his whole time to that job" (U.S. Senate 1947, 66; emphasis mine).

Even military experts within the legislature—those national security intellectuals—shied away from challenging War and Navy Department officials. Representative Clare Hoffman (R-Mich.) underscored this point during the House unification hearings of 1947, remarking that "if Congress ventures to suggest . . . any change, if it has to do with national defense, immediately the individual Member of the Congress is charged by commentators or columnists or somebody with being against national defense, with being against the Government" (U.S. House 1947a, 172). Little wonder members preferred to let the military take the lead role in shaping the postwar national security apparatus. With such high stakes and such deep divisions within the armed forces, Congress could not win. For a legislator to take *any* stand was to risk angering at least one military service and igniting public criticism. As Bridges ruefully put it, Congress was "rather behind the eight ball" (U.S. Senate 1947, 66).

Finally, War and Navy officials took deliberate steps to keep Congress out of the game during its closing minutes. Once the services reached a compromise, they closed ranks; in congressional hearings, the vast majority of soldiers, sailors, and airmen expressed unwavering support for the plan. More important, they took pains to highlight the tenuous and delicate nature of the compromise. With such hard-won agreements and such a fragile framework, they argued, any single change could unravel the entire plan. Consider these comments from both War and Navy Department representatives:

GENERAL LAURIS NORSTAD: I believe this is the best bill—I think this is a good bill; it is sound, it is workable. I have no fears about any of it; I personally would not change a word, a period, or comma. (U.S. House 1947a, 226)

ADMIRAL FORREST SHERMAN: I am afraid if you start to change one part of the structure, you will get demands to change another part of the structure and then you will have divergent views, much as they were a year ago. (U.S. House 1947a, 185)

Such a strategy proved effective—so effective, in fact, that it drew angry outbursts from a few frustrated legislators. In perhaps the most testy exchange, Representatives Porter Hardy (D-Va.) and Carter Manasco (D-Ala.) blasted both Army and Navy representatives for their unwillingness to criticize the bill. "How in the world are we going to arrive at the truth of this thing and get this bill in the kind of shape it ought to be in if people are not going to be willing to tell us where the corrections need be made?" Hardy asked in exasperation. When Admiral Sherman responded by suggesting one addition—a legislative preamble that he and the War Department had already drafted—Manasco sarcastically thundered, "But we dare not touch the sacred document you gentlemen have agreed to" (U.S. House 1947a, 185). These were words of angry defeat. Facing the military's united front, Hardy, Manasco, and others had nowhere to go. On July 16, 1947, their committee favorably reported the administration's unification bill, with few changes.

In sum, it appears that expecting Congress to play even a modest role in JCS design would have been asking too much. Ironically, military divisions kept Congress on the sidelines in the early going, and military cohesion had the same effect in the end. With weak electoral incentives, with high risks, and with sharp splits among military experts, legislators had rational reasons to take no role at all. The Joint Chiefs of Staff was an executive branch creation.

Overview: Unification and the Joint Chiefs of Staff

The original wartime Joint Chiefs of Staff was an easy target. Thrown together by President Roosevelt just two months after Pearl Harbor, this first JCS operated in the rush of war. Procedures were decided, organizational arrangements were made, and jurisdictions were established with little thought to long-term consequences. As the official JCS history notes, "The Joint Chiefs of Staff came into being to meet an immediate need, without a background of long study and specific decision within the US Government regarding the most effective form of higher military organization for war" (JCS 1980, 1). Operating without so much as a presidential directive or charter, the JCS emerged from World War II with no firm legal grounding. This tenuous legitimacy, coupled with the JCS's short history and unwritten rules, made for an uncertain postwar future.

The War Department lost no time in seizing the initiative. Realizing the potential for postwar gains, leaders began issuing calls for radical military integration even before the war's end. All of these calls included plans for a revamped, revitalized Joint Chiefs of Staff with broad statutory duties and specific procedures.

The opening salvo came during the congressional hearings of 1944 and 1945. General Joseph T. McNarney and Lieutenant General Lawton Collins presented two specific plans to unify the armed forces. The details varied between the two plans, but the core JCS provisions did not. Both proposals recommended fixing key wartime JCS functions into law: the new JCS, like the old, would be responsible for advising the president on crucial issues of military policy and strategy. In addition, the McNarney and Collins plans recommended some dramatic changes. They called for creating a new chief of staff or military commander to "head" the Joint Chiefs of Staff and to exercise overall command of the armed forces. They implicitly suggested replacing the wartime JCS's unanimous agreement rule with majority voting.[12] Perhaps most important, both plans proposed adding a substantial new power to the Joint Chiefs: to formulate a central military budget. As the McNarney Plan put it, the new Joint Chiefs of Staff would have the "sole duty" of advising the president on "the general determination of budgetary needs and allocations" (U.S. House 1944a, 35). With decisive rules, a strong head, and principal authority over service budgets, the postwar Joint Chiefs of Staff would be a powerful body.[13]

If the War Department's fortunes hinged on strengthening the wartime JCS, the Navy's fate lay in its continued weakness. From the start, Navy leaders pressed for maintaining the essential features of the old JCS system. In the early days of 1944, Navy officials openly challenged the idea of JCS budgetary authority. In a disingenuous but effective move during the Woodrum Committee hearings, Forrestal "wondered" aloud whether Congress would want the military budget determined chiefly by the Joint Chiefs of Staff. "I do not know. I just raise the question," Forrestal mused, adding, "It runs somewhat counter to our concept, I think, of government" (U.S. House 1944a, 133). Assistant Secretary Artemus Gates underscored the point. Arguing that Congress had properly placed funding authority "in civilian hands for 150 years," Gates concluded that he could "not favor such a radical change" as McNarney's Joint Chiefs of Staff (U.S. House 1944a, 233). Such complaints did the trick. Concerned about potential Navy opposition, Congress postponed all consideration of military unification until after the war.

When hearings resumed in the fall of 1945, Navy leaders took the offensive, issuing a lengthy and serious counterproposal to War Department plans. Known as the Eberstadt Report, this study included very specific provisions for postwar JCS organization—provisions that aimed to minimize the agency's power and effectiveness. For starters, the Eberstadt Report placed budget authority not in the JCS but in the civilian National Security Council; there the Navy secretary could directly (and, if past experience were any guide, successfully) lobby for his own programs before the president. The report also insisted on writing the old JCS unanimous decision rule into law. Although this proposal would increase the likelihood of indecision and gridlock, it would maintain the Navy's critical veto against an emerging and ever-threatening Army/Air Force coalition. As further protection of the Navy's autonomy and influence, the Eberstadt study rejected the idea of a supreme military commander or a JCS chairman of any sort.[14]

Finally, and most important, the report institutionalized conflict of interest at all levels of the organization. At the top, Army, Air Force, and Navy chiefs were charged with producing sound overall military advice and strategy within the JCS. But these same officers were also supposed to head their own services, promoting service-specific interests and satisfying service-based needs. Lower-level JCS officials faced similar tensions between joint and service responsibilities. Though a new Joint Staff was to have responsibility for staffing joint projects, and was expected to bring joint perspectives to the table, it would consist of detailees from the individual military services. In essence, these Navy provisions guaranteed that all JCS personnel would serve two masters. Given that chiefs and staffers alike depended on just one master—their parent service—for promotions and assignments, the outcome was clear. JCS personnel had little incentive to put joint interests ahead of parochial ones.

Thus, with no head, no budget authority, no means of forcing decisions or action, and no structural incentives to foster truly joint recommendations, the Eberstadt Report's Joint Chiefs of Staff hardly appeared destined for success. This is exactly what the Navy wanted.

Despite the Navy's efforts, President Truman initially sided with the War Department. In a special message to Congress on December 19, 1945, the president called for nothing short of unified command—complete with a ranking chief of staff and a powerful JCS organization with budget authority and majority rule. Criticizing the original Joint Chiefs of Staff as an "expedient" of war, the president remarked, "This kind of coordination was better than no coordination at all, but it was in no sense a unified command." Peacetime conditions, he argued, would only make matters worse. With declining resources, rising interservice rivalries, and new military challenges, the old JCS system would have a harder time reaching agreement, forging policies, and offering coherent, useful advice to the president. As Truman put it, "During the war period of extreme national danger, there was, of course, a high degree of cooperation. In peacetime the situation will be different. It must not be taken for granted that the Joint Chiefs of Staff as now constituted will be as effective" (Truman 1961–66, 1: 548, 550).

Truman's speech dealt a serious blow to the Navy and ignited a round of furious lobbying and debate. Privately, Navy Secretary Forrestal confronted the president head-on, calling his unification plan "completely unworkable" (Forrestal 1951, 148). Publicly, Navy leaders launched a massive media campaign and pressed friends on the Senate Naval Affairs Committee to hold a fresh round of hearings (Caraley 1966, 132).[15] At these hearings, Navy officials mounted a vigorous new attack against the president's plan, giving particular attention to the Joint Chiefs of Staff. A rough survey of witnesses suggests just how much the Navy's postwar hopes hinged on maintaining a weak central military organization. Considering the most senior civilian and military officials who testified—Secretary Forrestal; Ferdinand Eberstadt, author of the report that bears his name; Chief of Naval Operations Chester Nimitz; and Fleet Admiral Ernest King—we find 41 percent of the testimony devoted to the Joint Chiefs of Staff (see Table 3).

TABLE 3.   Number of Pages of Testimony Devoted to Joint Chiefs of
           Staff by Top Civilian and Military Officials at Senate Naval
           Affairs Committee Hearings, 1946

Witness	Pages Devoted to JCS	Total Pages of Testimony
Ferdinand Eberstadt	8	20
James Forrestal	6	23
Ernest King	16	19
Chester Nimitz	5	24
TOTAL	35	86

SOURCE: Data from U.S. Senate, Committee on Naval Affairs, *Unification of the Armed Forces: Hearings on S. 2044* (79th Cong., 2d sess., 1946).

The attention was hardly positive. Nimitz called the chief of staff one of the four "major defects" of the president's plan (U.S. Senate 1946, 94). Admiral King launched a more philosophical attack, criticizing the president and his War Department allies for confusing unified field command with unified command at home. "There are positive dangers in a single command at the highest military level," King declared. "I consider this fact the most potent argument against the concept of the single department" (U.S. Senate 1946, 128). Forrestal reserved some of his harshest criticism for the War Department/Truman JCS, calling it an effort to "emasculate and destroy" a wartime system that had been proved in battle (U.S. Senate 1946, 41).

By May 1946, Navy objections had so inflamed the unification debate that White House officials began to worry. Clark Clifford notes in his memoirs, "On May 12, I told President Truman that I had concluded the Army's position might be correct on its merits, but was politically out of reach. Our real choice, I said, was between concessions to the Navy or no bill at all" (Clifford 1991, 150). The president's predicament was clear: yield on the JCS or risk losing the entire unification bill. The following day, Truman called Forrestal,

Secretary of War Patterson, and other military leaders into his office, dropped his support for the chief of staff proposal,[16] and strongly urged the two departments "to sit down together and work out their points of agreement and disagreement" (Truman 1956, 50). This move broke the impasse. Sensing the shifting winds, Patterson declared that he was not prepared to "jump into the ditch and die for the idea" of a chief of staff (Forrestal 1951, 161). Compromise negotiations began.

JCS design was settled almost immediately, and to the Navy's satisfaction. On May 31, 1946, just two weeks after negotiations began, Patterson and Forrestal sent President Truman a letter declaring "agreement" on eight major issues, including the Joint Chiefs of Staff.[17] This was no surprise. With a chief of staff now out of the question, War Department officials had little to gain by digging in their heels on other JCS provisions. Instead, they turned their attention and energies to other key unification issues, such as the civilian Department of Defense and service roles and missions.

By February 1947, the War and Navy departments reached final agreement on all aspects of postwar military organization. The JCS that emerged bore a striking resemblance to its wartime predecessor. It would consist of three statutory members—the ranking Air Force, Navy, and Army officers—who would both head their own services and furnish joint perspectives.[18] It would operate by unanimous consent, without a chairman. It would continue to advise the president, prepare strategic and logistical military plans, establish unified field commands, and formulate policies on other joint issues. Equally important, this proposed Joint Chiefs of Staff organization would have no hand in formulating military budgets. Budget authority would rest, as it had always done, in civilian hands.[19]

Over the next five months, Truman's War-Navy compromise proposal made its way through Congress with negligible changes. As for the Joint Chiefs of Staff, Congress appeared to follow General Lauris Norstad's advice, changing hardly a "word, a period or comma" (U.S. House 1947a, 226). Indeed, the JCS that Truman signed into law in July 1947 differed in only one minor respect from his own February compromise plan: Congress added a rather uncontroversial provision assigning the JCS responsibility for coordinating military educational policies.

In the end, Forrestal and his Navy colleagues got the Joint Chiefs of Staff they wanted. From the beginning, they were convinced that the Navy's strength lay in weak central military organization. The dual-department system of the previous 150 years had served the Navy well, enabling it to garner large pieces of the budgetary pie, to develop its own aviation and ground arms, and to wield substantial influence on strategic thinking. Without a Joint Chiefs of Staff, the Navy had become the preeminent service. With a weak Joint Chiefs of Staff in World War II, the Navy had been able to hold its own. But a strong JCS along War Department lines posed a grave danger to Navy interests. Little wonder Navy leaders set out to hamstring the postwar JCS from day one. They knew, as the War Department did, that their future depended on it.

Conclusions

If the propositions developed in Chapter 1 are on target, then we would expect to find two things in this case: minimal congressional involvement (proposition 1) and poor agency design (proposition 2). We find both.

The postwar Joint Chiefs of Staff was clearly a product of executive branch politics. Its membership, its jurisdiction, its capabilities, and its procedures were all determined by three actors: the president, the Department of War, and the Department of the Navy. There is no doubt that the bureaucratic politics was fierce. As the president himself remarked, "I have the feeling that if the Army and the Navy had fought our enemies as hard as they fought each other, the war would have ended much earlier" (quoted in Clifford 1991, 146).

Congress may have provided a forum for debate, but it never took the initiative. At every juncture, congressional committees followed the lead of the president and his feuding military departments. When War Department officials first pushed for unification in 1944, the House responded by creating a Select Committee on Post-War Military Policy. When Navy officials objected to the committee's study, it retreated, concluding that "the time is [not] opportune to consider detailed legislation which would undertake to write the pattern of any proposed consolidation" (U.S. House 1944b, 4). When the president presented his first unification proposal in a public address in December 1945, the Senate Military Affairs Committee began translating his ideas into legislative language. But when the Navy saw these proposals, they pressed the Senate Naval Affairs Committee to hold hearings that could publicize their objections and stem the unification tide. Only in the spring of 1947, once the warring military services settled their differences, did House and Senate committees resume action—and then they fashioned only minor changes to the administration's final unification plan. The Joint Chiefs of Staff that ultimately appeared in the National Security Act of 1947 was, line for line, almost identical to the one proposed by the Truman administration.

As we have seen, legislators had good reason to stay out of the fray. Without strong interest group involvement, potential electoral rewards were low. Yet the risks associated with challenging military expertise seemed high. As Senator Bridges explained during the 1947 hearings, any congressional action that questioned military advice laid the legislature open to public attack. "The accusation would go out that Congress was trying to interfere with the workings of the War and Navy Departments. . . . And we are told that General So-and-so, and Secretary So-and-so, who are devoting their whole time to it, should know more than the Congress" (U.S. Senate 1947, 66). In the JCS case, where any stand was bound to antagonize at least one military department, no stand seemed the wisest choice for rank-and-file members.

Evidence also suggests the Joint Chiefs of Staff was ill designed to serve national needs. Why? Because it was a creature of the Navy, and the Navy cared above all about its own future. Navy self-interest comes across loud and clear in Secretary Forrestal's own diaries. He writes:

> My own conduct in this matter [of military unification] has been governed by three main considerations: (1) to try to keep the Navy intact as a Service as distinct from a merely subordinate branch of a vast Department; (2) to obtain the improvements in our national defense organization which the war indicated should be made *but without sacrificing the autonomy of the Navy*; (3) to discharge my responsibilities to the President as a member of his Cabinet, which means that I must go as far as I can in accepting and promulgating his views, always having the alternative, when I can no longer do so honestly, of resigning. (Forrestal 1951, 167; emphasis his)

For Forrestal, the Navy came first.

Unfortunately, Navy interests did not coincide with national interests. At a minimum, the United States stood to benefit from a postwar military organization that could allocate limited resources effectively, eliminate unnecessary waste and duplication between services, provide coherent strategic planning, and offer sound and timely advice to the commander in chief. The Navy's idea of a Joint Chiefs of Staff was not designed to do any of these things. The budget process described in the National Security Act expressly provided multiple lobbying channels for each service to plead its own case. JCS veto rights granted the Navy protection, but at the risk of perpetual gridlock. Decentralized command gave the Navy more autonomy at the expense of service coordination. JCS structure provided strong incentives for chiefs and staffers alike to cast aside joint interests in favor of parochial ones. By maintaining control over individual assignments and promotions, the Navy ensured the loyalty of its JCS representatives. Under Secretary of War Kenneth C. Royall offered this candid assessment of the new national security apparatus: "It will not save money, will not be efficient, and will not prevent interservice rivalry" (quoted in Clifford 1991, 157).[20]

Certainly, it is possible that Navy officials did not see JCS design issues in such narrow terms. It is conceivable that they created an ineffective Joint Chiefs of Staff by mistake, and not by design. Yet two considerations cast doubt on such a claim. First, cleavage lines over JCS proposals—and unification in general—were sharp, with the vast majority of War Department officials on one side and the vast majority of Navy officials on the other. Both sides pushed agency models that all too conveniently protected their own missions, their own budgets, their own philosophies, and their own political power. If the War and Navy departments harbored any altruistic intent, it was hard to see.

Second, the Navy's own Eberstadt Report suggests that officials knew how to create a productive and powerful joint military agency, but chose not to. Eberstadt spends all of Chapter 2 drawing lessons from the wartime JCS experience. In doing so, he makes a point of analyzing why some JCS staffing committees worked better than others. Singling out the Joint Strategic Survey Committee for its "invaluable service," Eberstadt finds one key to success: a structural design that maximized the incentives for members to think in joint terms. His study notes:

> The members of the [Joint Strategic Survey] Committee attribute a substantial part of their success to the fact that from their inception they have been housed together and have no departmental duties assigned. This has enabled them to concentrate on joint problems which in turn has increased their individual knowledge of the problems and viewpoints of

the other services and has enabled them to develop an over-all joint view-point which has had great weight and influence. (Eberstadt 1945, 64)

As this passage suggests, Eberstadt and his staff saw at least the rudiments of successful agency design, and realized the consequences of ignoring it. They knew the dangers of asking joint committee members to split their duties between service and joint assignments. "Dual hatting" did more than just pit service interests against national interests. It gave service interests the upper hand, impeding the development of "an over-all joint viewpoint." Yet Eberstadt's proposed JCS invited that very outcome!

Ultimately, Navy leaders successfully hobbled the Joint Chiefs of Staff because they gave the president no other option. Three factors enabled the Navy to negotiate from a position of strength. First, Forrestal and his colleagues favored the status quo. In a political system that naturally made change difficult to achieve, this was a substantial advantage. Navy officials had only to muster one critical majority in one committee in one chamber of Congress to derail the president's entire unification effort. This low threshold was easily met. The Navy's public relations campaign tapped just enough congressional support to cast doubt on the National Security Act's chances of success.[21] Expertise was also a key ingredient here. Legislators stayed on the sidelines because they feared to oppose military experts on military issues. Thus the burden of proof was on unification supporters. To change the existing military system, Congress had to take action, it had to take a stand. But to take a stand was to oppose Navy war heroes—a situation that even congressional defense experts wanted to avoid. The structural realities of American politics appear to have worked against Truman from the start.

Second, even without the prospect of congressional opposition, President Truman had good reason to satisfy the Navy's demands: the Navy was simply too important to ignore. Forcing massive military reorganization against its will promised to entrench the Navy's opposition, not end it. Sailors, after all, were perfectly capable of resisting organizational changes and shirking new duties they disliked. Moreover, the department could retaliate against the president by withholding support on other key Cold War issues. With Soviet aggression, postwar economic conversion, and his own reelection campaign on the horizon, President Truman could not take that chance. Compromising on the JCS now appeared a much better option than dealing with Navy resistance later.

Third and finally, the distribution of preferences within the executive branch played into the Navy's hands. Though Truman and the War Department ideally wanted a complete merger of the War and Navy departments, they preferred any change to the status quo. Some unification was better than no unification at all. This gave the Navy Department tacit veto power. Forrestal knew he could push Truman and his War Department allies into a corner, presenting them with a stark choice: compromise along Navy lines or condemn unification on any basis. He was right. Truman eventually met Navy demands on a host of issues—including JCS design—because he knew he could do no better. As one War Department official put it, Truman signed the National Security Act because he "felt it was the best we could get under the circumstances and constituted an improvement over the system with which we had fought World War II " (Kenneth C. Royall, quoted in Clifford 1991, 157).

Juxtaposing this case against a realist model further underscores the usefulness of a new institutionalist approach. Recall that for realists, international factors are most important in explaining international outcomes. Though the theory remains silent about the formation and evolution of domestic-level foreign policy agencies, it implicitly assumes that these organizations are forged to meet international threats and are well designed to do so. Why? Realism demands that agencies such as the JCS be theoretically insignificant. To be theoretically insignificant, such agencies must not exert any meaningful independent influence over international outcomes. And this means they must be able to translate national needs seamlessly into policies that get carried out. In this case, realism would argue: first, that JCS design was determined by international rather than domestic political factors, and second, that the Joint Chiefs of Staff was optimally designed to serve U.S. interests. As we have seen, however, the facts call into question both hypotheses. A new institutionalist approach may be less parsimonious than a realist one, but ultimately it provides a more satisfying understanding of why national security agencies such as the Joint Chiefs of Staff look and behave the way they do.

CHAPTER 5

Evolution of the Joint Chiefs of Staff:
"The Swallows Return to Capistrano"

Criticism and stagnation are the two watchwords of JCS evolution. Since its statutory creation in 1947, the Joint Chiefs of Staff has been roundly attacked as unhelpful, unimaginative, and ineffective. Referring to the Pentagon in such derisive terms as "Disneyland East" and "Malfunction Junction," politicians, pundits, and professional military officers alike have launched a barrage of complaints about every aspect of JCS activity (Davis 1985, 155). Dean Acheson likened the agency's uncreative and untimely advice to his "favorite old lady who could not say what she thought until she heard what she said" (Acheson 1969, 243). Henry Kissinger dismissed JCS planning recommendations as "nonaggression treaties among the various services" that bore no relation to any coherent vision or strategy (Kissinger 1979, 398). Dwight Eisenhower said he found the JCS's direction of military operations so poor that "had I allowed my interservice and interallied staff to be similarly organized in the theaters I commanded during World War II, the delays and the resulting indecisiveness would have been unacceptable to my superiors" (Eisenhower 1958–61, 6: 282). In 1982, one defense expert noted that "recommendations about the JCS are as perennial as the return of the swallows to Capistrano" (U.S. House 1982, 514–

15). The Joint Chiefs of Staff stands among the most studied and criticized executive agencies in modern American history.

Criticism, however, has not led to action. Though every president, every secretary of defense, and many military leaders have believed the JCS to be seriously flawed since its inception, the agency remained virtually untouched for most of its life—with serious consequences. As the former JCS chairman Colin Powell writes, "These failings in the JCS were more than bureaucratic. In my judgment, this amorphous setup explained in part why the Joint Chiefs had never spoken out with a clear voice to prevent the deepening of the morass in Vietnam" (Powell 1995, 411). Only in 1986, with a once-in-a-lifetime political aligning of the stars, did the agency finally undergo substantial reform.

The largely unchanging state of JCS design and operation presents a sharp contrast to the NSC system case. The two agencies' evolutionary paths could hardly have diverged more. Whereas the NSC system underwent rapid and radical transformation, the Joint Chiefs of Staff organization seemed mired in its original design. In the NSC case, presidents had both the incentives and the capabilities to lead the reform charge. They were able effectively to pull foreign policy–making power into the hands of their NSC staff. But presidents have been handicapped when it comes to the JCS. Though Truman and Eisenhower attempted some major defense reforms after passage of the National Security Act, their proposals were watered down in form and thwarted in practice. No other chief executive has made the same mistake; since 1958, no president has ever initiated a major reorganization of the U.S. military establishment. Instead, as we shall see, presidents have found other ways of coping with an ineffective and intransigent defense apparatus.

Let us start with the evolutionary facts, tracing the JCS's organizational history through the early years of attempted reform in the Truman and Eisenhower administrations to the stagnation era of the 1960s and 1970s, then on to the sudden emergence of reorganization in the mid-1980s. Next, we pick up the analytic threads of the NSC evolution case—examining how JCS development was influenced by the agency's initial design in the 1947 National Security Act; by the ongoing interests and capabilities of bureaucrats, presidents, and legislators; and by exogenous events. Finally, we revisit the National Security Agency Model and I offer some conclusions that bring the JCS and NSC system cases together.

JCS Evolution

1947–1958: PRESIDENTIAL REFORM
ATTEMPTED AND THWARTED

The Joint Chiefs of Staff that emerged in 1947 was weak by design. It had no primary budget authority, no chairman, no action-forcing voting procedures, and it offered members no structural incentives to think in joint terms. As we saw in Chapter 4, the Navy Department wanted it that way. Ineffectual central military organization protected naval budgets, promoted naval autonomy, and guaranteed naval preeminence in an increasingly competitive military environment. For the Navy, poor centralization was the next best thing to no military centralization at all. For President Truman and his unification supporters, the 1947 National Security Act was the best they could do.

Though Truman lost the initial battle over JCS design, he believed the war was far from over. Reacting to the passage of the National Security Act, the president confided to a White House aide, "Maybe we can strengthen [the military organization] as time goes on" (Clifford 1991, 157). Two years later, Truman proposed and Congress passed a series of amendments to the National Security Act.

The National Security Act Amendments of 1949 sought to strengthen both the civilian Department of Defense and the military Joint Chiefs of Staff organization. On the civilian side, the amendments downgraded all three service secretaries, stripping them of Cabinet rank and removing them from the National Security Council. Legislative provisions also elevated the central "National Military Establishment" to the status of an executive Department of Defense, streamlined budget procedures, and augmented the direction, authority, and control of the secretary of defense over the individual military services. On the military organization side, changes to the Joint Chiefs of Staff were far less ambitious. The 1949 amendments created the new position of JCS chairman, increased the Joint Staff from 100 to 210 officers, and added the National Security Council to the list of those who would be advised by the JCS corporate body on military affairs (JCS 1980, 27; *U.S. Statutes at Large* 1950b, 578–92).

Two points should be noted about these amendments. First, Truman's drive for a stronger central military organization was propelled by the support of an unlikely ally—James Forrestal. As secretary of the Navy, Forrestal had led the charge *against* military unification. But in 1947, Forrestal became the first secretary of defense. This move prompted a sharp reversal in Forrestal's views of military organization. Almost immediately after assuming office, Forrestal began calling for a statutory JCS chairman to advise him on military problems, for an expanded Joint Staff, and for additional measures that strengthened his own authority over the military services. As the official JCS history concludes, "It is clear that the initiative for the 1949 reorganization came from Secretary Forrestal" (JCS 1980, 33).

The second point to highlight is that Truman's proposed changes to the Joint Chiefs of Staff were modest. Increasing the size of the Joint Staff and adding a nonvoting JCS chairman hardly compared to downgrading the individual service secretaries and bolstering the power of the defense secretary. In fact, evidence suggests that Truman explicitly rejected more far-reaching proposals to centralize the Joint Chiefs of Staff under a powerful military head. In February 1949, when the White House legislative drafting team presented its proposed amendments, Truman accepted every recommendation except one: the creation of a powerful, ranking military chief of staff. Why, especially given the president's preference for such a post, would he refuse to put it on the table for consideration? Because the president knew that a JCS chief of staff, more than any other proposal, would draw Navy fire (Clifford 1991, 161). Forrestal may have jumped on board the unification movement when he became secretary of defense, but the rest of the Navy did not. To avoid intense naval opposition, then, the president opted for the creation of a much weaker and more politically palatable JCS chairman—someone who would run JCS business and "be the principal military adviser" to civilian leaders but would not exercise any kind of military command (Truman 1961–66, 5: 163–66).

In the end, even this proposed chairman was too strong. The final National Security Act Amendments of 1949 explicitly confined the chairman's duties to expediting JCS business—setting agendas, presiding over meetings, and informing civilian leaders of JCS decisions. The corporate JCS, and not the chairman, would serve as "principal military advisers" to civilian leaders (*U.S. Statutes at Large* 1950b, 578–92). Such provisions guaranteed that the new JCS chairman would have little significance. As William Lynn and Barry Posen write, "The JCS continued to operate on the World War II model as a weakly led committee of service representatives, with only a small, service-dominated Joint Staff" (Lynn and Posen 1985, 73).

Like Truman, Dwight Eisenhower made military organization a central focus of his administration. In 1953 and again in 1958, he introduced what he hoped would become sweeping military reforms. Both efforts aimed to improve civilian control of the military, increase efficiency in military spending, and raise the quality of strategic planning (Eisenhower 1958–61, 1: 225–38). More specifically, they targeted four areas of JCS operation: (1) the chairman's lack of independent authority; (2) the conflict of interest between the chiefs' service and joint responsibilities; (3) the parochial character of the Joint Staff; and (4) the weakness of unified and specified commanders (Lynn 1985, 175). In all four areas, however, reforms failed to produce significant results. They were at once too limited and too ambitious. Strong measures were enfeebled in the face of Navy opposition. Weaker measures were simply circumvented once they became law.[1]

To bolster the chairman's power, for example, Eisenhower's 1953 Reorganization Plan gave the JCS chairman authority to help appoint and manage the Joint Staff (*U.S. Statutes at Large* 1953, 638–39). These moves soon proved inadequate. In 1958, Eisenhower requested the chairman be given voting rights in JCS deliberations, and that he be granted direct authority to assign Joint Staff duties and to select the Joint Staff director. In the end, however, voting rights proved inconsequential—JCS decisions continued to be determined by consensus, not votes—while the other measures never made it through Congress intact. Prompted by intense Navy pressure, legislators granted the JCS chairman only partial and imperfect control over the staff.[2] The final Defense Reorganization Act of 1958 charged the chairman with managing the Joint Staff "on behalf of the Joint Chiefs of Staff," required him to seek "consultation" with the chiefs and "approval" of the secretary of defense when selecting the Joint Staff director, and gave overall authority over Joint Staff activities to both the chairman *and* the corporate JCS (*U.S. Statutes at Large* 1959, 514–22). In short, the 1958 act ensured that the chairman could not exercise any authority, administrative or otherwise, without the consent of the other chiefs.

Eisenhower fared no better in his efforts to get JCS members to think in joint terms. Charged with both heading their respective services and serving on the JCS, the chiefs faced an inherent conflict of interest between their joint roles and their service responsibilities. Invariably, parochial concerns and views colored JCS deliberations. As the Center for Strategic and International Studies (CSIS) report put it in 1985: "Although the 1947 National Security Act mandates that a service chief's joint role should take precedence over his duties as leader of a service, this does not occur in practice—and for good reason. If a chief did not defend service positions in the joint forum, he would lose the support and loyalty of his service, thus destroying his effectiveness" (CSIS 1985, 12).

Eisenhower's solution to this "dual hatting" problem was to reduce the chiefs' service workloads. In 1953 he tried to put more administrative authority in the chairman's hands. The 1958 act took more direct aim, creating vice chiefs in the Army, Navy, and Air Force who would be primarily responsible for handling service issues.[3] All of these measures passed, but none worked in practice. Indeed, 22 years later, JCS Chairman David Jones still complained of rampant service parochialism among the chiefs. Testifying before a congressional committee, Jones remarked, "Individual service interests too often dominate JCS recommendations . . . because four of the five members are charged with the responsibility to maintain the traditions, esprit, morale and capabilities of their Services" (U.S. House 1982, 55). Eisenhower's vice chiefs never assumed principal authority for service duties because the chiefs never let them. As Lawrence Korb put it, "The man who spends nearly forty years as a follower in his service sees his appointment to the JCS as the opportunity to remake his service in his own image. He does not view it as an opportunity to serve as a principal military adviser to the President and the Secretary of Defense" (Korb 1976, 20). Service interests easily overwhelmed legislative dictate.

Eisenhower also missed his third target: service parochialism among the Joint Staff. Though the president succeeded in expanding the Joint Staff from 210 to 400 officers and in eliminating its committee system (which gave service representatives tacit veto rights over JCS proposals at all stages of deliberation), these measures had little effect. Staff officers continued to press the interests of their parent services and continued their cumbersome, veto-ridden committee system under a different name. They were rewarded for doing so; without more specific legislative reforms, Joint Staff members continued to be appointed and promoted by their respective services.

Fourth and finally, the president sought to create more integrated commands in the field. "Separate ground, sea, and air warfare is gone forever," Eisenhower declared in April 1958. "If ever again we should be involved in war, we will fight it in all elements, with all services, as one single concentrated effort" (Eisenhower 1958–61, 6: 274). Toward this end, Eisenhower sought to downgrade the JCS, and more specifically to reduce the military chiefs' command authority. The 1953 plan removed JCS members from the operational chain of command entirely, transferring executive authority over unified commands from the chiefs to the civilian-run departments of the Army, Navy, and Air Force. In 1958, Eisenhower removed even the service departments from the chain, while making the JCS a transmitter of military orders. Thus the operational chain of command ran from the president, to the secretary of defense, "through" the Joint Chiefs of Staff, and directly to the unified combat commanders. The 1958 Defense Reorganization Act also removed the chiefs' statutory operational authority, gave the president power to establish unified commands, and attempted to clarify the division of labor between military services and the unified commands in the field. In essence, Eisenhower's new proposals were to give the commanders in chief (CINCs) of the unified and specified services "full operational command" of their forces.

This did not happen. Statutory provisions withered in the face of entrenched service interests and power. Members of the JCS took full advantage of the blurry line between transmitting and issuing orders. Moreover, the Army, Navy, and Air Force continued to administer their respective "components" within each unified command, deciding vital questions of training, logistics, procurement, and maintenance. Except for purely operational matters, component heads still reported directly to their own services, bypassing the CINCs and the unified command structure. Finally, though the president now had official authority to establish all unified and specified commands, informally the services maintained a system in which each got its own piece of the command pie; the Air Force assumed a dominant role over the three specified commands,[4] while the Navy primarily controlled the Atlantic and Pacific commands and the Army served as the dominant influence over the European, Southern, Readiness, and Central commands. In reality, the CINCs never achieved anything close to the "full operational command" that Eisenhower desired.

In sum, the Eisenhower reforms of 1953 and 1958 were more far-reaching on paper than in practice. The president's efforts failed to get at the root problem: service power and interests. Eisenhower granted the JCS chairman voting rights in a system that had always operated informally by consensus. He created the positions of service vice chiefs and simply assumed they would be used to handle service issues and allow the chiefs to focus on more joint concerns. He eliminated the Joint Staff committee system but did nothing to change the incentives that compelled all staffers to favor parochial service interests over joint ones. He ordered the creation of truly integrated commands without creating compelling reasons or capabilities to achieve unified command in practice. As Lawrence Korb concludes, none of Eisenhower's measures had much impact "upon the manner in which the Joint Chiefs have operated" since 1947. "The problem areas that existed in 1947 still persist[ed] a generation later" (Korb 1976, 18).

1958–1986: STAGNATION AND CIRCUMVENTION

The 1960s, 1970s, and early 1980s were a period of stagnation for the Joint Chiefs of Staff. After Eisenhower's last stand, the JCS stood unchanged for the next 28 years. There were no new military reorganization plans, no new pieces of major legislation,[5] no major initiatives from either the White House, the military, or the Congress that reformed joint structure or operations.

JCS stagnation was not due to lack of attention. In fact, Eisenhower's successors thought a great deal about defense reorganization. John F. Kennedy considered the issue even before assuming office, initiating a wide-ranging study of defense organization during his 1960 presidential campaign. Chaired by Stuart Symington, the committee concluded that Eisenhower's efforts had failed and recommended massive reform. Among other things, the Symington Report called for eliminating the three separate military departments; empowering the JCS chairman, rather than the corporate JCS, to advise the president and secretary of defense; and stripping the military chiefs of all service-specific duties (Symington 1982). The Symington Report had good company. As Lynn and Posen note, "every time control of the White House has shifted from one political party to the other, a major study of the defense establishment has been initiated" (Lynn and Posen 1985, 75). In 1970, Richard Nixon fulfilled a campaign pledge to examine defense organization by appointing the Fitzhugh Committee.[6] In 1978, Jimmy Carter commissioned a series of studies on defense issues, including one—the Steadman Report—on the military command structure. While the specifics of these reports varied, their conclusion was the same: the American defense establishment was in need of extensive overhaul.[7]

None of these studies led to action. Kennedy, according to his personal lawyer, rejected almost all of the Symington committee's proposals "without serious discussion" (Clifford 1991, 330). Recommendations of the Fitzhugh and Steadman Reports also went unheeded. Instead of undertaking legislative reform, presidents lived with and worked around JCS weaknesses. Kennedy, Johnson, Nixon, Ford, Carter, and Reagan all used a variety of informal mechanisms to get military advice, to oversee military operations, and to guide strategic planning and budget allocations largely outside the JCS. To compensate for JCS shortfalls, presidents made do with what they had.

Chief executives during this period employed two basic strategies. First, they took steps to bring alternative sources of military expertise and advice into the White House. Truman, Ford, and Reagan all appointed high-ranking military officers to head their National Security Council staffs.[8] Eisenhower chose to be "his own Secretary of Defense" (Greenstein 1982, 136) and in addition relied heavily on his staff secretary—first General Pete Carroll and then General Andrew Goodpaster—to run his daily national security affairs. Kennedy, after the Bay of Pigs, appointed the revered soldier-statesman General Maxwell D. Taylor as a special independent "Military Representative to the President" (Smith 1987, 36). According to White House counsel Theodore Sorensen, Kennedy "was convinced after the Bay of Pigs that he needed military advice that neither Bundy's civilian [NSC] staff nor the holdover Chiefs of Staff were able to give" (Sorensen 1965, 607).[9] During the Nixon administration, General Alexander Haig served first as deputy national security adviser and then as chief of staff. Notably, when Haig became chief of staff to the president, he was replaced on the NSC staff by Air Force General Brent Scowcroft. In addition, over time, National Security Council staffs came to include special functional directorates for defense and arms control issues—directorates that provided the president an in-house source of information and advice on major military matters.[10]

In addition to bringing defense expertise into the White House,

presidents tried to get around the JCS system by relying more heavily on civilian officials within the Department of Defense. Reform
efforts during the 1940s and 1950s vastly strengthened the civilian
side of the defense apparatus while making more modest
proposals—and achieving even more modest results—on the military side (Davis 1985).[11] Not surprisingly, Eisenhower's successors
took advantage of what tools they had. The natural result was the
appointment of relatively strong secretaries who were given leeway
to assume more responsibility in advising, budgeting, and strategic
planning. Presidents Kennedy, Johnson, and Carter were the most
ardent supporters of this approach. Robert S. McNamara's appointment as secretary of defense in 1961 ushered in a fundamental shift
toward more centralized, rationalized budgeting procedures. Instead
of relying on the military chiefs to provide their own services'
budget wish lists, McNamara drew from a new group of brilliant
young civilians—the "whiz kids"—to develop procurement, budgetary, and strategic plans that cut across service lines. This systems
analysis approach changed over time, but McNamara's successors
continued to use its core elements.[12]

Why presidents employed these two strategies instead of instituting more wholesale reform and the costs that such strategies
entailed will be discussed more fully below. For now, the point is
that presidents during this period clearly saw JCS weaknesses, had
concrete reform proposals before them, and yet shied away from
sweeping reorganization. The period from 1958 to 1986 can rightly
be called a time of JCS stagnation and presidential circumvention.

1986–1999: REFORM FROM WITHIN AND WITHOUT

On October 1, 1986, the Goldwater-Nichols Department of Defense
Reorganization Act was signed into law (*U.S. Statutes at Large* 1989,
992–1075b). Its passage came without much fanfare or public attention; the *New York Times* covered the story in just four paragraphs
on a back page (Boo 1991). Yet Goldwater-Nichols marked a major
milestone in the history of JCS design and operations. *Congress and
the Nation* called it "the most sweeping reorganization of the U.S.
military establishment since the creation of the Department of
Defense in 1947" (Congressional Quarterly 1990, 299). Defense
expert Lawrence Korb hailed the act as "one of the primary con-
tributing factors to our success" in the Persian Gulf war (Boo 1991).
Senator Barry Goldwater (R-Ariz.) himself told reporters, "It's the

only goddamn thing I've done in the Senate that's worth a damn" (Wilson 1986a).

Succeeding where Eisenhower had failed, the Goldwater-Nichols Act instituted fundamental change on three fronts. First, the legislation bolstered the power of the JCS chairman. It granted him direct authority over the Joint Staff. It designated him, rather than the corporate JCS, the "principal military adviser to the President, the National Security Council, and the Secretary of Defense" (*U.S. Statutes at Large* 1989, 1005). It assigned him responsibility for strategic plans, military contingency plans, and budget estimates. And it created the position of vice chairman to assist him in running daily JCS business. These moves enhanced both the chairman's independence and his capabilities. Suddenly the JCS chairman could act on his own, unencumbered by service dissent, on a host of critical joint defense issues. As Colin Powell notes, "This act, for the first time, gave the Chairman of the JCS real power" (Powell 1995, 411).[13]

Second, Goldwater-Nichols vastly improved the composition and administration of the Joint Staff. By requiring joint service for promotion to flag or general officer rank, the act provided strong incentives to attract top-quality officers to Joint Staff postings. The act also weakened service parochialism by allowing the JCS chairman to make promotion decisions on his own, even over the objections of the parent service chief.

Finally, Goldwater-Nichols granted the unified and specified combatant commanders (CINCs) more autonomy and authority over their units. Clarifying the chain of command, the act expressly stated that operational orders ran from the president to the secretary of defense to the CINCs in the field. Moreover, within their respective commands, the CINCs were granted broader authority than ever before—authority that covered, among other things, all aspects of military operations, interservice training, and supplies. These and other measures loosened the services' grip on joint field commands.

This landmark legislation did not suddenly appear out of nowhere. On some fundamental level, it was 40 years in the making—achieving the kind of military centralization that Truman had fought so hard for in the mid-1940s. More directly, it is fair to say that Goldwater-Nichols was four years in the making, the culmination of a bitter fight between reformers and antireformers that began in 1982. Curiously, the battle lines were not nearly so sharp as they had been in 1947. While reformers were led by an Air Force general and an Army general, they soon became joined by think tank defense experts and key members of Congress—defense intellectuals such as Sam Nunn (D-Ga.), Les Aspin (D-Wis.), Barry Goldwater (R-Ariz.), and Bill Nichols (D-Ala.). This reform coalition encountered bitter resistance from the Office of the Secretary of Defense (OSD), by four of the five sitting chiefs, by many high-ranking officers in all three services, and especially by civilian and military officials in the Navy. Meanwhile, President Reagan and his White House aides sat this one out, taking no public stand until the legislation passed Congress decisively, by votes of 406–4 in the House and 95–0 in the Senate.

The opening salvo came from inside the JCS itself. In March 1982, two sitting JCS members—JCS Chairman (and Air Force General) David C. Jones and Army Chief of Staff General Edward "Shy" Meyer—published articles criticizing the joint military apparatus and calling for dramatic change (Jones 1982; Meyer 1982). Jones and Meyer were a powerful pair, well respected within the military, on Capitol Hill, and on Pennsylvania Avenue for their leadership and their intellect. As Admiral William Crowe, a future JCS chairman himself, noted, Meyer had a "reputation for knowing what he was talking about. No one concerned with the military was likely to dismiss his opinions outright" (Crowe 1993, 146–47). The result was dramatic. As Goldwater put it, these articles were like a flame-thrower, "scorching the seats of pants all over town" (Goldwater 1988, 351). JCS reform was suddenly on the agenda.

Within a month, in April 1982, Jones persuaded the House Armed Services Committee to hold hearings on military reform. Congress did not eagerly jump on the reform bandwagon at this point. Rather, the Armed Services Committee appeared an unenthusiastic partner, acquiescing in the chairman's request because of two background conditions or political contexts. First, there was widespread recognition that American military forces had not performed as well as they should have since World War II. The Korean war, Vietnam, the Bay of Pigs, the Iranian hostage rescue attempt of 1980—all of these episodes were hardly seen as stunning military triumphs. Stories of operational failures, mission blunders, and organizational snafus were well known.[14] The abortive Iranian mission, above all, stood as a searing reminder of the cost of poor military coordination. Occurring most recently, and in the midst of the year-long hostage crisis, Operation Eagle Claw lingered in the press, in the Congress, and in the public consciousness. Two investigations—one by the Senate and one by a special JCS commission—came to similar conclusions: the mission was, in one senator's words, "plagued with planning, training, and organizational problems" (Goldwater 1988, 344). Among other things, the operation went ahead with no centralized command, with no joint training drills among the various mission components, and with no thought as to which service was best equipped to perform which role.[15] In the end, eight team members were killed and the mission was aborted in the desert.[16]

House hearings also stemmed from concerns that Reagan administration defense budgets were bloating the federal deficit while producing only minor improvements in U.S. security. With spiraling defense budgets came reports of waste, fraud, and abuse in the military procurement system. Stories of how the Pentagon paid $110 for a 4-cent diode (Hiatt 1983) and $9,000 for an ordinary wrench made national headlines (Werner 1983). Reagan and his defense secretary, Caspar Weinberger, vowed to put an end to military financial mismanagement, but few appeared to believe them. In 1981, the Reagan administration's own budget director, David A. Stockman, called the Pentagon a "swamp" of waste and "contracting idiocy" that cost the taxpayers an unnecessary $10 to $30 billion each year (Webbe 1981a). A Republican congressional study came to the same conclusion, citing potential savings of $15 billion a year if the Pentagon put its house in order (Webbe 1981b). In the face of these reports, even hard-line defense advocates within Congress could not avoid turning an eye toward defense organization. Unprecedented deficits transformed Pentagon management into a salient domestic political issue. As Senator Charles E. Grassley, a Republican member of the Budget Committee, put it, "Why dump huge sums of money into the Defense Department when it is rotting with bad management?" (Roberts 1982).[17]

The 1982 hearings did not initially produce much in the way of results.[18] While reformers like Jones, Meyer, and former Secretary of Defense Harold Brown made their case, the antireform coalition issued a fiery protest. Led by Defense Secretary Weinberger, Navy Secretary John Lehman, and a number of high-ranking Navy officers, this group argued that the military establishment did not need fixing and that any potential cure would be far more dangerous than the illness it was meant to remedy. As Admiral Thomas B. Hayward, chief of naval operations, put it, "In my judgment the current organization is entirely adequate to the task and performs its functions well. I believe it would be effective in war and does not need major surgery at the present time." While admitting the need for "significant improvement" in planning, Hayward warned, "I have grave reservations that reorganization along the lines proposed would not move toward a more effective joint organization but would rather be the first, dangerous step toward a general staff" (U.S. House 1982, 100).[19] Such statements proved quite effective, stalling the reform movement in June 1982. Though House Armed Services Committee Chairman Les Aspin continued to hold hearings, it was clear that no major legislation stood a chance of passing during the 97th Congress (Perry 1989).[20]

Pentagon reform would have remained dead in the water had it not been for two military events that occurred within hours of each other. The first was the terrorist bombing of a Marine barracks in Beirut on October 23, 1983. One of the worst disasters in U.S. military history, the truck bomb killed 241 Marines and brought home in human terms the cost of confused chains of command. Though command responsibility lay with the unified European commander, General Bernard Rogers, operational authority over issues such as defense logistics rested in a separate Marine chain of command looping from Beirut to Norfolk, Virginia. In essence, Rogers was left with no authority to "run the show," to tell the Marines how to defend their position (Rogers, quoted in Boo 1991). Interservice rivalry and confusion ran so high in the immediate aftermath of the attack that the Navy and Air Force began fighting over which service would treat the wounded. While service officers squabbled aboard a transport helicopter, two of the injured Marines went into cardiac arrest (Perry 1989, 317–18).

The next day, in the early hours of October 24, American military forces launched an invasion of Grenada to rescue American medical students, restore democracy, and expel Cuban forces. Though hailed as a military success, the operation was riddled with problems.[21] Unable to agree on a unified command, the military services literally divided the island in half, with one side controlled by the Army and the other by the Marines. Army helicopter pilots were unable to evacuate wounded soldiers because they had never been trained to land on Navy ships. All in all, it took three days for 7,000 American troops to defeat 50 Cuban soldiers and a few hundred lightly armed construction workers (Goldwater 1988, 350). In the process, 18 U.S. troops were killed and 116 wounded. As one Pentagon official observed, the military "botched the whole operation. The result was easy to see, command and control, communications, planning and operations—it was just a disaster." He added, "Hell, we haven't had a successful military operation since Korea. Grenada should have been a walk" (quoted in Perry 1989, 321).[22]

The combination of Beirut and Grenada radicalized key members of Congress, and in so doing restarted the engines of reform. Senator Sam Nunn, Senator Barry Goldwater, Representative Bill Nichols, and former Senate staffer Barry Blechman all credit these twin military failures with catalyzing a renewed and reinvigorated reform effort. Nichols, a World War II veteran who had lost a leg in combat, had visited the Marine barracks in Beirut before the bombing and seemed particularly affected by the attack. "That picture became indelibly printed in my mind," he told a *Washington Post* reporter (Wilson 1986b). Though rank-and-file members were still a long way from embracing wholesale reorganization of the Pentagon, reform now drew support among some of the staunchest military advocates in the legislature.

What happened between the fall of 1983 and the passage of Goldwater-Nichols in October 1986 is a story of Congress—of how the hard-core reform advocates galvanized support from their legislative colleagues and how they overcame entrenched resistance from both military and civilian leaders in the Pentagon. Gaining legislative support and quelling bureaucratic resistance were two sides of the same coin. Indeed, to anyone looking in from the outside, reform leaders in late 1983 appeared to face an uphill battle. In the pages that follow, we will examine more closely the interests and incentives that have compelled average legislators to resist military centralization. Here it is worth pointing out that the typical district-oriented representative or senator clearly stood to profit from a decentralized military system; military duplication and inefficiency filled the trough of pork barrel politics. As Dan Morgan of the *Washington Post* put it, "The Pentagon is by far the largest governmental provider of contracts and employment, with virtually every congressional district beholden to it for jobs, money and patronage"

(Morgan 1982). Lest there be any doubt, Weinberger, Lehman, and others lobbied hard to make clear the political price of legislative overhaul.

Why, then, did reform ultimately succeed once it appeared on Congress's agenda?

There appear to be two reasons. First, by the fall of 1983, military reform had the backing of crucial leaders within the House and Senate. Goldwater and Nichols both had distinguished careers in the military, and Nunn, Aspin, and others were well-respected supporters of the military establishment. As defense stalwarts go, they had unparalleled and unassailable credentials. In the words of Senator Joseph Biden (D-Del.), "You know that old comment . . . that only Nixon could go to China. Only Goldwater could produce this. If anybody else had been the one who had been advocating this reorganization, every military man and woman at the Pentagon would have been down on our backs as 'communist sympathizers' " (Wilson 1986a). Such a hawkish reputation shielded other members from public criticism—and in the process lowered the cost of a pro-reform vote.

But reputation was not enough. Goldwater, Nichols, and other leaders made conscious use of their political prestige and capital to bring other members on board.[23] At this critical juncture, these national security intellectuals were convinced that reform was crucial to military effectiveness, and that military effectiveness was an issue worth fighting for. Theirs was a massive campaign, taking more than four years, 22 hearings, and hundreds of pounds of testimony and studies. Broad legislative support did not come easily. Goldwater wrote that as late as February 1986, during markup of the bill, the Senate Armed Services Committee "was split almost down the middle," with ten members supporting the reform bill and nine "against or leaning that way" (Goldwater 1988, 339).[24] The final overwhelming Senate and House votes for Goldwater-Nichols were thus quite deceiving. The Defense Reorganization Act of 1986 passed because some of Congress's most honored leaders and military supporters staked their careers on it. "Had there not been a swan song by the retiring Goldwater, all the 'anti-military' bluster of the opponents might have prevailed," noted Katherine Boo in the *Washington Monthly* (1991).

The second reason reform succeeded was that President Reagan stayed out of the political fray. He made no grand public stand, issued no strong personal appeals, and invested no major presidential capital in either opposing or promoting Pentagon reorganization. Why the president preferred the role of observer to actor on this issue is unclear. He may have chosen to let Defense Secretary Weinberger take the lead out of a philosophical commitment to Cabinet government. He may have deliberately chosen to sacrifice Weinberger in order to focus his attention on other military issues, such as the Strategic Defense Initiative, arms control negotiations with the Soviets, or the then-brewing Iran-Contra initiative. He may have felt, as Weinberger did, that reform would only codify existing practices and consequently had no "monumental significance or importance."[25] Whatever the reason, one thing is clear: Reagan was never a large part of the political equation.[26] This presidential absence substantially reduced the political power and influence of his military bureaucracy. Whether he intended it or not, Reagan's apparent indifference to reform undercut the Defense Department's position, giving Congress room to maneuver without fear of a presidential veto.

In sum, Goldwater-Nichols became a reality because all of the right factors converged. The 1986 act was one of those rare and unpredictable moments when the political stars aligned. Forty years of military deficiencies set the broad backdrop for reform. The history of military operations led many observers to wonder how well-equipped American forces actually were: if U.S. troops could not perform well in small-scale conflicts such as Grenada and Iran, how could they be expected to win the big one? Reagan defense increases, coupled with scandalous reports of Pentagon waste and fraud, provided a more immediate context. When the administration's own budget director charged the military with "contracting idiocy" worth $30 billion a year, legislators and voters began to take notice. JCS members David Jones and Shy Meyer also played pivotal roles. Their articles and testimony marked the first time in JCS history that acting chiefs had openly criticized the military system. Coming from within the organization itself, their charges catalyzed the reform movement. Without them, Goldwater-Nichols would never have gotten off the ground. The timing of tragic events was also fortuitous for JCS reform; the Beirut bombing and Grenada invasion came at just the right moment to restart reform after it had stalled. Even so, Goldwater-Nichols still required an all-out campaign by national security intellectuals to win the support of rank-and-file legislators. Had Barry Goldwater not been freed of electoral concerns by his impending retirement, had he not made JCS reform his swan song, had other defense stalwarts not used their political chits to rally their colleagues behind them, the bill would have gone down to defeat. Finally, President Reagan's low profile quelled the possibility of a strong, sustained executive opposition. All of these factors were necessary to make JCS reform a reality.

SUMMARY

Constancy, not change, has been the hallmark of JCS evolution. From its statutory creation in 1947 until the Goldwater-Nichols Act of 1986, the organization remained virtually untouched. The $64,000 question is not why the Joint Chiefs of Staff finally underwent reform in 1986 but why it was not overhauled earlier. For almost 40 years, during the darkest days of the Cold War, political leaders knew about serious organizational flaws in the American military and even had recommendations about how to redress those problems. Although Presidents Truman and Eisenhower attempted reform, in the end they did not succeed. Subsequent presidents did not make the same mistake. Rather than take on Pentagon reorganization, these leaders chose informal, low-cost ways of coping with JCS deficiencies. By bringing military expertise into the White House and by relying on civilian officials within the Department of Defense, chief executives sought makeshift ways to improve strategic planning, to get better military advice, and to streamline military budgets. Only in the 1980s, after a long line of problematic military operations—including recent embarrassing failures in Iran, Beirut, and Grenada—after widespread reports of the Pentagon's financial incompetence, after unprecedented personal pleas by two sitting JCS members, after an aggressive lobbying effort by congressional national security intellectuals, and after the president got out of the way, did Congress reluctantly and gradually take up the reform banner. If anything, Goldwater-Nichols suggests just how difficult it was to change this agency.

Explaining Evolution

JCS evolution presents a stark contrast to the NSC system case. Rather than undergoing rapid radical transformation, the Joint Chiefs of Staff organization seemed stuck in its original design. If the National Security Council system shows how powerful presidents can be in shaping their foreign policy apparatus, the JCS case shows just the opposite: here, presidents were frustrated at almost every turn. The agency proved remarkably resistant to reform.

Yet these different outcomes can be explained by the same set of variables. Here, too, we can understand why the agency developed as it did by examining three basic factors: its initial design, the ongoing interests of relevant political players, and critical events.

INITIAL DESIGN

The Joint Chiefs of Staff was not originally destined for success. A creature of the Navy, the JCS was meant to exercise little authority or influence over military affairs. NSC provisions of the 1947 National Security Act were part of a long-forgotten compromise, but JCS provisions were not. The Joint Chiefs of Staff organization was made weak in explicit, positive, statutory provisions. This made all the difference (*U.S. Statutes at Large* 1948, 495–510).

The JCS was statutorily encumbered in two fundamental ways. First, the National Security Act vested authority not in any individual office or position but in the corporate JCS body as a whole. Every provision relating to the JCS made clear that the chiefs could act only in unison. The chiefs together would serve as the "principal military advisers" to the president and secretary of defense (*U.S. Statutes at Large* 1948, 505). The Joint Chiefs of Staff as a unit would be responsible for appointing the Joint Staff director and for directing the staff's work. Noticeably absent were any references to a JCS chair, or to any action-forcing procedures or voting rules. By providing no way to surmount internal dissent, the act virtually guaranteed that JCS recommendations would be watered-down, least-common-denominator agreements between the services. A Hydralike corporate body, the Joint Chiefs of Staff was given authority but no real power.[27]

Second, the act demanded that each service head wear two hats: one as service chief and one as JCS member. This requirement built conflict of interest into every aspect of JCS activity. The chiefs were expected to defend the interests of their services *and* to make recommendations from a broader national perspective. It did not take much guesswork to see which hat would be tossed aside. General Shy Meyer captured the essence of the problem. "It should not . . . be surprising," he wrote in 1982, "that the four Service Chiefs found it somewhat difficult to sit down three times a week and act as a corporate body against some of the very remedies they individually were seeking to apply within their respective Services." Indeed, in a world of limited military budgets, to act responsibly was usually to act to the detriment of one's own service. "This 'dual-hatting,' " Meyer concluded, *"dictated by law,* confers real power with the Service Chief hat and little ability to influence policy, programming and budget issues with the joint hat. This is the root cause of the ills which so many distinguished officers have addressed these past 35 years" (Meyer 1982, 9–10; emphasis mine). As Meyer suggests, the National Security Act of 1947 made it structurally impossible for the Joint Chiefs of Staff to promote national interests.

These two features of JCS design were not easily altered. The National Security Act's JCS provisions were written in a way that made it essentially impossible to improve agency operations short of wholesale legislative reform. For one thing, JCS design was spelled out in detail. Compare, for example, the NSC staff to its JCS equivalent, the Joint Staff. Both organizations were designed to backstop the activities of their parent agencies, but their similarities end there. The NSC staff is mentioned only briefly and vaguely. Nothing is said about the staff's size, its composition, its activities, or its management. The only specific provision concerning the NSC staff—that it be "headed" by a civilian "executive secretary" appointed by the president—gives the president legal grounds and legal room to change the agency unilaterally. The Joint Staff, by contrast, is ridden with statutory specifications. Its size is limited to 100 officers, with "approximately equal numbers" from the three armed services. Its head, the Joint Staff director, serves the corporate JCS and directs staff activities according to their wishes. Such a setup leaves no room for president-led reform (*U.S. Statutes at Large* 1948, 495–510).

What's more, the JCS was not a stand-alone organization. It was part and parcel of a much broader "National Military Establishment." Thus questions of JCS design and operation unavoidably affected interservice relationships and civil-military relations. JCS operations could not be changed without somehow affecting the distribution of power among the Army, Navy, and Air Force. Nor could the agency be altered without addressing the relationship between the military chiefs and the civilian secretaries of the Air Force, Army, Navy, and Defense. By law, tackling the JCS involved taking on these broader and thornier relationships.

From the outset, then, the Joint Chiefs of Staff was hobbled and well insulated from future political interference. Its corporate character and dual hatting stacked the deck in favor of parochial service interests. At the same time, the specific nature of JCS provisions left little room for interpretation or for maneuvering around the law. Reform, if it came at all, would have to come from new legislation. Because of Congress's multiple veto points, this was a difficult task under ordinary circumstances. In this case, statutory reform seemed a monumental task; with repercussions for interservice relationships and civil-military relations, legislative changes to the JCS could not be narrowly targeted. For presidents, this was the worst of all worlds. The National Security Act itself posed serious obstacles to improving JCS design and operations.

ONGOING INTERESTS AND CAPABILITIES
OF POLITICAL ACTORS

Initial agency design left open only one viable path to JCS reform. The interests and capabilities of political players made sure this path would be exceedingly difficult to take. Though presidents certainly wanted to improve jointness within the Joint Chiefs of Staff, bureaucrats and legislators did not. This combination of bureaucratic and congressional resistance proved so devastating that it overpowered any moves toward reform legislation for nearly 40 years.

Presidents.   We already know that presidents deliberately avoided reorganizing the military establishment, choosing instead to bring military expertise into the White House and to rely on civilian Defense Department officials. The question here is why they chose such ad hoc strategies in lieu of more thoroughgoing legislative reform.

The answer is that presidents were long on motive but short on capabilities. Presidents of all stripes had the same aims: to create an unsurpassable, unified fighting force; to ensure civilian (presidential) control over the military; to maximize efficient allocation of defense resources; and to have at their disposal top-notch military advice from professional officers who considered national interests above all else. These aims, they all knew, could best be met by amending the National Security Act.

But presidents also knew that legislative reform of the military was a costly venture. It required substantial investment of three scarce resources: political capital, energy, and time. To devote these

resources to organizational reform was to take them away from other initiatives—initiatives that were far more likely to advance a president's policy agenda, to improve a president's electoral prospects, and to satisfy a president's desire for an honored place in history. Success was by no means guaranteed. JCS reform meant taking on Congress, the civilian Department of Defense, and the military services, all of whom had good reasons to resist any kind of centralization and all of whom could punish the president by withdrawing support from other initiatives. In Kennedy's case, for example, evidence suggests the president sidestepped reform recommendations precisely because he anticipated fierce military resistance and political controversy (Sorensen 1965, 238; Clifford 1991, 330). Even winning did not promise much in the way of rewards. Truman and Eisenhower may have secured new legislation, but they paid a high price and received little benefit (Steadman, in U.S. House 1982, 851). Their reform efforts of 1947, 1953, and 1958 alienated the services, divided the Congress, and drained their political capital. In short, major legislation offered presidents high risks, high costs, and low returns.

Bureaucrats.   Two bureaucratic groups vehemently opposed any moves to improve the Joint Chiefs of Staff: civilian officials within the Department of Defense and officers in the individual military services.

Defense Department officials saw that a weak Joint Chiefs of Staff allowed interservice rivalries to flourish, a situation that opened the door for greater civilian influence and control.[28] Samuel Huntington recognized this dynamic as early as 1961. "Interservice rivalry," he wrote, "not only strengthened the civilian agencies but also gave them a whipping boy upon whom to blame deficiencies in the military establishment for which just possibly they might be held responsible" (Huntington 1961, 380). Without an effective Joint Chiefs of Staff, Defense Department officials were left with the task of resolving interservice disputes and with providing coherent, broad-based recommendations to the secretary on military matters. JCS reform threatened this civilian primacy and power. Not surprisingly, civilian authorities sounded the alarm quickly and loudly when major reform initiatives surfaced. In 1982, for instance, during the early days of the Goldwater-Nichols debates, General Meyer testified that he had "already seen some comments from that group." He explained, "Under the top level, civilians within the Defense

Department . . . see their role, which has been to provide military advice in lieu of the advice of the military, threatened" (U.S. House 1982, 29–30).

The three military services also stood firm in resisting JCS legislative reform. At first glance, this may seem surprising. After all, the original JCS arose over the objections of the Army and Air Force, both of which preferred a strong central military agency. Yet, once the National Security Act of 1947 became law, the game changed. In relatively short order, Army and Air Force officers came to embrace the status quo. In part, this stance stemmed from military culture, which tended to view any change with suspicion. Army doctrine, for instance, defended the necessity of the horse cavalry until 1940 (John Kester in U.S. House 1982, 512). In part, support for the existing system also arose from the services' deep-seated distrust of one another. Vincent Davis writes, "A truly effective set of JCS mechanisms would have clearly required that senior officers receive and obey orders from other senior officers not of their own service" (Davis 1985, 159). Especially troubling was the notion of a powerful JCS chairman with authority independent of the other chiefs. As Colin Powell explained, "it was bureaucratic. The chiefs did not want their prerogatives subordinated to the chairman. This would give too much authority to one individual."[29]

Mostly, however, support for the existing JCS system arose out of the rapid realization that it fostered a mutually beneficial live-and-let-live arrangement between the services. With weak central military control, each service could and did secure for itself a place in the sun. "By the end of the Eisenhower administration," Davis notes, "each of the services had won enough rounds to at least assure its survival in an acceptable form" (Davis 1985, 157). The budget data shown in Table 4 confirm this conclusion. Given the greater technological needs of the Air Force, service shares of the budgetary pie were relatively equitable.

Moreover, budget disparities between the Army, Navy, and Air Force grew smaller over time. As Table 5 shows, between 1951 and 1960 the Air Force received the greatest budgetary allocation—an average of 42.11 percent of the budget—while the Navy received the lowest—28.16 percent. Taking the difference between these averages, we get a gap between the richest and poorest service of 13.95 points. During the following decade, that margin shrank to 9.85 points. By 1980, the gap closed even further, to 7.25 points. The

TABLE 4.   Average Shares of U.S. Military Budget Allocated to the Three Armed Services, 1951–85 (percent)

Service	Average Budget Share
Army	29.4%
Navy	32.6
Air Force	38.0
All services	100.0%

SOURCE: Data from C. W. Borkund, *U.S. Defense and Military Fact Book* (Santa Barbara: ABC-CLIO, 1991), 54 – 57.

TABLE 5.   Disparity Between Shares of U.S. Military Budget Allocated to the Three Armed Services, 1951–60 to 1971–80

Service	Budget Share		
	1951–60	*1961–70*	*1971–80*
Army	29.73%	29.65%	29.55%
Navy	28.16	30.85	36.80
Air Force	42.11	39.50	33.65
Disparity (points)	13.95	9.85	7.25

SOURCE: C. W. Borkund, *U.S. Defense and Military Fact Book* (Santa Barbara: ABC-CLIO, 1991), 54 – 57.

trend here is clear: Army, Navy, and Air Force budgets were becoming more even over time.

An enfeebled JCS also ensured that each service shared in the action. It is no coincidence that control over unified and specified commands was split fairly evenly among the Army, Air Force, and Navy. Nor is it a coincidence that military operations usually provided a major role for each service, even at the expense of overall effectiveness and efficiency. The five separate air wars in Vietnam and split command in the Grenada invasion were not isolated events. They were direct results of a Joint Chiefs of Staff system that was structurally incapable of exerting discipline over its service members. As Richard Steadman noted in 1982, the JCS system was "designed to minimize controversy and to reach compromise at the lowest possible levels, and it remains like this because such a system protects the interests of the individual services" (U.S. House 1982, 845).

In short, civilian officials and the military services all came to favor the 1947 JCS organization because it protected and promoted their individual interests.

Legislators.   Congress's role in JCS evolution can be understood as a classic collective action problem. Though Congress as a whole has held a strong interest in providing the best possible defense apparatus, most individual members have not. To be sure, congressional national security intellectuals such as Stuart Symington, Sam Nunn, and Barry Goldwater had long seen the need for JCS reform. But these members constituted a tiny minority within the House and Senate. For average members, those traditional reelection-seekers, three factors provided overwhelming incentives to protect the status quo JCS system.

First, military decentralization enhanced congressional power. Brent Scowcroft captured the situation well:

> One of the things you have to remember about the Hill is that it is useful to the Congress to have the services, or any subordinate agencies, separated, because the Congress then can get inside the harmony between the Army, Navy, and the Air Force. . . . The Congress plays a role in that. It helps them, because they can balance off people and it lets them play a much stronger role than if you have this monolithic department that they just can't get a handle on.[30]

Division within military ranks was good for Congress. Not only did it reinforce civilian control of the military, but it enabled individual members to exercise substantial influence over military policies and weapons programs.

This suggests a second, more important reason why average legislators favored the status quo: pork. A decentralized, inefficient military meant more defense spending. And more defense spending provided more jobs to more voters in districts back home. Goldwater noted that "historically, Congress . . . has been a foe of centralized leadership of the military and its branches. . . . This was to attract military bases and spending contracts to their states and congressional districts" (Goldwater 1988, 340). Military spending was in-

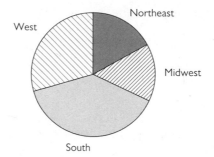

FIGURE 10.   *Defense Contracts Awarded in FY 1994, by Region*

NOTE: For exact percentage and dollar breakdowns, see Appendix D.
SOURCE: *Statistical Abstract of the United States, 1995* (Washington: U.S. Department of Commerce, 1995), 358.

deed big business. In 1985, during the Goldwater-Nichols reform discussions, the Pentagon spent $261 billion on American defense. The military's budget constituted 26.7 percent of all federal outlays and 6.4 percent of the gross domestic product (*Statistical Abstract of the United States, 1995, 336*).

Though the precise relationship between military budgets and political patronage is difficult to prove, general indicators and anecdotal evidence are compelling. Consider, for example, the distribution of military installations and defense contract awards. In a truly efficient military system, basing and contracting should be relatively concentrated. Ground troops might be somewhat dispersed, but domestic Navy bases should cluster along coastlines and Air Force installations should be located in more inland, protected locations. Generally, we would not expect to see large areas with installations of all three services. Similarly, an optimal defense contracting system would not scatter contracts to an array of manufacturers, but would channel awards to a few cost-effective, reliable producers. The market should reward companies that possess a comparative advantage.

But this is not what we find. In 1991, 30 of the 50 American states housed facilities of all three military services. Nearly 90 percent of all states—44 of 50—contained installations of two or more services. Navy facilities did tend to cluster along the coasts, but they

against national defense, with being against the Government" (U.S. House 1947a, 172). Senator Joseph Biden made the same point in 1986 during the Goldwater-Nichols debates.

In sum, maintaining the status quo military system provided large benefits for average members. A weak JCS bolstered civilian control of the military—and congressional power in particular—by allowing Congress to play the three services against one another. Military inefficiency meant big business for congressional districts; one legislator's waste was another's service to his constituents. Supporting the military also offered more reputational advantages than supporting military reform. As Les Aspin put it, "When it comes to national security matters, there is a tendency to 'play it safe.' Playing it safe usually means buying more" (Aspin 1975, 157). These three considerations made Congress a forceful ally of the military services and Defense Department officials.

All of these players had good reason to prefer the devil they knew to the devil they did not know. Even Goldwater did not champion reform legislation until his impending retirement, when the costs of taking on the Pentagon, his colleagues, and his constituents became negligible. Obviously, history shows that the interests and capabilities of these actors did not freeze JCS design forever. Yet presidential, bureaucratic, and congressional incentives and tools go a long way toward explaining why it was so difficult to change the Joint Chiefs of Staff for so long. To succeed, reform had to come through major legislation. And it had to contend with opposition on three fronts: from average legislators, civilian officials, and the military services.

EVENTS

The most stunning thing about political events is how little they influenced JCS development. It is no secret that the Joint Chiefs of Staff operated poorly from 1947 to 1986. Indeed, if performance in combat is the ultimate test of military organizational design, then the JCS system consistently scored low marks. During the Korean war, interservice rivalry extended to conflicts over which service would operate a laundry in Alaska (Dickson 1983). The Joint Chiefs of Staff signed off on Kennedy's Bay of Pigs plan despite serious reservations about its chances for success. "The advice of every member of the Executive Branch brought in to advise was unanimous," Kennedy remarked, "and the advice was wrong" (Sorensen 1965, 305). The military's lackluster performance in Vietnam has been the subject of myriad examinations. More recently, even small-scale operations in Iran, Grenada, and Beirut suffered from planning, command, and coordination problems. As Colin Powell concluded, JCS performance before the Goldwater-Nichols reforms of 1986 was "barely adequate."[31]

Reform did come in the end, but it came more than 10 years after Vietnam, 25 years after the Bay of Pigs, and 40 years after the start of the Cold War. Examining the role of events in JCS evolution reveals the agency's remarkable resilience when it was subjected to exogenous shocks. It took 40 years of mounting pressure to move the agency toward reform. Even then, success was by no means guaranteed; without the timely and tragic occurrence of the Beirut bombing and Grenada invasion in 1983, or the sustained leadership of key national security intellectuals within Congress, Goldwater-Nichols almost certainly would have failed.

SUMMARY

Odds were against the Joint Chiefs of Staff from the start. The JCS provisions of the National Security Act fulfilled the Navy's wildest dreams, hamstringing the Joint Chiefs at the outset and making future modifications nearly impossible. The statute conferred authority on a corporate JCS but gave it no power. It created conflicting interests at all levels of activity. It insulated the agency from presidential meddling by spelling out JCS features in explicit statutory language and by embedding the agency in a web of intricate and delicate relationships. All of these features ensured that changing the JCS would be difficult; to succeed, reform would have to be sweeping and it would have to come through legislation.

The ongoing interests and capabilities of relevant political players also worked against improving JCS design after 1947. Civilian Defense Department officials, the military services, and average legislators all stood to gain from a weak Joint Chiefs of Staff. Poor central military organization enhanced civilian control, ensured service survival, and provided electoral benefits to reelection-minded legislators. Presidents had the incentive to reform JCS design but lacked the capability to do so. Congress had the capability but lacked the incentive. With bureaucrats and legislators supporting the status quo, there was little presidents could do.

These two factors—initial design and the constellation of political interests—made the Joint Chiefs of Staff particularly resistant to the pressures of events. For decades, the JCS system was buffeted by operational shortcomings and by calls for reform. Yet nothing happened. No single event, not even the Vietnam war, could break through this wall of resistance. Reform required a massive accumulation of *all* these events and a crusade by some of Congress's most venerated leaders. Even then, it nearly failed.

Conclusions

We know from Chapter 4 that the National Security Agency Model provides a more satisfying explanation of JCS origins than the realist alternative. The Joint Chiefs of Staff was by all accounts inadequately designed at the outset—hardly the well-oiled Cold War military organization realism would expect to find. In this chapter, we see that new institutionalism offers a more complete account of JCS evolution as well. It turns out the JCS didn't just get off to a bad start. Its design flaws lasted for 39 years, during the most protracted and threatening period of international conflict in U.S. history. Amazingly, the Joint Chiefs organization remained unaltered despite nearly four decades of Cold War tension, despite an unprecedented shift from a multipolar to a bipolar distribution of international power, and despite military engagements that indicated grave organizational problems. Change did come, but it came when it was least expected. Nineteen eighty-six was no magic year. Certainly, events such as the Grenada invasion, the Beirut barracks bombing, and the failed hostage rescue attempt contributed to JCS reform. As in the NSC system case, events played a part in shaping the organization's development. But as any realist would quickly point out, events are not the same as changes in the international system. From a realist perspective, 1986 was just like any other Cold War year. The system was a bipolar one. The Soviet threat loomed large. The Cold War's end did not come for five more years—and when it did, nothing happened to the Joint Chiefs of Staff. In short, we find agency change in a time of systemic constancy and agency constancy at a time of systemic change.

By contrast, the new institutionalist National Security Agency Model proposed the following general hypotheses about the evolution of national security agencies: (1) agency evolution should be driven by the executive branch; (2) congressional oversight should be sporadic and largely ineffectual; and (3) specific agency trajectories can be explained mostly by initial agency design, and to a lesser extent by the ongoing interests and capabilities of political actors, and by world events. The JCS case fits fairly well with all three claims.

Though Congress has undoubtedly gotten more involved in defense budgets and issues since the Vietnam war (Blechman 1990), it has not done much to improve the workings of the Joint Chiefs of Staff. In fact, Congress's assertiveness on budget issues places its indifference to organizational issues in stark relief. After Vietnam, Authorization and Appropriations committees may have kept a closer eye on Pentagon expenditures, but they turned a deaf ear to complaints about basic problems of military organization. The Joint Chiefs of Staff was left to sputter along.

What few changes were made to the Joint Chiefs of Staff came from executive branch initiatives. Defense Secretary Forrestal was the driving force behind the 1949 National Security Act Amendments, Eisenhower pressed for reforms in 1953 and 1958, and JCS Chairman General David Jones set the reform ball rolling in the early 1980s.

Finally, examining initial agency design, actors' preferences, power, and outside events gets us a long way toward understanding precisely how and why the Joint Chiefs of Staff evolved in the way it did. A broad view of JCS evolution finds an overwhelming pattern of stasis. The Joint Chiefs of Staff was born a hard target: its initial design favored the status quo and gave bureaucrats and legislators little reason to change it.

JCS reform in 1986 stands as the exception that proves the rule. The truth is Goldwater-Nichols should never have happened. No theory or general explanation could have predicted its passage. Reform succeeded only because a series of factors converged at just the right moment, in just the right way. Had any one of them been missing, the Joint Chiefs of Staff would still be hobbled today.

CHAPTER 6

Origins of the Central Intelligence Agency: "Those Spooky Boys"

When most Americans think of the Central Intelligence Agency, they conjure up images of a rogue elephant, a supersecret organization gone out of control.[1] "Those spooky boys," as Secretary of State Dean Rusk called them (Leary 1984, 6), designed exploding Cuban cigars to assassinate Fidel Castro, mined Nicaraguan harbors, planted Soviet moles, and sponsored coups from Guatemala to Vietnam. The ultimate Cold War agency, the CIA became best known for its covert, subversive operations abroad.

But this Central Intelligence Agency looks nothing like the one created by the 1947 National Security Act. When Truman submitted that draft legislation in February 1947, he meant to create an intelligence confederation. Conforming to his military's wishes, the president sought a small central intelligence agency that would coordinate, evaluate, and disseminate intelligence, but not collect it. The original CIA was never supposed to engage in spying. It was never supposed to sponsor coups, influence foreign elections, or conduct any other kind of subversive operations. It was never supposed to be more than an analysis outfit, coordinating the information gathered by preexisting intelligence units in the Army, Navy, FBI, and State Department.[2] To put it plainly, the CIA was supposed to be weak. Its provision in the National Security Act was among the least noticed and least debated of all.

At the outset, it is also important to bear in mind that the CIA's origins were much more complicated than those of the NSC system or the Joint Chiefs of Staff. There were many more bureaucratic actors on the scene who had a stake in the creation of a central intelligence organization. Despite the popular perceptions generated by Tom Clancy novels and James Bond movies, American intelligence gathering was not a Cold War invention: it has existed since the Republic's founding. George Washington organized his own intelligence unit during the Revolutionary War, sending spies behind enemy lines and overseeing counterespionage operations. In 1790, just three years after the Constitutional Convention, Congress acknowledged an executive prerogative to conduct intelligence operations and gave President Washington a secret unvouchered fund "for spies, if the gentleman so pleases" (Andrew 1995, 11). Intelligence has been a component of American foreign policy ever since.

More important for our purposes, America's growing involvement in world affairs during the late nineteenth and early twentieth centuries led to the establishment of several permanent intelligence organizations. In 1882, the Office of Naval Intelligence (ONI) was created and charged with collecting technical data about foreign naval ships and weapons. Three years later, the Department of War established its own intelligence unit, the Military Intelligence Division (MID). In 1908, the Federal Bureau of Investigation opened its doors. By the 1930s, the FBI had become the nation's paramount counterespionage agency and had branched into running intelligence activities in Latin America. The State Department, meanwhile, had developed an expertise and a mission that focused on overt information collection. Finally, Japan's stunning surprise attack on Pearl Harbor sparked the creation of a new wartime central intelligence agency under the Joint Chiefs of Staff, the Office of Strategic Services (OSS), which collected information, analyzed raw intelligence, and carried out a range of covert subversive operations abroad, from propaganda to sabotage to paramilitary operations. By the end of World War II, these five bureaucratic actors were vying for their own places in the postwar intelligence arena. This was hardly the same straightforward War Department versus Navy Department environment that gave rise to the National Security Council system or the Joint Chiefs of Staff.

In addition, although the CIA's statutory charter can be found alongside provisions that established the NSC system and the Joint Chiefs of Staff, questions of postwar intelligence were peripheral to the unification debate. Political players, particularly the president, were far more concerned with consolidating the military services than with establishing any kind of peacetime central intelligence agency. The JCS and even the NSC system figured directly in War-Navy unification discussions. But postwar intelligence issues were mostly hashed out along a separate, parallel negotiating track. Indeed, these issues appeared to be settled in January 1946, a full year before the Truman administration presented Congress with its final version of the National Security Act: in an executive directive, the president signaled his acceptance of a hard-won compromise intelligence plan. The arrangement protected all existing intelligence units by granting each exclusive control over its own sphere of activity and by creating a new, weak, central coordinating body called the Central Intelligence Group (CIG). All sides expected this arrangement to be simply and automatically codified in the forthcoming National Security Act.

To everyone's surprise, however, the new Central Intelligence Group quickly took on a life of its own, pressing the administration for broader jurisdiction, more autonomy, and stronger legal foundations in the National Security Act. The timing could not have been worse. The warring military services were just now edging toward a comprehensive compromise unification bill. Reopening intelligence discussions at this point threatened to rekindle military opposition and derail the entire legislative package. Facing this specter, Truman and his aides were in no mood to compromise with CIG. Determined to get a military consolidation bill through Congress in 1947, the White House rejected all of CIG's demands and kept intelligence provisions as brief and as uncontroversial as possible. The administration's proposed National Security Act included the barest mention of a central intelligence agency. Ironically, such thin, vague provisions opened the door for subsequent CIA abuses. Truman's uncontroversial language would become the proverbial wolf in sheep's clothing.

The Players

WILD BILL DONOVAN AND THE OFFICE OF STRATEGIC SERVICES

Called an empire builder by some and Wild Bill by most, William J. Donovan began floating radical ideas for a powerful central intelligence organization as early as 1940 (Troy 1981, 74). During a European tour for President Roosevelt, Donovan became convinced that the existing intelligence system—which left War, Navy, State, FBI, and other intelligence units to their own devices—was incapable of providing the president with integrated intelligence analysis or operations. With U.S. involvement in the war imminent, Donovan began pressing Roosevelt for an agency that would not only coordinate these disparate intelligence components but combine intelligence collection, analysis, and subversive foreign operations under a single roof (Karalekas 1984). Events soon played into Donovan's hands. The surprise Japanese attack on Pearl Harbor gave rise to the Office of Strategic Services (OSS). With Donovan at its helm, the OSS was directed to "collect and analyze . . . strategic information" and to "plan and operate . . . special services" (Franklin D. Roosevelt, "Military Order of June 13, 1942: Office of Strategic Services," in Troy 1981, 427). The agency quickly evolved. By the end of the war, the OSS was engaged in a range of activities—from guerrilla warfare to clandestine activities to strategic analysis—and employed over 1,200 people (Yergin 1977, 215–16).

Still, the OSS was far from the all-encompassing, powerful central intelligence agency that Donovan envisioned. Placed under the Joint Chiefs of Staff, OSS faced stiff competition and firm resistance from both the Office of Naval Intelligence and the Army's G-2 intelligence branch. Anne Karalekas writes, "From the outset the military were reluctant to provide OSS with information for its research and analysis role and restricted its operations" (Karalekas 1984, 17). General Douglas MacArthur, she notes, excluded the OSS from the Pacific theater. FBI Director J. Edgar Hoover prohibited the OSS from conducting any domestic espionage activities and maintained the FBI's tight control over all intelligence activities in Latin America. In short, with no direct access to the president, with relatively limited autonomy, and with little cooperation from other intelligence components, the Office of Strategic Services contributed only modestly to the wartime intelligence effort (Lowenthal 1992).

The OSS experience was central to Donovan's thinking about postwar intelligence organization. In the fall of 1944, Donovan once again took the initiative, proposing a new and improved OSS to meet American peacetime intelligence needs. According to Donovan's memo to Roosevelt of November 18, 1944, this proposed central intelligence agency would report directly to the president. It would have its own budget. It would be able to call on other intelligence agencies for personnel and information. And it would have explicit authority to gather its own intelligence, to conduct its own subversive activities abroad, and to coordinate the intelligence functions and policies of all other intelligence agencies. In short, the Donovan proposal called for a truly centralized system, dominated by a single agency.[3]

THE MILITARY, THE FBI, AND THE DEPARTMENT OF STATE

Donovan's strong central intelligence agency plan ran up against serious opposition. The Navy Department, the War Department, the Justice Department's FBI, and the Department of State all conducted intelligence activities of their own. Without objecting outright to the idea of a central coordinating agency, these actors sought to protect their own turf. As former CIA Deputy Director Ray Cline writes, "The one thing that Army, Navy, State, and the FBI agreed on was that they did not want a strong central agency controlling their collection programs" (Cline 1981, 112). A common enemy forged common bonds. Though the specific motivations and plans varied among these actors, their objective was the same: maintaining the maximum power and independence of their own intelligence operations. In an unusual coalition, sailors, soldiers, G-men, and diplomats came together and lobbied for a decentralized, confederal intelligence system. Nominally coordinated by a small central organization, the system would allow each department to run its own intelligence affairs.

The Department of the Navy. The Navy Department led the charge against Donovan's idea of a powerful central intelligence agency. This should not come as a surprise. A decentralized intelligence system fitted nicely with the Navy's unification proposals and philosophy. Decentralization and loose coordination served the Navy's interests on all fronts. Navy leaders knew that confederal organizations—be they the National Security Council, the Joint Chiefs of Staff, or some diluted central intelligence agency—offered the best odds of maintaining the department's unparalleled status, power, and influence. That was exactly what they wanted. In Cline's words, the Navy "sought a central [intelligence] structure strong enough to prevent any other agency from dominating everything but weak enough to present no threat to Navy's control of its own affairs" (Cline 1981, 112).

But there was more to the Navy's motives than naked self-interest. As Ferdinand Eberstadt's 1945 report suggests, the Navy, War, and State departments had very different informational needs—needs that could not easily be combined or even understood by a central intelligence apparatus. Developing Navy strategy, tactics, weapons programs, and force structure required detailed technical information about enemy and allied naval forces. Similar considerations applied to the Army and Air Force. As for the State Department, diplomatic moves required both military information and intelligence about broader economic and political conditions abroad. "Each of these departments," Eberstadt concludes, "requires operating intelligence peculiar to itself. Intimate and detailed knowledge of the objectives and problems of each service is obviously indispensable to successful operation" (Eberstadt 1945, 163). For all three departments, collecting the right information and interpreting it in the right way required specialized expertise. Such skills, they believed, were most efficiently developed and used by their own, in-house intelligence components.

The Department of War.   War and Navy department interests coincided. While the two departments fought tooth and nail over almost every other provision of the National Security Act, they formed a united front against a strongly centralized intelligence system. Like the Office of Naval Intelligence, the Army's G-2 served the unique needs of its parent department. Operations, intelligence gathering, and analysis were all undertaken with an eye to improving War Department strategy and tactics. Though military consolidation promised a multitude of benefits for the War Department, intelligence consolidation did not. In this one area, War Department leaders willingly chanted the Navy's mantra: the more organizations, the better.

The Federal Bureau of Investigation.   The FBI, like the Navy and War departments, had good reasons to resist a highly centralized intelligence system. Initially established as the Justice Department's basic federal law enforcement agency, the bureau quickly extended its activities to counterterrorism and counterintelligence. During the 1930s, J. Edgar Hoover's G-men were responsible for rooting out spies, for investigating sabotage, and for hunting down communist and fascist operatives within the United States. It was not long before the ever-ambitious Hoover began pushing for more. In 1939, the FBI assumed responsibility for collecting foreign intelligence in Latin America. With President Roosevelt's blessing, the bureau created a Special Intelligence Services whose 360 agents controlled Western Hemisphere intelligence activities throughout the war (Richelson 1989, 136). By 1945, Hoover's FBI had become the nation's primary counterespionage agency, with near total control over domestic activities, and had begun venturing into overseas operations. As the war's end drew near, the bureau was naturally reluctant to cede either of these hard-won gains to Donovan's OSS or to any other organization.

An Uneasy Partner: The Department of State.   The State Department sat more tenuously in this coalition. It appeared to be caught between two countervailing pressures.

On the one hand, Donovan's idea of a strong central intelligence agency threatened the secretary of state and his colleagues. As State saw it, the line between analyzing intelligence and providing foreign policy advice was a thin one. Indeed, the State Department largely saw its mission in terms of intelligence; what else did Foreign Service officers do but collect information and use it to develop workable policy proposals and programs? For diplomats, information was power. Donovan's new agency, with its broad information-gathering mandate and direct access to the president, posed a direct challenge to the State Department's influence in foreign affairs.

On the other hand, the department's own cultural norms and organizational structure pulled in the opposite direction. Disdain for all things covert ran deep within the diplomatic corps. As Secretary of State Henry L. Stimson once put it, "gentlemen do not read each other's mail." Such sentiment had prompted the department to disband its code-breaking joint venture with the Army and Navy in 1929 and to resist creating an internal clandestine intelligence unit until after World War II. For these officials, intelligence was supposed to be gained openly, by trained diplomats who spent their time monitoring foreign news, socializing with foreign diplomats, and cabling their impressions back home to Washington (Cline 1981, 30–37). If clandestine activities had to be performed at all, the feeling ran, it was better to let some other organization take responsibility. By this reasoning, a powerful central intelligence agency might not be a bad thing. At the very least, it kept the dirty business of spying from sullying the hands of diplomats.

The department's centrifugal organization only added fuel to the fire. Regional bureaus dominated the State Department's power structure. Rooted in this division was the idea that all activities, including overt intelligence collection, should be scattered across the various country and regional offices rather than concentrated in any kind of department-wide functional bureau. This resistance to creating an in-house, State Department intelligence outfit weakened the department's hand in the broader executive branch battle.

As we shall see, these countervailing pressures led the State Department to move in and out of its alliance with the Navy, the War Department, and the FBI. At first, fears of Donovan's all-powerful agency drove the department into their arms. Once Donovan's plan was off the table, however, Secretary of State James Byrnes tried to break away from the coalition and take control of *all* intelligence activities in the executive branch. But Byrnes soon found himself waging a two-front war—one against his coalition partners in the executive branch and the other against his own department. Byrnes eventually conceded, rejoined the War/Navy/FBI coalition, and lived to fight another day.

A LATE ARRIVAL: THE CENTRAL INTELLIGENCE GROUP

The Central Intelligence Group was never supposed to become an actor in the intelligence conflict. When Harry Truman created CIG by executive directive on January 22, 1946, he believed the bureaucratic battle to be over: CIG's design represented a decisive victory for proponents of decentralized intelligence. Surrounded by superintending and advisory bodies, dependent on other departments for budgets and staffing, and limited to coordinating, correlating, evaluating, and disseminating the intelligence collected by others, CIG was designed to be a clearinghouse without strong central authority or power.[4]

Truman expected to codify this language eventually (and easily) in the National Security Act. The Central Intelligence Group had different ideas. Within six months of its creation, the agency began pushing for wide-ranging changes. Complaining about its "stepchild" status, CIG Director Hoyt S. Vandenberg mounted a campaign to win his agency greater autonomy, broader jurisdiction, and more power, and to enshrine all of these gains in a new statutory charter. Rather than ending the intelligence controversy, CIG's creation added one more voice to it.

THE PRESIDENT

For Harry Truman, creating a strong peacetime central intelligence agency was never a high priority. Publicly, he remained relatively detached from intelligence hostilities, refusing to take a firm position or get out in front of the issue.[5] When moments of decision did arrive, however, the president sided with his military services. At every critical juncture of the intelligence debate, Truman opted for the weaker central intelligence agency proposed by the military. There were three major moments of decision. The first came in September 1945, when Truman chose to disband the wartime Office of Strategic Services instead of maintaining it during peacetime, as Donovan wanted. Second, in January 1946, the president opted to coordinate intelligence through an emasculated Central Intelligence Group rather than through a much stronger State Department apparatus. Finally, in 1947, Truman proposed a CIG-like agency for the National Security Act instead of the more powerful agency recommended by CIG Director Vandenberg.

These choices may seem surprising at first. After all, we would expect any president, *ceteris paribus*, to prefer more information to less, and to favor centralized control over decentralized arrangements. By this reasoning, Truman should have been driven by the imperatives of office to *reject* the military's intelligence plans. However, Truman's position makes more sense when placed in context. For this president, no organizational issue appeared more important than consolidating the War and Navy departments into an effective, efficient military apparatus. As he explained in his 1945 special message to Congress:

> We would be taking a grave risk with the national security if we did not move now to overcome permanently the present imperfections in our defense organization. However great was the need for coordination and unified command in World War II, it is sure to be greater if there is any future aggression against world peace. . . . Our combat forces must work together in one team as they have never been required to work together in the past. (Truman 1961–66, 1: 549)

Unification of the armed forces was Harry Truman's crusade. For two years, the president marshaled all the energies and powers of his office to make this idea a reality. Eyeing the unification prize, Truman had little patience for anything that might jeopardize his campaign.

A new, powerful central intelligence agency threatened to do just that. Intelligence was one of the few issues on which the warring Navy and War departments actually agreed. From the start, both services resisted any proposal that sought to concentrate intelligence authority in a single organization—be it the OSS, the State Department, or a Central Intelligence Agency. From the president's vantage point, opposing the military on this issue posed high risks and promised low rewards. Given the delicate nature of unification negotiations, Truman needed all the help he could get.[6]

TWO MISSING PIECES: INTEREST GROUPS AND CONGRESS

Just like the NSC system and the JCS, the CIA was created without much input from interest groups or members of Congress. The absence of interest groups in this case is understandable. We already know that the foreign policy interest group scene was rather sparse. In addition, intelligence operations and organizations were, by nature, shrouded in secrecy. With no way to know what the issues were, even interested citizens naturally found it difficult to organize and try to influence the debate.

Legislators also played minor parts in the CIA's creation. Between 1944 and 1947, substantive debates about postwar intelligence organization stayed within the confines of the executive branch. Though House and Senate committees held a string of hearings during that time about military unification, questions of intelligence organization were rarely raised and hardly discussed. Tellingly, Truman succeeded in disbanding the wartime OSS and creating the Central Intelligence Group without any congressional involvement at all. Both changes were made by unilateral executive action.[7] Moreover, legislators appeared to duck the intelligence question even when they had an opportunity to tackle it. In 1947, the intelligence provisions of Truman's National Security Act sailed through the House and Senate with little controversy. Though the House Committee on Expenditures in the Executive Departments insisted on specifying the CIA's functions, they adopted the president's old CIG directive almost word for word. No one ever seriously considered what this new agency would or should be doing. The question hinged on whether the CIA's powers should be spelled out in legislation, not on what those powers should be (Troy 1981, 385; Lowenthal 1992, 17). Thus, National Security Act provisions ended up creating a CIA that closely resembled its CIG predecessor. This was precisely what the Truman administration wanted.

Congress acquiesced on CIA design for many of the same reasons it did on the NSC system and the JCS provisions of the National Security Act. First and foremost, average members had no real incentives to take charge of the issue. If anything, electoral considerations militated against challenging the executive branch on national security organization. There were no strong organized interests that could reward legislators for their votes. Conversely, broad-based public opinion could easily be turned against members who challenged military experts on American national security issues. Against the Cold War backdrop, these considerations prevented even congressional national security intellectuals—that is, leading legislators who tackled national issues for nonelectoral reasons—from taking a prominent role. With dim prospects of rallying their colleagues to action, congressional leaders sat on the sidelines.

The administration also made it difficult for Congress to join the intelligence debate. For one thing, placing intelligence provisions in the omnibus National Security Act deflected attention from the CIA and toward other more contentious issues such as the secretary of defense's powers or the Navy's autonomy. For another, White House aides deliberately adopted a strategy of "the less said, the better," making CIA provisions brief and vague (Troy 1981; Clifford 1991). Fearing that any more detailed language might reopen bureaucratic conflict or invite closer congressional scrutiny, administration officials kept controversial provisions to a minimum, presented them as stopgap measures, and promised Congress a second, separate intelligence bill in the future (Admiral Forrest Sherman, in U.S. House 1947a, 174).[8] The approach worked: all but a few legislators were content to let the National Security Act's intelligence provisions stand unchallenged.

In sum, like the National Security Council system and the Joint Chiefs of Staff, the Central Intelligence Agency was forged out of conflict in the executive branch. A host of bureaucratic actors—the wartime OSS, the military, the FBI, the State Department, the Central Intelligence Group—all held substantial stakes in postwar intelligence organization. Each fought to achieve its own goals. President Truman was a reluctant arbiter. Preoccupied with military unification, the president took action only when necessary and always sided with his military departments. Legislators, for their part, had little reason to get involved. Flexing congressional muscles on this issue offered little in the way of electoral rewards and much in the way of potential public criticism.

Overview: Unification and the Central Intelligence Agency

The intelligence battle was a three-round affair. All rounds were fought within the executive branch, but they did not involve the same actors or the same options. Round 1, which lasted from late 1944 to the fall of 1945, pitted Wild Bill Donovan and his OSS against a coalition of the Navy, War, Justice, and State departments. At issue was whether to transform the wartime Office of Strategic Services into a powerful, independent peacetime central intelligence agency. When the round ended, Donovan had lost. Not only did the president reject Donovan's vision of a central intelligence agency, but he disbanded OSS altogether, transferring its divisions to the departments of War and State like spoils to the victors. In round 2, it was State versus the military; suddenly, without the OSS as a common enemy, the Navy/War/Justice/State coalition began to fray. While Secretary of State Byrnes pressed for a new State Department–controlled intelligence system, War and Navy officials stuck to their guns, continuing to support the old coalition plan for a Central Intelligence Group under joint State/War/Navy control. In the end, State conceded and CIG was established by executive directive. Round 3 featured two new players—the freshly minted Central Intelligence Group and the White House. Between January 1946 and February 1947, CIG pushed for more power and for stronger statutory foundations in the National Security Act, while Truman and his legislative drafting team, mindful of the military's position, desperately tried to quell their demands. With the entire unification bill hanging in the balance, CIG did not have much chance. The CIA that emerged from the National Security Act of 1947 satisfied the War and Navy departments. It was weak by design.

ROUND I: NOVEMBER 1944–SEPTEMBER 1945

Wild Bill Donovan kicked off the conflict in November 1944 with a memo to Franklin Roosevelt (printed in Troy 1981, 445–47). In it,

Donovan urged the president not only to keep OSS after the war but to vastly increase its autonomy, capabilities, and jurisdiction.[9] Whereas the wartime OSS had to report to the Joint Chiefs of Staff, Donovan's postwar agency would be led by a director who reported directly to the president. Whereas the OSS had to make do with budgets from other departments and agencies, the postwar intelligence agency would have an independent budget. Whereas the OSS's mandate was limited, Donovan's new agency had wide-ranging authority to run its own spies and conduct subversive operations, as well as to analyze and disseminate intelligence gathered by State, ONI, G-2, the FBI, and any other governmental intelligence unit. With its own money, its direct access to the president, and its broad authority, Donovan's new agency would be suffused with power. It was designed not to coordinate existing intelligence agencies but to dominate them.

Naturally, the departmental intelligence services resisted Donovan's plan. As Thomas Troy notes, the OSS's "pretensions to permanence and power" generated "intense hostility" among other intelligence producers, particularly those in the departments of War, the Navy, and Justice. "These had not wanted . . . OSS in the first place, had never become reconciled to it, and were determined it would never attain what they were sure it aspired to, namely, control over their intelligence and their intelligence departments" (Troy 1981, 278). In their view, effective intelligence gathering and analysis could be realized only by a decentralized system in which each department trained its own experts and developed its own priorities.

Politics made for strange bedfellows. Between November 1944 and September 1945, the departments of State, War, the Navy, and Justice joined forces against the Donovan plan. They counterattacked along several fronts. The military spearheaded the effort, working within the JCS to develop constructive alternatives to the Donovan plan. They finished in a matter of weeks. Their counterproposal, which was issued as JIC 239/5 on January 1, 1945, diluted much of the central agency's power.[10] Instead of reporting directly to the president, the agency's director answered to a "National Intelligence Authority" (NIA) consisting of the secretaries of state, war, the Navy, and a representative from the Joint Chiefs of Staff. This NIA was a far more powerful superintending authority than anything Donovan had envisioned, with nearly total control over the new agency's budgets, jurisdiction, and activities. The JCS plan also called for an intelligence advisory board, filled with the heads of all the major intelligence units, which would advise the new central agency's director. In essence, this scheme sought to create an intelligence system that was centralized in name only; sandwiched between the NIA and the advisory board, the proposed central intelligence agency would have minimal authority and power (Troy 1981, 151).

Meanwhile, Hoover's FBI worked behind the scenes to sabotage the OSS effort. In February 1945, news of Donovan's plan made front-page headlines in three leading anti-Roosevelt papers—the *Chicago Tribune*, the *New York Daily News*, and the *Washington Times Herald*. The articles, written by Walter Trohan, carried classified details of the Donovan plan and denounced them all. "Donovan Proposes Super Spy System for Postwar New Deal; Would Take Over FBI, Secret Service, ONI and G-2 to Watch Home, Abroad," ran the *Times Herald* story. The *Chicago Tribune* declared, "New Deal Plans Super Spy System; Sleuths Would Snoop on U.S. and the World" (quoted in Troy 1981, 255). Calling the proposed central intelligence agency "an all-powerful intelligence service to spy on the postwar world and to pry into the lives of citizens at home" (quoted in Troy 1981, 255), Trohan inflamed public fears of a U.S. Gestapo. Though J. Edgar Hoover never admitted responsibility, many observers, including Donovan and White House aide Clark Clifford, believed him to be the source of the leaks (Darling [1953] 1990; Troy 1981; Clifford 1991).

As the JCS counterproposal made its way to the president's desk and as press leaks made Donovan's plan increasingly untenable, the departments of State, Justice, War, and the Navy embarked on a diplomatic initiative to stall consideration of the entire intelligence issue. On April 5, 1945, just before his death, President Roosevelt asked Donovan to canvass the heads of all intelligence services about the establishment of a postwar central intelligence agency. Secretary of War Henry L. Stimson responded by sending a letter to Donovan. His position was firm and clear: as the primary protectors of U.S. national interests abroad and at home, the departments of State, War, the Navy, and Justice had to retain complete control over their own intelligence operations. Stimson also made clear that the War Department was not standing alone. "State, War, Justice and the Navy have together examined the proposed central intelligence service and are in substantial agreement that it should not be considered prior to the termination of hostilities against Germany and Japan," he wrote (quoted in Troy 1981, 269). The meaning of this sentence could not have been lost on Donovan: the four most powerful executive departments had already forged a coalition against him (Darling [1953] 1990; Troy 1981). Delaying the intelligence issue was merely a polite—and effective—signal of their intentions.

Donovan and the Office of Strategic Services had no chance against such odds. Indeed, as Troy writes, the agency "was in a fundamentally weaker position than all its rivals and foes" (Troy 1981, 277). Forged in wartime, without any statutory authority, OSS was never intended to be anything more than a temporary creation. As such, the agency lacked institutional strength. It had no alumni to speak of, few congressional supporters, and no real broad public support. As the war wound down, public sentiment favored a quick return to business as usual, including the demobilization of wartime agencies.

This first round of conflict ended five months later, on September 20, 1945, when President Truman issued an executive order disbanding the Office of Strategic Services and transferring its divisions to the departments of State and War. With the big four executive departments on the offensive, with public criticism on the rise, and with Donovan against the wall, the president's choice was easy. When the dust cleared, OSS was dead and Donovan's hopes for a strong postwar central intelligence agency were dashed.

ROUND 2: SEPTEMBER 1945–JANUARY 1946

Round 2 began immediately. With OSS gone, the locus of conflict moved inside the Navy/War/Justice/State coalition. On September 20, the same day Truman eliminated OSS, he asked Secretary of State James Byrnes to "take the lead in developing a comprehensive and coordinated foreign intelligence program" ("Letter from President Truman to Secretary Byrnes Concerning the Development of a Foreign Intelligence Program," in Troy 1981, 463). Why the president handed this responsibility to the State Department remains unclear; what is clear is that Byrnes and his acolytes seized the opportunity. They soon began lobbying for a State Department–controlled postwar intelligence system. The State Department plan, developed by Byrnes's special assistant for research and intelligence, Alfred McCormack, called for housing an overarching national intelligence authority within the State Department, under the exclusive authority and direction of the secretary. Under the McCormack plan, State would be the sole conduit of intelligence reports to the president (Troy 1981; Jeffreys-Jones 1989; Clifford 1991).

McCormack's proposal touched off a new and bitter, struggle between the Department of State and the military. To War Department and Navy Department officials, a State-run intelligence system was no better than Donovan's independent central intelligence organization. Both threatened departmental prerogatives. Both promised to undermine military control over military intelligence units. Both guaranteed outside interference in Army, Navy, and Air Force intelligence activities. As Rhodri Jeffreys-Jones put it, "The services wished to keep their own intelligence arms intact. If there had to be a central system, they demanded a major say in it" (Jeffreys-Jones 1989, 34).

War and Navy leaders quickly forged an alliance to resist this new threat. On October 13, 1945, Navy Secretary James Forrestal wrote Secretary of War Robert Patterson a memo that, among other things, praised the old JCS intelligence plan and suggested the two secretaries "push it vigorously at the White House" (Troy 1981, 316). Days later, the Navy Department publicly released its lengthy study of military unification, the Eberstadt Report. In forceful prose, the report reiterated the Navy's support for a weakly centralized intelligence system. "Complete merger of the intelligence services of the State, War and Navy Departments is not considered feasible," the report declared (Eberstadt 1945, 163). On November 3 the War Department concluded its own internal study of intelligence issues. The department's final report differed in some details but agreed in principle to JCS and Navy proposals for a confederal intelligence system with minimal central control. As Troy concludes, "With these two reports in hand . . . the two secretaries had both a common position and a common front . . . and their alliance presented a serious challenge to the Secretary of State" (Troy 1981, 319).

State leaders also found themselves facing fierce opposition within their own department. Regional division heads feared the proposed State Department national intelligence authority would interfere with their own intelligence efforts. Jealously guarding their prerogatives, these Foreign Service officers wanted no part of McCormack's plan. As Under Secretary of State Dean Acheson recalled, the geographic divisions, led by Latin American Division chief Spruille Braden and Near Eastern Division chief Loy Henderson, "were moving into solid opposition to intelligence work not in their organizations and under their control." Braden later described it as a "knockdown, dragout fight" (Acheson 1969, 159–60).

The combination of internal and external resistance proved devastating. With a two-front war on his hands, Secretary of State Byrnes did not last long. In mid-November, Byrnes began to move toward accommodation with the secretaries of war and the Navy. In December, the military turned up the heat, sending the president copies of the State and JCS plans, along with a cover memo by Admiral Sidney Souers outlining why the president should adopt the military's proposal.[11] The critical moment came on January 6, 1946, when Byrnes, Forrestal, and Under Secretary of War Kenneth Royall met at the Shoreham Hotel. In their meeting, Forrestal reportedly told Byrnes, "Jimmy, we like you, but we don't like your plan. Just think what might happen if another William Jennings Bryan were to succeed you in the State Department" (Darling [1953] 1990, 70). Byrnes capitulated. Before the meeting ended, he agreed to rejoin the coalition and renew his support for a decentralized intelligence system (Darling [1953] 1990; Troy 1981).

Three weeks later, President Truman made the deal official. His executive directive of January 22, 1946, created a central intelligence system that closely followed the military's recommendations. Under the directive, each department retained almost complete autonomy over its own intelligence services. A new Central Intelligence Group was created, but given no real autonomy or power. Instead of reporting directly to the president, as Donovan had wanted, CIG served under a National Intelligence Authority—a board that included the secretaries of state, war, the Navy, and a presidential appointee. Sitting above the central agency, the secretaries of state, the Navy, and war were in an ideal position to protect the interests of their own intelligence components. That was not all. Truman's directive created an Intelligence Advisory Board consisting of all intelligence agency heads to "advise" the new CIG director. The presidential order also guaranteed the continued existence of departmental intelligence agencies, provided no authority for CIG to collect intelligence or conduct covert operations, and explicitly prohibited the new agency from exercising any "internal security functions" that might infringe on the FBI's jurisdiction. Truman even gave the State, War, and Navy departments control over CIG budgets and staffing. As Anne Karalekas notes, this was a recipe for feeble centralization. "Through budget, personnel, and oversight," she writes, "the Departments had assured themselves control over the Central Intelligence Group. CIG was a creature of departments that were determined to maintain independent capabilities as well as their direct advisory relationship to the President." She concludes that "they succeeded in doing both" (Karalekas 1984, 21).

ROUND 3: JANUARY 1946–FEBRUARY 1947

At this point, all sides thought the intelligence battle was over. Donovan and his OSS were out of the picture, the State Department had come back into the fold, and the president had created a Central Intelligence Group that left each department to run its own intelligence affairs. As Truman and his warring military services now turned to drafting a compromise military unification bill, the intelligence consensus was clear: any legislation should include provisions codifying the president's CIG directive.[12] Doing so would freeze the existing intelligence system into law, insulating it from the whims or desires of future political players. On this much, at least, the War and Navy departments agreed.

The Central Intelligence Group did not. Ink on the CIG directive had hardly dried before the agency began taking on a life and agenda of its own. CIG's problems were apparent from the start. During the early months of 1946, departmental intelligence services readily bypassed the central agency, sending their information and taking their case directly to the president. They provided CIG with a small budget and a meager, mediocre staff. They refused to share raw intelligence and ignored the agency's efforts to reconcile or synthesize conflicting information. As Anne Karalekas writes, the intelligence units "jealously guarded both their information and what they believed were their prerogatives in providing policy guidance to the President, making CIG's primary mission an exercise in futility" (Karalekas 1984, 24). The problem was simple: CIG's success hinged on the generosity of those who wanted it to fail. Truman's directive appeared to be working too well.

Frustrated by their agency's impotence, CIG officials soon began pressing for substantial changes. In their capacity as National Intelligence Authority members, the secretaries of war, the Navy, and state granted some significant concessions.[13] But these were not enough. In July, CIG General Counsel Lawrence R. Houston sent a draft "Bill for the Establishment of a Central Intelligence Agency" to the White House that sought to transform CIG from a small planning staff to "a legally established, fairly sizable, operating agency" (Elsey Papers, Box 56).

This move came as an alarming surprise to the White House, which was now deeply embroiled in the unification conflict. As Troy writes, "In this perspective, where the White House had the difficult problem of getting generals and admirals to agree on a fundamental reorganization of their services, the legislative problem of the CIG must have seemed . . . an unwelcome detail" (Troy 1981, 371). As the War and Navy departments moved toward compromise, the president and his legislative drafting team hardened toward CIG. By January, when the military finally agreed to a comprehensive unification bill, the White House was in no mood to humor the Central Intelligence Group's demands that the legislation specifically outline CIA functions, make the director of central intelligence a statutory nonvoting member of the NSC, provide procurement authorities, or grant the CIA power to "coordinate" foreign intelligence activities and "operate centrally" where appropriate. Such controversial measures threatened to reignite military opposition and reopen the entire unification conflict (Troy 1981). Thus, as CIG pressed for more, the White House responded with less. On February 26 the president submitted his draft National Security Act to Congress. It included only the barest mention of the CIA—enough to transform the CIG directive into law and nothing more. In just 30 lines the CIA section established the agency, placed it under the National Security Council, gave it a director appointed from civilian or military life by the president (with the Senate's consent), and authorized it to inherit the "functions, personnel, property, and records" of the Central Intelligence Group (U.S. House 1947b, 10). Round 3 was over. CIG had lost.

EPILOGUE: CONGRESS CONSIDERS THE NATIONAL SECURITY ACT

The CIA provisions of the National Security Act went relatively unnoticed and unaltered in Congress. Legislators concentrated instead on the more hotly contested aspects of merging the two military departments—such issues as the power of the new secretary of defense and the protection of the Navy's Marine Corps and aviation units. In the Senate, Armed Services Committee deliberations resulted in only two relatively minor changes to the proposed CIA, neither of which dealt with its functions or jurisdiction.[14] In fact, the committee's final report specifically noted that the agency would continue to perform the duties outlined in Truman's CIG directive until Congress could pass permanent legislation at a later date (Troy 1981). In the House, members of the Committee on Expenditures in the Executive Departments raised more questions and concerns about the CIA's "Gestapo" potential and about its unspecified functions. But transcripts clearly show such questions and concerns were overshadowed by other unification issues. Discussion of the CIA occupied just 29 out of 700 pages of House committee testimony.[15] The committee's probing did not go far or produce far-reaching changes to the bill. Quite the opposite: when House members finally decided to list CIA functions in greater detail, they simply cut and pasted from Truman's existing CIG directive.

The CIA that arose from the National Security Act of 1947 closely resembled its CIG predecessor. Like CIG, the CIA was supposed to "correlate," "evaluate," and "disseminate" intelligence from other services, but was given no authority to collect intelligence on its own or to engage in any covert operations. Like CIG, the CIA operated under the vigilance of other intelligence producers; where CIG reported to a National Intelligence Authority, the CIA operated under the National Security Council—a committee including the secretaries of war, the Navy, state, and defense and the president. Mimicking the CIG directive, the National Security Act protected existing intelligence components with explicit guarantees. In deference to the FBI, the law barred the CIA from exercising any "police, subpena, law-enforcement powers, or internal-security functions." It also provided that "the departments and other agencies of the Government shall continue to collect, evaluate, correlate, and disseminate departmental intelligence." Finally, the act borrowed two broad clauses from Truman's directive that were to have a profound impact on the CIA's subsequent development. The new agency was charged with conducting "such additional services of common concern as the National Security Council determines" and with performing "such other functions and duties related to intelligence affecting the national security as the National Security Council may from time to time direct" (*U.S. Statutes at Large* 1948, 497–99). Taken together, these CIA provisions created an agency that suited the War and Navy departments to a T. If CIG were any guide, the CIA would pose no threat to departmental intelligence agencies.

Conclusions

Here, too, it appears that a major national security agency was forged without much congressional input and without much consideration of the national interest. Like the National Security Council system and the Joint Chiefs of Staff, the Central Intelligence Agency took shape almost exclusively within the executive branch, where bureaucratic players cared first and foremost about their own institutional interests.

The CIA was clearly a product of executive branch discussions and decisions. All three rounds of the postwar intelligence battle were fought among bureaucratic actors and were ultimately decided by the president. Round 1, which pitted OSS chief Donovan against the Navy/War/Justice/State department coalition, ended with an executive order disbanding the OSS and transferring its functions to the departments of State and War. Round 2 featured internecine warfare between top State Department officials and the military. It, too, ended with unilateral presidential action: an executive directive that implemented the military's recommendations for a weak Central Intelligence Group. In round 3, it was CIG against the White House. With the entire unification bill hanging in the balance and with military preferences about postwar intelligence well known, Truman and his legislative drafting team took decisive action. Rebuffing CIG's advances, they introduced a national security bill that included brief, vague CIA provisions. Their aim was to continue CIG under new, statutory authority while generating as little controversy as possible.[16]

Truman succeeded, thanks in large part to congressional indifference. Legislators in both chambers accepted the CIA provisions with little comment or debate. Though a few members raised alarms about the agency's potential police power and broad jurisdiction, these voices were whispers against the wind.[17] Average legislators had little incentive to probe deeply into the CIA's design, and national security intellectuals had bigger fish to fry in the unification bill. Tellingly, even those who pressed for a more specific CIA mandate ended up simply copying from Truman's CIG directive of 1946. It seems that even here, legislators were content to defer to the executive. The CIA that emerged bore an uncanny resemblance to the Central Intelligence Group. Truman himself writes that the National Security Act succeeded in "renaming" the Central Intel-

ligence Group—implying that the act made no substantive changes
to CIG's design or operations at all (Truman 1956, 57–58).

There can also be little doubt that the Central Intelligence Agency
was forged out of parochial rather than national interests. Creating
any kind of postwar central intelligence apparatus inevitably benefited some bureaucratic actors and threatened others. While the OSS
and CIG had much to gain by a strongly centralized system, the
departments of State, Justice, War, and the Navy all stood to lose.
For these "big four" departments, promoting U.S. national security
was never a paramount concern. Instead, these departments sought
a central intelligence system that, above all, insulated their own
intelligence services from outside interference. Paradoxically, their
vision of an "effective" central intelligence agency was one without
strong central control or coordination. The ideal CIA was a weak
CIA.

But why did these departments succeed? Why did the president so
readily accept their vision of postwar intelligence organization? The
short answer is that Harry Truman needed the military services
more than they needed him. Propelled by national interest, the president had placed military consolidation at the top of his political
agenda. To him, no issue was more vital to American postwar security than unifying the War and Navy departments into a single
Department of Defense, and no price was too great to achieve success. In this context, Donovan's vision of a powerful statutory CIA
never had a chance. From day one, War and Navy leaders strenuously opposed such a scheme. With no political capital to spare, the
president went along. His executive actions and legislative recommendations all sought to create a central intelligence apparatus that
protected departmental intelligence units rather than to ensure that
the new central agency would function well.

Evolution of the Central Intelligence Agency: "One of the Weakest Links in Our National Security"

The evolution of the CIA bears a remarkable resemblance to that of both the NSC system and the Joint Chiefs of Staff. At first glance, this may seem peculiar. After all, the NSC system is a case of rapid and radical president-led reform, while the JCS appears a model of agency stagnation. For presidents, changing the NSC staff came easily. Almost overnight, they were able to turn an insignificant staff provision of the National Security Act into a powerful presidential foreign policy organization. This was hardly true of the Joint Chiefs of Staff organization, which remained impervious to presidential reform efforts and hobbled by its ineffective design for four decades. The NSC system and JCS evolutionary patterns appear to be polar opposites.

How could the CIA have been radically transformed and mired in its original design at the same time? The answer is that the Central Intelligence Agency really contains two organizations in one: a coordinating/analysis unit and a clandestine service.[1] With separate personnel, vastly different cultures and missions, and rigid organizational barriers, these two sides of the CIA have evolved in separate ways along separate tracks. The CIA's schizophrenic nature has led to schizophrenic development.

The covert wing—now called the Directorate of Operations—has developed much like the NSC staff. It first arose and flourished because presidents wanted it to. Covert action was never explicitly authorized by the National Security Act or any subsequent legislation. Clandestine intelligence gathering and secret political activities have been conducted solely on the basis of presidential orders, memos, and directives.[2] What's more, this covert branch has remained well insulated from congressional oversight or reform, even through the scandals of the 1970s and 1980s.

At the same time, the CIA's analysis and coordination efforts—now housed in the Directorate of Intelligence and the office of the director of central intelligence (DCI)—have floundered. Like the JCS, these offices originally arose out of intense bureaucratic conflict. CIA design pitted a Navy/War/Justice/State department coalition against OSS founder Bill Donovan and various incarnations of his wartime intelligence service. Above all, coalition members wanted the CIA to be a coordinating agency that left them alone—one that did not actually coordinate much at all. They got what they wanted in the 1947 National Security Act. Statutory provisions created a Central Intelligence Agency that was incapable of centralizing intelligence. Truman and his successors naturally disliked such an unwieldy decentralized system, yet they could do little about it. As in the JCS case, presidents have been stymied by congressional acquiescence and by anticipated as well as actual threats of bureaucratic resistance. Thus, instead of pressing for major CIA reforms, chief executives have developed alternative ways of centralizing and analyzing critical intelligence.

As we shall see, CIA evolution provides a third supporting case for the general propositions of the National Security Agency Model. Here, too, the executive branch shaped agency evolution. Here, too, Congress paid little attention and exerted little influence. When it came to oversight, Congress's bark proved worse than its bite. And here, too, agency evolution can be understood by examining initial design, the interests and capabilities of political actors, and events.

Below I track the development of both CIA branches through the decades, offer a new institutionalist explanation, and assess how well this case fits my general claims about the evolution of American national security agencies.

CIA Evolution

1947–1974: THE SPOOKS REIGN SUPREME

The Central Intelligence Agency was never supposed to amount to much. The departments of State, War, Justice, and the Navy wanted it that way. A central intelligence organization with no real central authority and limited power guaranteed that each department could continue to develop its own intelligence priorities and maintain its own intelligence capability.

Two points about initial CIA design should be underscored. First, *the agency was given no authority to engage in covert activities of any sort—be it collecting intelligence or conducting subversive political activities abroad.* This was no accident. Evidence strongly suggests that, with the exception of OSS chief Bill Donovan, nobody wanted or intended the Central Intelligence Agency to undertake covert action. Of all the proposals, only Donovan's 1944 memo called for direct intelligence "collection" and for "subversive operations abroad" (text in Troy 1981, 445–47). The JCS plan,[3] the Navy's Eberstadt Report (1945), Truman's 1946 Central Intelligence Group directive,[4] and successive drafts of the National Security Act all mention "intelligence collection" only when they discuss the activities of existing departmental services, not the CIA. And they all avoid mentioning covert operations altogether. The bureaucrats were not alone. It seems that back-alley warfare never received serious consideration in the halls of Congress, either. As the Senate's CIA investigating committee concluded in 1976, "There is no reference to covert action in the 1947 National Security Act, nor is there any evidence in the debates, committee reports, or legislative history of the 1947 Act to show that Congress intended specifically to authorize covert operations" (U.S. Senate 1976, 149).[5] Nor did Truman anticipate or sanction the idea. Thomas Troy writes, "It is quite likely true that on July 26, 1947, when he signed the act, he had no thought of the new agency conducting subversive operations against foreign governments. As far as evidence goes, no one did" (Troy 1981, 413).[6]

This leads to the second point. *Ostensibly, the CIA's primary responsibility was coordinating the disparate elements of the intelligence community. Yet, as we saw in Chapter 6, the agency was not designed to do this job well.* The CIA provisions of the 1947

National Security Act clearly show an agency whose mandate far exceeded its capacity to perform. The act charged the CIA with "coordinating the intelligence activities of the several Government Departments and agencies" but provided no language compelling these various agencies to cooperate. The director of central intelligence, who headed the agency, had no levers—no general budget authority, no overall intelligence personnel authority, no exclusive access to the president—to force interagency collaboration on his own. In addition, the act explicitly protected existing intelligence components by barring the CIA from domestic law enforcement activities and by providing that other agencies "shall continue to collect, evaluate, correlate, and disseminate departmental intelligence." Even more important, the Central Intelligence Agency was placed "under the direction of the National Security Council." Since the NSC's members included the secretaries of state, defense, the Army, the Navy, and the Air Force, this provision gave departmental intelligence services a court of final appeal. In reality, the CIA sat beneath the very agencies it was supposed to coordinate (*U.S. Statutes at Large* 1948, 497–99). Taken together, these provisions created an intelligence apparatus that was centralized in name only. That was precisely the point. CIA design reflected the interests and desires of existing intelligence organizations—the very actors who most wanted it to fail.

It turns out that the National Security Act only half succeeded in restraining this new intelligence agency. Between 1947 and 1974, the CIA ventured into a range of unforeseen clandestine activities. Yet as the covert side of the agency ballooned into a powerful and large organization, its coordination functions suffered. Analysis and coordination offices languished, forcing presidents to devise new ways of centralizing intelligence.

The Covert Side.   Ink had no sooner dried on the National Security Act than policy makers began contemplating covert action. By 1947, Communists had assumed power in Poland, Hungary, and Romania and were making electoral inroads in Western Europe. As Anne Karalekas (1984, 38) notes, Truman and his advisers viewed these developments as a grave global threat to American security that demanded "new modes of conduct in foreign policy to supplement the traditional alternatives of diplomacy and war." On December 14, 1947, at its very first meeting, the NSC granted the CIA authority to perform psychological activities throughout

Eastern Europe.[7] One week later, the agency created a Special Procedures Group that, among other things, laundered over $10 million in captured Axis funds to influence the election that would determine the next Italian prime minister (Andrew 1995, 172). In June 1948, an NSC directive made the CIA's covert unit permanent and official. NSC 10/2 charged the Central Intelligence Agency "with conducting espionage and counter-espionage operations abroad" (text in Leary 1984, 131).

The CIA's covert office immediately took off. In 1949, the euphemistically named Office of Policy Coordination (OPC) employed a staff of 300 in seven overseas offices with a budget of $4.7 million. In 1952, thanks in large part to the Korean war, OPC agents numbered almost 6,000. Their activities spanned 47 countries and used an annual budget of $82 million (Karalekas 1984, 43–44). With more resources came greater reliance on paramilitary operations and other intrusive political activities. In 1948, CIA subversive ventures in Italy had been confined to dropping leaflets, spreading anticommunist propaganda, and financing the Christian Democratic Party. In 1953 and 1954 the agency successfully sponsored antileftist coups in Iran and Guatemala. It is fair to say that by the mid-1950s, the Office of Policy Coordination had been transformed from a small office that conducted ad hoc political information activities to a vast organization that performed ongoing covert operations on a massive scale (Karalekas 1984, 43). Clandestine activities had become the CIA's dominant mission.

Covert intelligence collection and action continued to flourish throughout the 1960s. In the early part of the decade, attention turned toward Cuba and efforts to oust Fidel Castro. During the summer of 1960, CIA Deputy Director Richard Bissell developed a series of assassination plots that ranged from hiring Mafia hit men to poisoning Castro's favorite cigars (Andrew 1995, 252–53). Ironically, the Bay of Pigs debacle did nothing to dampen the enthusiasm for covert activities. Though President Kennedy requested a thorough review of paramilitary operations, the aim was to improve such activity, not to abolish it. After 1961, counterinsurgency operations spread to other parts of Latin America, the Far East, and Africa. The CIA's Laos operation became one of the largest paramilitary efforts in postwar history. Covert action peaked between 1964 and 1967 (U.S. Senate 1976, 148). Though reliance on intrusive covert action declined in the late 1960s and early 1970s, clandestine operations still occupied a central place in the CIA's identity and in its resource allocation. As of 1973, the CIA's covert side had a budget of $440 million (Richelson 1989, 17). Between 1961 and 1974, the CIA conducted over 900 major covert action projects and thousands of smaller ones (U.S. Senate 1976, 445).

The Coordination/Analysis Side.   While the CIA's covert side prospered, its coordination and analysis side floundered. Ostensibly, the CIA had been established to provide thorough, objective intelligence analysis for senior policy makers and to eliminate duplication among the various military intelligence services. Producing interagency intelligence estimates and coordinating the broader intelligence community were two sides of the same coin. Without exercising direction over departmental intelligence units, the CIA could not hope to provide the president with high-quality, coherent intelligence.

But this was not meant to be. In 1948, just one year after the CIA's birth, the *New York Times* called it "one of the weakest links in our national security" (Ranelaugh 1986, 113). The agency's problems were endemic, part and parcel of the bureaucratic rivalry that surrounded its creation. Karalekas notes: "From the outset no Department was willing to concede a centralized intelligence function to the CIA. Each insisted on the maintenance of its independent capabilities to support its policy role. With budgetary and management authority vested in the Departments, the Agency was left powerless in the execution of interdepartmental coordination" (Karalekas 1984, 103).

Faced with determined departmental resistance, the agency quickly abandoned its clearinghouse role and began producing its own intelligence analysis based on its own sources. But this only added to the intelligence cacophony, duplicating the efforts of other intelligence agencies and expanding the overall intelligence paper flow to senior policy makers. The CIA's transformation from intelligence coordinator to intelligence producer, in turn, hindered the efforts of the director of central intelligence to manage the overall intelligence community. "The DCI," concludes Mark Lowenthal, former director of the House Intelligence Committee staff, "was no longer a fully independent agent in dealing with other intelligence agencies—especially in analytical disputes—because he sometimes had to defend 'his agency' " (Lowenthal 1992, 106).

We can see this trend clearly in the evolution of national intelligence estimates. In 1947, the CIA established an Office of Reports and Estimates (ORE) to issue longer-term, broad-based reports on major intelligence issues. Initially, the ORE was to synthesize the ideas, information, and predictions that flowed from the various intelligence agencies. Departmental resistance, however, quickly stymied its efforts. Forced to rely on its own research and analysis, the ORE produced reports that remained insignificant. In January 1949, just eighteen months after the CIA's creation, a presidential commission delivered a harsh attack on the ORE and the CIA in general. The report concluded:

> The principal defect of the Central Intelligence Agency is that its direction, administrative organization and performance do not show sufficient appreciation of the Agency's assigned functions, particularly in the fields of intelligence coordination and the production of intelligence estimates. The result has been that the Central Intelligence Agency has tended to become just one more intelligence agency producing intelligence in competition with older established agencies of the Government departments. (Leary 1984, 134–42)

As Karalekas notes, by 1950 "it was clear that the CIA's record in providing national intelligence estimates had fallen far short of expectation" (Karalekas 1984, 28). The situation was so bad that in October 1950, three months after American troops landed in Korea, the agency still had no current coordinated analysis of the war. Subsequent organizational reshuffling and reform had little effect. Despite the creation of a new Office of National Estimates in 1952, national intelligence estimates were not consistently read by high-level officials. By the end of the 1960s, such analyses still had not achieved the consistent policy support role that had been the primary purpose of the CIA's creation. It would take twenty more years, a former CIA director in the Oval Office, and the physical relocation of the NIE office outside the CIA to make national intelligence estimates true interagency products.

Presidents responded to the CIA's coordination problems much as they did to the Joint Chiefs of Staff. Instead of reforming the CIA, they tried to bypass it, devising new mechanisms to compensate for the agency's deficiencies. They did so in two ways—by creating additional intelligence centralizing organizations and by developing an intelligence analysis capability in the NSC staff. Harry Truman was the first to farm out CIA management duties to other agencies.

In 1952, frustrated by reports criticizing the CIA's coordination of signals intelligence, Truman created a separate National Security Agency (NSA). Issuing a secret executive order, the president gave the NSA responsibility for all communications intelligence such as eavesdropping and code breaking. In doing so, he made sure to give the new agency undisputed direction over all departmental signals activities. Within five years, the NSA had almost 9,000 employees and ran the most sophisticated computer complex in the world (Andrew 1995, 216). Today it is estimated to be the single largest American intelligence agency, with a staff of somewhere between 80,000 and 120,000 (Lowenthal 1992, 134).

Truman was not alone. During the Kennedy administration, Secretary of Defense Robert McNamara ordered the creation of a Defense Intelligence Agency (DIA) to reduce the overlap and parochialism among the various military intelligence services. Duplication and bias, it seems, had gone largely unchecked by the Central Intelligence Agency. Nixon went even further, setting up his very own intelligence arm—the "plumbers"—in the White House basement.

In addition to founding new intelligence organizations, presidents tried to offset CIA shortcomings by placing intelligence experts directly inside the White House. Truman's first executive secretary of the National Security Council, Sidney Souers, had been deputy chief of naval intelligence during World War II and had served as the first director of CIG, the CIA's immediate forerunner. President Kennedy had raw intelligence sent directly to the West Wing, where he, National Security Adviser McGeorge Bundy, and a small NSC staff could interpret the information themselves (Schlesinger, 1965, 391–97). Kissinger's memoirs tell how Nixon's national security adviser actively recruited intelligence officials to serve on the NSC staff. Presidents continued this strategy long after 1974. Records show that every NSC staff from Carter to Clinton has included a functional directorate specifically devoted to intelligence issues.

These presidential efforts were better than nothing, but they fell far short of creating a truly unified intelligence apparatus. In 1974, as in 1947, intelligence continued to be collected and analyzed by a wide array of organizations, each with its own priorities and inter- ests. While Army intelligence officers sought information about enemy ground forces and strategies, for example, Navy intelligence tended to focus exclusively on Navy needs. The development of a

Defense Intelligence Agency made only marginal headway toward integrating military efforts: as the Church Committee put it, "DIA has met this need [for strong analysis] better than the service intelligence organizations which preceded it, but . . . has not fulfilled expectations that it would provide a coordinating mechanism for all defense intelligence activities and information" (U.S. Senate 1976, 463). Such a system created serious inefficiencies—duplication in some areas, neglect in others.

Congressional Undersight.   As the Central Intelligence Agency's covert side blossomed and its coordination side withered, one political actor remained conspicuously silent: Congress. Barry Blechman (1990) aptly calls the 1947–74 period an era of "Congressional undersight." For 27 years, oversight was splintered among subpanels of the Appropriations and Armed Services committees in both the House and Senate. These subpanels had little time for or interest in the CIA's activities. They usually met just two or three times each year. At these rare meetings, legislators seldom questioned CIA representatives about agency programs or problems. As CIA legislative counsel Walter Pforzheimer remarked, "We briefed in whatever detail they wanted. But . . . you couldn't get Congress to get interested" (Smist 1994, 5). Pforzheimer's recollection is supported by Senator Leverett Saltonstall (R-Mass.), who served on both the Senate Appropriations and Armed Services committees during the 1950s. "It is not a question of reluctance on the part of the CIA officials to speak to us," Saltonstall remarked in 1956. "Instead it is a question of our reluctance, if you will, to seek information and knowledge on subjects which I personally, as a Member of Congress and as a citizen, would rather not have" (*Congressional Record* 1956, 5924). In such an atmosphere, CIA budgets were routinely approved, CIA coordination flaws routinely ignored, and covert actions routinely executed without prior notification of Congress (Smist 1994).

It is important to stress that Congress sat on the sidelines by choice, not by chance. Legislative majorities voted repeatedly and overwhelmingly against bills to consolidate their fragmented intelligence oversight system. Of more than 150 oversight reform measures proposed during this period, only 2 made it past the committees to floor votes—Mike Mansfield's 1956 resolution for a joint Senate-House intelligence oversight committee and Eugene McCarthy's 1966 proposal for a general Senate intelligence oversight committee. Both measures were soundly and easily defeated.

Executive opposition played some role; Eisenhower is said to have commented privately that Mansfield's bill "would be passed over my dead body" (Ambrose 1981, 187). However, it was the senior congressional leadership that proved decisive. Unwilling to cede their own committees' jurisdiction, senators such as Armed Services Committee Chairman Richard Russell (D-Ga.) and Leverett Saltonstall (R-Mass.) mounted a powerful opposition campaign.[8]

Even after the 1961 Bay of Pigs operation, legislators shied away from challenging or changing the CIA. Reaction was limited to a single set of hearings by the Senate Foreign Relations Committee. Though the committee called Secretary of State Dean Rusk, Director of Central Intelligence Allen Dulles, and Deputy Director Richard Bissell to testify, the tone of these meetings was friendly, even jovial. Bissell and the committee members exchanged pleasantries. Chairman Wayne Morse (D-Ore.) expressed some surprise at some of the support logistics, but left it at that. The CIA emerged without a scratch (Jeffreys-Jones 1989).

Congress even gave itself low marks for the period. The Church Committee's final report merits quoting at length:

> The legislative branch has been remiss in exercising its control over the intelligence agencies. For twenty-five years Congress has appropriated funds for intelligence activities. The closeted and fragmentary accounting which the intelligence community has given to a designated small group of legislators was accepted by the Congress as adequate and in the best interest of national security. There were occasions when the executive intentionally withheld information relating to intelligence programs from the Congress, but there were also occasions when the principal role of the Congress was to call for more intelligence activity, including activity which infringed the rights of citizens. In general, as with the executive, it is clear that Congress did not carry out effective oversight. (U.S. Senate 1976, 11)

For 27 years, Congress was content to avert its eyes.

Summary.   For the Central Intelligence Agency, 1947–74 was a time of lopsided development and congressional undersight. Covert activities, which had never been planned or expressly authorized by the National Security Act, quickly became the agency's dominant mission. By the 1960s, the covert Directorate of Plans claimed more than half of the CIA's budget and personnel. While the covert side took off, the CIA's coordination and analysis functions never got off the ground. The root of the problem was structural. No department was willing to bow to centralized control; the Navy, War, Justice, and State departments sabotaged CIA design at the outset. This was bad news for presidents. After 1947, coordinating central intelligence became an exercise in damage control. Congress, meanwhile, did nothing. The spooks reigned supreme.

1974–1999: THE MORE THINGS CHANGE . . .

The mid-1970s ushered in a period of unprecedented congressional activism, particularly in foreign affairs. Gone were the days when legislators automatically deferred to the executive branch. With Vietnam and Watergate dominating the headlines, a resurgent Congress started flexing its muscles. Since 1974, legislators have taken aim at a host of executive branch offices and agencies—none more than the CIA.

However, targeting and hitting an agency are two different matters. A longer view of the past two decades suggests the oversight revolution has been short-lived and ultimately unsuccessful. For all the hearings, scandals, investigations, and bills, congressional resurgence has not seriously constrained covert activities or fostered more integrated intelligence analysis. Even the Cold War's end has yet to produce fundamental legislative reform. The years since 1991 have brought major changes in the CIA's intelligence priorities but relatively minor changes in its basic design and operations.[9] Today's CIA may focus on nuclear terrorism instead of Soviet aggression, but it does so in a decentralized intelligence system that still prizes clandestine action and intelligence collection over coordinated analysis.

Congress Targets the Covert Side.   Nineteen seventy-four was not a good year for the Central Intelligence Agency. In August, President Richard Nixon resigned amidst deepening suspicion that he had obstructed Watergate investigations and had used the CIA to do it. In September, press headlines revealed the CIA was undertaking a deliberate covert action to "destabilize" Salvador Allende's Marxist government in Chile. The real blow came on December 22, with a front-page *New York Times* article by Seymour Hersh. Citing "well-placed Government sources," the article chronicled a "massive illegal domestic intelligence operation during the Nixon Administration against the antiwar movement and other dissident groups in the United States." The CIA had been spying on American citizens since the 1950s, in direct violation of its statutory charter.

Hersh's allegations were like sparks igniting a prairie fire. Within days, Congress passed its first oversight measure, the Hughes-Ryan Amendment to the Foreign Assistance Act. Initially drafted in response to the CIA's secret activities in Chile, Hughes-Ryan required presidents to issue "findings" certifying that each covert operation was "important to the national security of the United States" and to report those findings to six congressional committees "in a timely manner" (*U.S. Statutes at Large* 1976, 1804). In January, the Senate went even further, establishing a Select Committee to Study Governmental Operations with Respect to Intelligence Activities under the chairmanship of Frank Church (D-Idaho).[10] The committee's mandate was to examine allegations of "illegal, improper, or unethical" intelligence activities and, if necessary, to recommend appropriate remedies (U.S. Senate 1976, 2). It was without a doubt one of the most sweeping congressional investigations in American history.[11]

Notably, it was intelligence abuses, not inefficiencies, that prompted Congress to act. Responding to press reports, legislators were principally concerned with protecting American civil liberties rather than with devising ways of making the intelligence machinery work better.[12] Senate Resolution 21, which established the Church Committee, clearly emphasized domestic and foreign "dirty tricks" over broader coordination and management issues. Of the fifteen "specific areas of inquiry and study" listed in the Church Committee's mandate, nine involved illegal secret activities at home and abroad. Only two mentioned management issues such as agency overlap and cooperation (U.S. Senate 1976, 2–3). As the Church Committee's final report put it, "The purpose of [our] inquiry into the intelligence activities of the United States has been to determine what secret governmental activities are necessary and how they best can be conducted under the rule of law" (U.S. Senate 1976, 423). The Senate inquiry targeted the clandestine side of intelligence but left the coordination/analysis side mostly alone.

The Church Committee's focus on covert activities should not be surprising. Tackling the unglamorous and knotty coordination problems of intelligence analysis was hard enough under ordinary circumstances. In times of public spy scandals, it was virtually impossible. With the camera lights on, Congress's attention naturally gravitated to covert activities, and for good reason: investigating and reforming the CIA's covert arm offered political dividends. Scandalous spy schemes made for sexy work and great publicity.

Legislators who investigated press reports of clandestine abuses were considered "players." They appeared important, at the center of action—and this appearance appealed to voters. Indeed, when Frank Church entered the 1976 presidential election, he was quick to highlight his credentials as a CIA covert action watchdog. As one campaign brochure declared, "In 1976 vote for the man who saved us from 1984" (Olmsted 1996, 155). Focusing on more nitty-gritty organizational issues instead of Orwellian specters offered no such political rewards.

Fifteen months, 800 interviews, 110,000 pages of documents, and 126 meetings later, the Church Committee issued its final report (U.S. Senate 1976, 7; Smist 1994, 28). It did not mince words: the intelligence community required major and immediate reforms to bring covert activities under congressional and constitutional control. The committee's centerpiece recommendation called for developing a new comprehensive legislative intelligence charter. There were four parts to this plan: (1) new legislation that would spell out the responsibilities and functions of each intelligence agency; such legislation would replace the presidential directives that had previously determined the development of the CIA, DIA, NSA, and other intelligence services, and would offer stronger, more specific statutory protection of American civil liberties; (2) new omnibus legislation that would replace the 1947 National Security Act and that would clarify relationships among the various intelligence agencies, the president, and the Congress; (3) a statutory ban on many covert activities, such as political assassinations; and (4) stronger congressional oversight mechanisms, including a new permanent Senate intelligence committee whose prior approval would be required for all covert activities.

As it turns out, these recommendations failed on two levels. On a broad level, the Church Committee's recommendations slanted Congress's intelligence reform agenda. Directing Congress's attention and energies toward covert operations, these proposals all but ignored the CIA's broader coordination functions. Even a cursory glance reveals the skewed focus of the committee's agenda. Three of the four major recommendations—agency charters, covert activity bans, and new congressional reporting requirements for clandestine operations—targeted the covert side of the intelligence community. The fourth, a recommendation for omnibus legislation, made some headway toward clarifying the roles and responsibilities of the various intelligence agencies, but it hardly constituted a ringing endorsement of or mandate for management reform. Taken together, these recommendations had serious long-term implications for congressional reform of the CIA. The Church Committee had been specifically established to provide an intelligence reform agenda. In performing that task, Church and his colleagues unwittingly ensured that more fundamental coordination issues would be kept off the table for the next twenty years.

On a second level, the Church Committee's recommendations failed in their own terms. Most of these proposals never made it off the starting block. Those that did were grossly delayed and diluted.

This was not inevitable. Momentum from the 1976 report was enormous and the newly elected president, Jimmy Carter, harbored a well-known hostility toward the intelligence community. At first, the Senate responded quickly, establishing a permanent Select Committee on Intelligence and charging it with implementing the Church Report recommendations. Yet the new Senate committee soon bogged down. Chairman Walter Huddleston (D-Ky.) took a full year to draft a National Intelligence Reform and Reorganization Bill. When he finished in 1978, the bill was a behemoth spanning 263 pages and containing a host of controversial provisions. Under fire from the intelligence community and the president, Huddleston's committee had to go back to the drawing board.

In the interim, their window of opportunity closed. Between 1978 and 1979, Soviet-backed subversive activities were discovered in Ethiopia, Angola, and Mozambique; Islamic fundamentalists overthrew the shah of Iran, seized the American embassy, and took more than 50 Americans hostage; and Soviet tanks rolled into Afghanistan. Robert M. Gates, director of central intelligence (DCI) in the Bush administration, writes, "Moscow's assertiveness, compared to American impotence in Iran and apparent lack of response elsewhere, kindled growing resolve in Washington to counter the Soviets, to again strengthen the U.S. military and CIA as the most suitable instruments to combat Soviet ambitions" (Gates 1996, 118). Press reports began to reflect this shifting consensus. On May 7, 1979, a *U.S. News & World Report* article spoke of "plummeting morale" in the CIA. An October *Wall Street Journal* headline read, "Experts Fear that U.S. Loses Espionage Battle with the Soviet Union." The *New York Times*, which had led the charge against the CIA just a few years earlier, ran a column by Ray Cline that called for "rebuilding American intelligence" (Cline 1981, 274–75). Even President Carter changed his mind, increasing CIA budgets, ramping up covert activities, and defending the agency publicly. By 1980, attempts to restrain and reform the intelligence system had become politically untenable.

When Huddleston's bill finally passed in October 1980, it was a shadow of the original. Stripped from 263 pages to 4, the Intelligence Oversight Act no longer included any legislative charter, any language about managing the intelligence community, or any ban on covert activities. Instead, it provided a set of loose, weak reporting requirements for covert activities. Though calling on presidents to keep the two permanent intelligence committees "fully and currently informed," the act did not require congressional *approval* for these activities (*U.S. Statutes at Large* 1981, 1981). Moreover, it allowed presidents to withhold congressional notification altogether in certain circumstances.

The Church Committee's recommendations never recovered. Charter legislation, which the panel had called "urgent" in 1976 and whose passage it had urged "in the coming year," did not pass until 1992 (U.S. Senate 1976, 426). By that time, the Cold War's end had made such agency charters moot; the collapse of the Soviet Union had thrown into question the very functions, responsibilities, and missions this legislation sought to nail down. New omnibus framework legislation for the intelligence community did not see the light of day until the mid-1990s and was ultimately scuttled. As for covert activities, Congress never succeeded in passing any outright bans. Instead, the scope of covert operations continued to be determined by executive orders that were easily changed. Indeed, President Carter attempted to aid the Church Committee in 1978, issuing an executive order that tightly restricted covert activities.[13] The order lasted just three years. In 1981, Ronald Reagan drafted Executive Order 12333, which granted broader powers to the CIA, including the authority to conduct domestic covert operations (Leary 1984, 8).

The Church Committee's final recommendation—that Congress enhance its oversight of intelligence agencies—also sputtered. Originally, oversight was to be strengthened in two ways: by the creation of permanent select intelligence committees in both houses and by passage of legislation that required the consent of Congress before the initiation of any covert activity. Both chambers did establish permanent intelligence committees, but Congress never passed the prior consent legislation. The Intelligence Oversight Act of 1980 required only that Congress be *informed* of covert activities, and deliberately left room for presidents to approve operations in some cases without any congressional notification at all.

Though the Iran-Contra scandal in 1986–87 ultimately produced some tightening of these reporting requirements, the result was not nearly as far-reaching as the Church Committee had envisioned. In fact, Congress's reaction to the arms-for-hostages scheme was surprisingly restrained, given that press reports, congressional investigations, and the president's own special review board catalogued a litany of Reagan administration breaches in the intelligence reporting process.[14] As Barry Blechman notes, David Boren (D-Okla.) and William Cohen (R-Me.), respectively chairman and vice chairman of the Senate Intelligence Committee, were reluctant at first to legislate any changes to the intelligence community, preferring instead to arrange more informal changes with the White House. The administration's response was a new national security decision directive (NSDD) that included some more refined reporting requirements but still made it possible for the president to delay indefinitely reporting covert actions to Congress (Blechman 1990). Cohen and Boren could not get legislation passed to close this loophole before the end of the congressional session. Meanwhile, House Speaker Jim Wright rekindled fears of congressional security lapses when he leaked secret information about covert operations in Nicaragua. The moment had passed. Efforts to enact the legislation continued for the next two years, but as one Intelligence Committee staffer remarked, "The further you got from Iran-Contra, the less political steam you had" (Smist 1994, 273). As the scandal receded, public attention and Congress's political will dwindled. New reporting requirements were codified in the 1991 Intelligence Authorization Act, but these provisions still allowed presidents to initiate covert actions without congressional approval and still left open the possibility that presidents could legally authorize clandestine activities without ever notifying a single member of Congress.[15]

In sum, the Church Committee's four major reform proposals were short-lived and watered down. Three of the four never got far, and the fourth was so long delayed that it became irrelevant. Congressional reform of the CIA's covert side left the shadow warriors virtually untouched.

Congress (Unsuccessfully) Considers Management Reform.   Paradoxically, the Church Committee's success in shaping Congress's intelligence agenda kept more wholesale reform of the intelligence community off the table until the mid-1990s. In fact, it took the Cold War's end, the worst spy scandal in U.S. history, and the discovery that one intelligence agency had misplaced billions of dollars in congressionally authorized funds to prompt the only serious consideration of intelligence management reform in the CIA's 50-year existence.

The first reformist rumblings could be heard in late 1991, with the fall of the Soviet Union. Amidst cries to cut U.S. defense-related spending, David Boren and David McCurdy (D-Okla.), chairmen of the Senate and House intelligence committees, respectively, introduced separate bills that called for restructuring the entire intelligence community. Both plans recommended consolidating all analytical programs, including the CIA's analysis branch, into a single National Intelligence Center. Even more important, both plans also recommended creating a new "director of national intelligence" who would have clear statutory authority over *all* intelligence agencies and budgets throughout the community. This was a major departure. Under existing arrangements, the director of central intelligence had virtually no control over any intelligence organization except the CIA. Budgets provide the clearest illustration. In 1996, of an estimated total intelligence budget of $29 billion, roughly $20 billion went to Pentagon intelligence agencies that were outside the DCI's reach. The intelligence director actually controlled only about 10 percent of the budget—the $3 billion allocated directly to the Central Intelligence Agency (Pincus 1996e).

The Boren-McCurdy plan did not last long. According to one study, the bill's sponsors never took its passage seriously. Boren apparently instructed his general counsel to draft a provocative piece of legislation primarily to stimulate executive branch thinking (Smist 1994, 286). In any case, the House and Senate intelligence committees quickly tabled the more sweeping provisions of the bill once DCI Robert Gates presented his more modest alternative plan in April 1992. Gates's recommendations succeeded in making some improvements to overall community processes but did not produce any major structural changes (Brown 1996). The legislation was left to codify existing arrangements by writing into law charter statements of all intelligence organizations.[16]

The real push for fundamental reform began in 1994 with the

arrest of CIA officer Aldrich H. Ames, the highest placed Soviet mole ever caught penetrating the U.S. intelligence establishment. Ames had been selling secrets to Moscow for nearly a decade, compromising dozens of agents and causing the execution of at least ten (Wise 1996). Soon after, reports surfaced that the National Reconnaissance Office (NRO), the agency that builds and maintains U.S. spy satellites, had secretly funneled $300 million in congressionally authorized, classified funds to a new headquarters and had lost track completely of more than $1 billion. Most disturbing was the fact that the NRO's loss of the money was discovered by chance, during an internal audit ordered by DCI John Deutch.

Together, the Cold War's end, the Ames spy scandal, and the NRO's financial mismanagement catalyzed a concerted congressional effort to review and reform the entire intelligence establishment. In October 1994, Congress established by statute a presidential panel—the Commission on the Roles and Capabilities of the United States Intelligence Community (the Brown Commission)[17]—to review "the efficacy and appropriateness" of U.S. intelligence activities in the post–Cold War era and to report its findings by March 1996 (*U.S. Statutes at Large* 1995, 3457–59). About the same time, the House Permanent Select Committee on Intelligence initiated a lengthy staff study of its own.[18] By the end of 1996, these reviews were joined by Senate proposals, presidential proposals, and plans from nongovernmental organizations such as the Council on Foreign Relations and the Twentieth Century Fund. Reform was in the air.

Once again, however, reformers did not succeed. House and Senate efforts to centralize intelligence collection and analysis faced entrenched opposition from two sides: Defense Department officials who wanted to maintain control over their own intelligence agencies and congressional defense committee members who wanted to keep a tight hold on these agencies' purse strings. This resistance proved fatal. The Intelligence Authorization Act that President Clinton signed into law in 1997 was more notable for the provisions it dropped than for the ones it enacted.

Action began on March 1, 1996, when the Brown Commission issued its report. Though the report was considered "the most comprehensive, high-level government review of U.S. intelligence-gathering to be conducted in nearly 20 years" (Smith and Pincus 1996), its recommendations proved surprisingly timid. Though the panel called for public disclosure of annual intelligence authorizations, for example, it never asked what the appropriate post–Cold War intelligence budgetary level should be (Wise 1996). Similarly, the report offered a few ways to bolster the director of central intelligence but did not seriously consider reshaping his role in any fundamental way or granting him greater control over community budgets and personnel. Quite the contrary. The commission concluded that "the DCI's existing legal authorities with respect to the Intelligence Community are, on the whole, sufficient" (Brown 1996, chap. 5, 7). As a *New York Times* editorial put it on March 3, 1996, the commission left "a flawed system essentially intact."[19]

Four days later, Larry Combest (R-Tex.), chairman of the House Intelligence Committee, issued his committee's year-long study. Declaring that "everything is on the table," Combest unveiled a series of recommendations that were by his own admission "radical" (Pincus 1996f). Among them were consolidation of all human clandestine operations currently housed in the Pentagon and CIA into a new, separate Clandestine Service directly under the DCI; reconfiguration of all technical intelligence collection into two new agencies; and the granting of broad powers to the director of central intelligence—assisted by a new deputy director of intelligence for community management[20]—to veto top-level appointments and to transfer budgets and personnel between agencies of the intelligence community, even those agencies housed in the Defense Department. The aim was to create a more "corporate" intelligence community, "a more closely integrated enterprise working towards a highly defined common end: the delivery of timely intelligence to civilian and military decision makers" (U.S. House 1996, "Overview and Summary," 5).

Though the Senate Intelligence Committee was unwilling to go as far as its House counterpart, it, too, offered a reform plan that centralized human clandestine activities (in the CIA, not a new clandestine service) and augmented substantially the DCI's budgetary, personnel, and appointment powers (Pincus 1996d, 1996e; Congressional Quarterly 1998).

Such radical proposals triggered strong reactions from Defense Department officials, the House National Security Committee, and the Senate Armed Services Committee. On April 29, Deputy Secretary of Defense John White sent a letter to Strom Thurmond (R-S.C.), chairman of the Senate Armed Services Committee, detailing his objections to the reform proposals now contained in the 1997

Intelligence Authorization Bill. White raised fears that greater intelligence centralization would create a Frankenstein "monolithic" intelligence structure. In particular, he argued against provisions granting the DCI power to transfer funds in and out of Pentagon intelligence agencies and providing for DCI approval of the defense secretary's top appointments to key Defense Department intelligence agencies (Pincus 1996d).

House and Senate Defense Department oversight committees also stepped in. On the House side, the National Security Committee stripped the bill of virtually every measure designed to increase the DCI's power over military intelligence agencies. With such opposition, Combest did not even move to send the bill to the floor (Congressional Quarterly 1998). Debate in the Senate proved even more acrimonious. Claiming it was too soon after the Cold War's end to make such dramatic changes, the Armed Services Committee asked Arlen Specter (R-Pa.), chairman of the Intelligence Committee, to delay consideration for a year. Specter refused. When it became clear that Armed Services would not back down, Specter took the unprecedented step of getting the 1997 defense authorization bill referred to his committee sequentially—in essence, holding it hostage. Armed Services countered by getting Specter's intelligence authorization bill held up (Pincus 1996c). Once the dust had settled, the National Security and Armed Services committees had taken the teeth out of intelligence reform. Gone was the proposal to consolidate human clandestine operations. Gone was the DCI's power over general budget management. Gone was his right to veto appointments to key intelligence agencies.[21] None of these provisions made it back into the bill before the president signed it in October 1996 (*U.S. Statutes at Large* 1997).

Why intelligence reform got derailed is no great mystery. Defense Department officials clearly and correctly saw any effort to enhance the DCI's power as a threat to their own. It was exactly this kind of thinking that originally hobbled the CIA's analytical/coordination branch in 1947. In this case, they were aided by a president who was unwilling to enter the fray. Though Clinton never articulated his reasoning, his passivity makes sense. Any president naturally would be reluctant to press an issue against the vehement objections of his own Department of Defense. And this particular president, with his Vietnam draft deferral and his early fumbling about homosexuals in the armed forces, came to the table weaker than most.

Finally, any true overhaul of the intelligence community posed the unpopular prospect of realigning congressional committee jurisdictions. Moving budgetary authority of Defense Department intelligence programs from the Pentagon to the DCI meant transferring congressional oversight from the defense to the intelligence committees. Such a power shift was bound to provoke resistance from those committee members who stood to lose. Thus, with the Defense Department on the move, with the president out of the picture, and with internecine warfare in the capitol, reform did not stand much chance. Richard Haass, who served in the Bush White House and led the 1996 Council on Foreign Relations study of intelligence reform, summed up the situation well: "Everyone who looked at [intelligence reform] came out with the question of how to strengthen the DCI, but no one was willing to do what it takes to give him real control. That was too much for the system to bear and they will end up only tinkering" (quoted in Pincus 1996b).

Thus it appears that congressional activism has not proved all that active. Certainly, legislators are more involved in intelligence matters today than they were in the past. But the absolute level of congressional oversight remains unremarkable. Indeed, it took a blatant, massive, illegal clandestine scheme in the executive branch to revive consideration of covert action reporting requirements in the mid-1980s, and it took a trifecta of events—discovery of Soviet spies, budgetary bungling, and the Cold War's end—to spark a serious debate about reforming intelligence coordination and analysis a decade later. Given the well-known problems in intelligence analysis and coordination, one major reform effort in over 50 years hardly seems the stuff of a resurgent Congress.

Perhaps more important, congressional efforts have not produced much in the way of results. Church aimed at and missed covert operations in 1974. Despite some new legislation, today's presidents can still undertake clandestine operations without legislative approval or, in some cases, notification. Church set aside the more intractable problems of intelligence coordination and analysis altogether. Though major reform made a brief appearance in 1996, it faded again in the face of bureaucratic resistance, congressional infighting, and presidential passivity. Today, with all the new challenges, threats, and uncertainties of the post–Cold War world, we are left with an intelligence apparatus that never managed to overcome its most serious Cold War deficiencies.

Presidents and the CIA: The Pattern Continues.   Presidents have continued the pattern of the 1947–74 period: they have relied heavily on CIA covert operations. At the same time, they have employed a variety of informal coping mechanisms to coordinate analysis of the broader intelligence community.

At first, the CIA's covert days appeared numbered. In 1976, not only was the agency embroiled in public scandal and congressional investigations, but it became a prime target for Jimmy Carter's presidential campaign. Condemning the national disgraces of "Watergate, Vietnam and the CIA," Carter made no secret of his distaste for secret activities (Andrew 1995, 425). Carter's first nominee for director of central intelligence, Theodore Sorensen, was considered so anti-CIA that the Senate Intelligence Committee forced his withdrawal (Lowenthal 1992; Andrew 1995). Despite this setback, Carter's early actions supported his rhetoric. In January 1978, the president issued an executive order that placed pervasive restraints on covert activities. The order was intended to be a stopgap measure, restricting covert activities until Congress could pass more permanent legislation.

The next 21 months, however, produced a complete reversal in Carter's attitude toward covert activities. In November 1978, in the wake of Iran's Islamic revolution, Carter sent a note to his secretary of state, national security adviser, and director of central intelligence that declared, "I am not satisfied with the quality of our political intelligence. Assess our assets and, as soon as possible, give me a report concerning our abilities in the most important areas of the world" (Turner 1985, 113–14). In 1979, the Iranian hostage crisis and the Soviet invasion of Afghanistan completed Carter's transformation. By the end of his administration, Carter had authorized covert activities from Afghanistan to Nicaragua to Iran to Yemen, and his CIA agenda had shifted from regulating the CIA's covert side to revitalizing it (Gates 1996). As the president himself remarked in his final State of the Union address, "We need to remove unwarranted restraints on America's ability to collect intelligence" (quoted in Lowenthal 1992, 62).

Ronald Reagan continued the trend, expanding covert operations, approving dramatic increases in foreign intelligence budgets, and drafting a new executive order that, as we have seen, increased the CIA's power and jurisdiction, particularly in covert activities. The details of the Reagan administration's ventures into covert activities have been much discussed elsewhere.[22] Here, suffice it to say that the president made clandestine programs a centerpiece of his anti-communist policy, launching more than a dozen major covert operations from Latin America to the Middle East to Africa.[23] Foreign intelligence budgets followed suit, increasing by more than 300 percent during Reagan's first term—a rate that exceeded that of even the Pentagon's budget increases (Jeffreys-Jones 1989, 234). Covert activities may have declined from their peak in the late 1960s, but in 1988 they still accounted for half of the CIA's total budget (Richelson 1989, 13, 17).

Evidence from the Bush and Clinton administrations is harder to come by. Nevertheless, it appears that those two presidents continued to protect and use covert operations, despite the Soviet Union's collapse and the end of the Cold War. Rather than eliminating or drastically reducing U.S. clandestine capabilities, George Bush fought to retain them, directing CIA director Robert Gates to rethink the agency's intelligence priorities for the post–Cold War world. And while Clinton promised substantial cuts in intelligence budgets during the 1992 presidential campaign, as president he made no move to implement them. Instead, Clinton has used covert action as a tool to aid new democratic regimes and to combat terrorism, drug trafficking, and the proliferation of weapons of mass destruction (Smist 1994; Johnson 1996).

As the CIA's covert activities have continued to thrive, the agency's coordination functions have continued to suffer. Like their predecessors, presidents have refrained from initiating fundamental organizational reform of the intelligence community, using informal coordination mechanisms instead. They, too, have used the same two dominant strategies—delegating coordinating functions to new organizations and pulling intelligence expertise into the White House. The Reagan/Bush years saw the rise of "fusion centers"— community-wide analytical clearinghouses that focused on long-term issues such as weapons proliferation, terrorism, and international narcotics trafficking. Bush, in particular, tried to exercise more discipline over intelligence analysis by developing new independent interagency units. In November 1991, he moved the National Intelligence Council and the national intelligence officers who produce national intelligence estimates out of the CIA and into a building of their own. At the same time, he authorized the creation of a National Human Intelligence Tasking Center to improve coordination of intelligence collection. Centralizing intelligence expertise in the White House has been a more popular strategy. Every administration from Carter to Clinton has created an NSC staff directorate specifically devoted to intelligence issues.

Summary.   Since 1974, when back-alley warfare began to make front-page headlines, activity has swirled around the Central Intelligence Agency. Yet all this attention has produced little change in the agency's broad evolutionary pattern. Congressional reform efforts have proved elusive—primarily targeting only one half of the agency and failing to achieve results even there. As a result, CIA covert operations have never been seriously constrained by legislators. Today, presidents still use clandestine programs as a major foreign policy instrument, and still authorize them without congressional approval. At the same time, an activist Congress has overlooked the thornier and more troublesome management problems of the CIA. Substantial reform on this front appeared only once, and unsuccessfully at that. In the 1990s as in the 1940s, presidents have had to cope with CIA coordination deficiencies on their own. The CIA has continued to develop in a lopsided fashion.

Explaining Evolution

CIA evolution was neither preordained nor haphazard. As in the NSC system and JCS cases, development of the Central Intelligence Agency can be understood as a product of three related factors: its initial design, the ongoing interests of political actors, and exogenous events. The 1947 National Security Act contained structural choices that ruled out some developmental paths while making others more likely. The interests of presidents, bureaucrats, and legislators helped narrow these possibilities even further. Events had a reinforcing effect, entrenching the agency along its particular trajectory. Together, these factors made it likely that the CIA's covert capabilities would prosper and its coordination capabilities lapse.

INITIAL DESIGN

The CIA's schizophrenic development had roots in its schizophrenic design. In a very real sense, the CIA provisions of the National Security Act laid the groundwork for the agency's subsequent evolution. These provisions allowed for the development of covert activities while impairing the development of the agency's coordination and analysis functions.

Vagueness was the critical factor. The National Security Act made no specific mention of covert activities anywhere. As noted earlier, policy makers saw no need to continue widespread clandestine activities after the war. Nevertheless, the act included two broad, catchall provisions that ultimately opened the door for covert operations. First, the act charged the CIA with performing "such additional services of common concern as the National Security Council determines can be more efficiently accomplished centrally." Second, and more important, the legislation authorized the new agency "to perform such other functions and duties related to intelligence affecting the national security as the National Security Council may from time to time direct" (*U.S. Statutes at Large* 1948, 498). It was these two provisions, along with the executive's general constitutional foreign policy prerogatives, that presidents later used to justify the creation of the CIA's clandestine service.

No such vague phrases came to the aid of the CIA's management functions. Quite the opposite. The National Security Act listed and limited CIA coordination provisions with precision. Military, State Department, and FBI intelligence units received protection from CIA interference with the provision that "The departments and other agencies of the Government shall continue to collect, evaluate, correlate, and disseminate departmental intelligence" (*U.S. Statutes at Large* 1948, 498). In addition, these agencies were given the ultimate trump card against the new Central Intelligence Agency: a National Security Council comprising their department heads with supervisory authority over the CIA. Specifics meant trouble. Initial agency design did not rule out improving the CIA's management capabilities, but it did make reform an uphill battle. The CIA's coordination/analysis side was hobbled at birth.

ONGOING INTERESTS AND CAPABILITIES
OF POLITICAL ACTORS

The CIA's original design made it relatively easy to create covert capabilities and relatively difficult to centralize intelligence analysis. The interests and capabilities of political actors turned these possibilities into reality.

Presidents.   One of the most striking aspects of CIA evolution is how presidents of all stripes have protected and promoted CIA clandestine operations. Truman, who distrusted secret ventures, became the first postwar president to use them. Kennedy insisted on increasing covert activity even after the Bay of Pigs disaster. Ford went to great lengths in his efforts to protect the agency in the 1970s. He tried to stave off congressional investigations by appointing his own blue-ribbon commission. He then narrowly restricted the commission's inquiry to those abuses that had already been reported in the press (Andrew 1995). Fully disclosing all of the CIA's abuses, he feared, "could cripple [its] effectiveness" (Ford 1979, 230). Even Jimmy Carter, who entered office intent on downgrading and reigning in the spies, embraced clandestine activities by the end of his administration.

Two factors explain why every postwar president has supported and relied on the CIA's covert branch to such a great extent. First, all presidents in all ages have strong natural incentives to develop foreign policy tools directly under their own control. Held uniquely responsible for foreign policy successes and failures, presidents have good reason to crave responsive weapons wherever and whenever they can get them. Thanks to the National Security Act, Truman and his successors could easily develop a covert capability that responded to their own policy needs—without congressional interference.[24] They readily took advantage of the opportunity. Since 1947, the CIA's covert side has developed on the basis of NSC directives and executive orders. Even today, presidents can authorize clandestine activities unilaterally, over the objections of CIA directors and legislators.

Second, the Cold War exacerbated these natural imperatives. With nuclear war hanging in the balance, Soviet-American conflict moved into a kind of twilight zone where each power sought to gain maximum advantage over the other without triggering overt military confrontation. Countering Soviet aggression and subversion required new weapons somewhere between diplomacy and war (Karalekas 1984). Clandestine operations filled this need. Robert Gates writes, "The national interest, as perceived by the President, sometimes can be protected or advanced only by action in the gray areas—somewhere between the politically acceptable and unacceptable." In the Cold War, such gray areas were everywhere. More than ever before, presidents needed options, they needed flexibility, they needed programs that coped with foreign policy problems in incremental steps, away from the public eye. Clandestine activities filled the bill. As

Gates (1996, 568) concluded, "In the real world, if CIA were to disappear, Presidents would create some entity to take its place." Presidents were driven to champion the CIA's covert branch because it was easy to do and because covert operations gave them what they wanted most in foreign policy making: flexibility and control.

On the coordination/analysis side, presidents were well aware of the CIA's deficiencies. Since its founding, the agency has been the subject of sixteen investigations and studies, half of them undertaken by the executive branch (U.S. House 1996, Appendix C). Yet we know that Truman and his successors avoided major reform measures, choosing instead to create new coordinating agencies and to draw intelligence expertise directly into the White House. The question here is why. If presidents had powerful incentives to centralize and coordinate foreign policy making, why did they avoid tackling CIA management deficiencies head-on?

In part, the answer is that major reform efforts require presidents to devote tremendous political capital, energy, and time, all of which are in short supply. Creating a new agency is almost always easier than reforming an existing one, particularly when the new agency can be created without legislation, as the NSA and DIA were. Presidents undoubtedly knew this, and opted for those strategies that produced maximum returns for minimal effort. Clinton's reluctance to place post–Cold War intelligence reform on his agenda or to support it when confronted by Pentagon resistance speaks volumes about the chief executive's political equation. When it comes to organizational overhauls, the right thing is not easily done.

Presidents also shied away from CIA management reform because it risked exposing the CIA's covert side to scrutiny and reorganization as well—a risk they could ill afford. The problem was not just Congress; presidents could have improved the agency's coordination capabilities on their own, through executive orders and directives. Rather, the bigger problem lay within the executive branch, in the numerous agencies of the intelligence community. State, Defense, and FBI intelligence units had both the interests and the capabilities to resist intelligence reorganization. As we saw in Chapter 6, these agencies succeeded in hamstringing CIA coordination capabilities in the first place. After 1947, these same intelligence outfits tolerated and even promoted the CIA's covert arm. They did so largely for rational reasons. Strengthening the CIA's clandestine service kept the agency busy and out of the coordination business. And so long as the CIA stayed out of the coordination business, each intelligence service could continue setting its own priorities and conducting its own activities. By contrast, revamping the CIA's coordination and analysis branch threatened to upset the entire arrangement. By jeopardizing what these agencies prized most—autonomy—major management reform promised to open up a Pandora's box of jurisdictional issues. Faced with a battle royal, other intelligence agencies might very well fight for pieces of the covert action pie. This was bad news for presidents, who knew that CIA control over covert activities meant presidential control. In sum, strengthening the CIA's coordination capabilities left the agency's covert side vulnerable to bureaucratic attack. The Central Intelligence Agency's coordination/analysis side was hardly ideal, but it was not worth the price of reform.

Bureaucrats. Above all, bureaucrats in the broader intelligence community wanted to be left alone. They fought for a decentralized intelligence system in 1947, and they tolerated the CIA's development so long as it allowed them to run their own affairs with their own budgets and their own people. Though all organizations generally prefer more autonomy to less, these intelligence agencies had other, performance-based reasons for maintaining their independence. As Ferdinand Eberstadt first observed in 1945, each organization had intelligence needs that were "peculiar to itself" (Eberstadt 1945, 163). Military intelligence units in particular feared that nonmilitary personnel would be unqualified to set defense intelligence priorities, unfit to interpret military intelligence data, and unable to make good use of them.

Thus intelligence organizations in the Army, Navy, Air Force, Defense, State, and Justice departments accepted the CIA's development without much opposition. Indeed, during the late 1940s, they even encouraged the agency to acquire covert capabilities. For one thing, none of these services wanted to be bothered with clandestine activities that could sully their hands and detract from their own work. For another, as mentioned above, involving the CIA in covert affairs directed its attention away from analysis and coordination.

Admittedly, these intelligence bureaucrats never expected the CIA's covert arm to grow as large or as powerful as it ultimately did. Evidence strongly suggests that when George Kennan, James Forrestal, and others pushed for the creation of the CIA's first clandestine unit in 1948, they believed the office would be small and used

on an infrequent, ad hoc basis. As Anne Karalekas writes: "Clearly
. . . policymakers intended to make available a small contingency
force that could mount operations on a limited basis. Senior officials
did not plan to develop large-scale continuing covert operations.
Instead, they hoped to establish a small capability that could be acti-
vated at their discretion" (Karalekas 1984, 43).[25]

Nevertheless, as the CIA's clandestine activities mushroomed
during the early 1950s, other intelligence agencies did not mount
much resistance.[26] Nor did they move off the sidelines when these
same kinds of covert actions came under attack in the 1970s and
mid-1980s. It was only in 1996, when reform threatened to alter the
broader distribution of power, budgets, and autonomy throughout
the intelligence community, that Defense Department officials
jumped in. This was no coincidence. Lopsided CIA development
suited the needs and interests of bureaucratic players quite well.

Legislators.   The role of legislators in the CIA's evolution has
been a bit more complex. We know that for the first half of the
Central Intelligence Agency's life, the vast majority of members of
Congress remained blissfully ignorant of the agency's covert activities and managerial shortcomings. Oversight subcommittees of the
Armed Services and Appropriations committees paid little attention
to either side of the CIA. Beginning in the 1970s, however, Congress
appeared to take a more active role, investigating CIA abuses, establishing new select oversight committees, attempting to pass legislation reforming the agency's covert side, and even considering more
fundamental management reform. Yet this activism has been more
apparent than real. Press reports and public scrutiny of CIA abuses
during the 1970s, 1980s, and 1990s gave legislators strong incentives
to investigate the CIA, but not to change it. For all the hoopla about
the "oversight revolution," Congress has been content to stay out of
the action most of the time. It has allowed the agency's covert side
to blossom and its coordination side to wither.

The truth is that average legislators have never had strong incentives to exercise vigilant oversight of the Central Intelligence
Agency. Under ordinary circumstances, delving into covert affairs
offers little in the way of electoral rewards. Intelligence issues do not
provide any tangible benefits for voters back home. As one Senate
Intelligence Committee senior staffer put it, "You don't make any
brownie points with constituents by serving on this committee. You
get nothing for your state" (Smist 1994, 92). Legislators cannot use

national security affairs for grandstanding purposes, either; discussing covert activities would mean divulging classified information and jeopardizing U.S. national security. Moreover, as Blechman notes, playing an active role in intelligence matters brings substantial political risks. "In the event an operation failed and embarrassed the United States . . . the legislators might share in the administration's culpability," he writes (Blechman 1990, 144).

Legislative incentives for dealing with the agency's coordination/analysis side are even lower. Spies are at least interesting and glamorous. There is some political cachet in appearing to be involved in high-level decisions about covert operations. But no one much cares about improving the CIA's management capabilities. Organizational details such as the CIA's specific statutory authorities are never burning election issues. Throughout the CIA's history, Congress has only once seriously considered management reform legislation.

Effective oversight also requires legislators to make substantial investments of their time and energy to develop expertise. But expertise in intelligence matters does not translate well on the campaign trail or in the town hall. Little wonder the National Reconnaissance Organization was able to stash and then lose billions of dollars in authorized funds for several years without triggering any congressional alarms. In the highly technical world of satellite intelligence, congressional committee members were in no position to review what spending levels were appropriate.

These disincentives are compounded by two other factors: the paucity of information about intelligence affairs and presidential resistance. Even those legislators who serve on the select intelligence committees have a hard time getting information about the agency's activities and deficiencies. Classification restrictions, the absence of interest groups, and bureaucratic self-interest all work against them. During the Reagan administration, for example, Representative Norman Y. Mineta (D-Calif.) made this remark about CIA Director William J. Casey: "I've often said that if you were talking to Casey, and your coat caught fire, he wouldn't tell you about it unless you asked" (Congressional Quarterly 1985b, 120). While Casey may be an extreme case, the fact is that CIA directors and their subordinates have good reason to keep information to themselves. As a result, legislators have little way of knowing what they do not know. Information asymmetries make it even more difficult and costly for Congress to take on the Central Intelligence Agency.

Presidents do not help, either. Their unique responsibility for American foreign policy gives them strong incentives to control and protect national security agencies whenever possible. Presidents may not go to the mat for the Federal Communications Commission, but they will for the CIA. Legislators know this. The anticipated threat of presidential resistance is a powerful deterrent to legislative reform.

We can see the presidential threat at work in almost all of Congress's major intelligence reform efforts. The first push for charter legislation fizzled in the face of Jimmy Carter's opposition. When legislation finally did pass in 1980, it was a hollow shell of the original. Fearing a presidential veto, Congress did not even try to legislate strict prior notice for all covert operations (Blechman 1990; Smist 1994). In 1991, Congress tried again. This time, it took seven months of negotiations with the White House to produce a bill that ultimately changed reporting requirements in minor ways. As one key participant bluntly remarked, "You cannot legislate in this area without the president. There are not enough votes to override a veto" (Smist 1994, 279). Congress's most successful legislative initiative—the 1992 passage of charter legislation for all intelligence agencies—went through only after the House received assurances from President George Bush that he would not veto the bill (Smist 1994, 286).

That said, there is one exception to the general rule of congressional inattention. When spy scandals surface, even reelection-minded legislators have powerful incentives to jump into the fire. We have seen such sudden intelligence activism on four occasions: after the Bay of Pigs in 1961, after press revelations of CIA domestic and foreign espionage abuses in 1974, after Iran-Contra in 1986, and after Aldrich Ames's arrest in 1994. At these rare moments, betrayals, snafus, and abuses in CIA clandestine operations captured the headlines and the public's attention. Congress reacted quickly, mounting special investigations.

Yet in all four cases, investigation did not lead to action. Legislators devoted vast amounts of time and resources exposing "what went wrong," but never succeeded in making it right. No major proposals emerged out of the Bay of Pigs hearings in 1961. The Church

Committee's recommendations sputtered and died soon after their 1976 debut. Iran-Contra did not produce significant new legislation, even though Reagan officials had been found skirting existing reporting requirements and directly violating statutes that prohibited aid to the Nicaraguan rebels. Nor did the Ames spy scandal succeed in generating meaningful reform. Why?

Two reasons. First, members of Congress get rewarded for rooting out abuses, not for rectifying them. What counted for Frank Church was that he led the investigation into CIA wrongdoing. He was at the center of action. When the cameras were rolling, he was there, fighting for American civil liberties. But once the investigation ended and the hard work of drafting reform legislation began, the cameras disappeared. As scandal faded from the public eye, so did Congress's political steam.

The link between public attention and congressional action is apparent in even the most basic aspects of congressional oversight. Consider, for example, participation on the House and Senate intelligence oversight committees. Created with great fanfare in the 1970s, these committees were originally considered plum assignments. Senator Daniel Inouye (D-Hawaii), the Senate committee's first chairman, considered committee membership to be "very prestigious in the Senate" (Smist 1994, 86). During the 1980s, however, intelligence committees became less and less attractive. "Increasingly," Smist writes, "members of Congress . . . have failed to devote the time and attention necessary for the committees to oversee properly" (Smist 1994, 320). By the 1990s, participation had become so problematic on the House side that Speaker Thomas S. Foley (D-Wash.) and Republican Leader Robert H. Michel (R-Ill.) sought strict assurances from the class of 1993 that they would take their intelligence duties seriously (Smist 1994, 321).

Second, overhauling the intelligence community threatened to upset Congress's own jurisdictional apple cart. Redistributing power and responsibility within the executive branch meant recasting oversight authority among House and Senate committees. In the legislative arena, where power is the most prized currency and jurisdictional battles are fought with all the zeal of a Darwinian drama, major reform was bound to run into major trouble. In 1996, it did. When House and Senate intelligence committees finally got around to CIA management reform, they could not get their proposals past defense committee colleagues.

In sum, rational self-interest helps explain Congress's protracted period of "undersight" as well as its periodic bouts of seeming activism. Average, district-oriented legislators stood to gain by staying out of the intelligence fray as much as possible and jumping into it only when they had to, only when the public was watching, and only as much as other congressional committees would allow.

Summary.   Presidents, bureaucrats, and legislators all propelled the CIA along its evolutionary path. Presidents had strong incentives to develop the CIA's covert side and avoid taking on the agency's coordination problems directly. Bureaucrats were content to let well enough alone, so long as the CIA did not infringe on their own priorities, programs, and needs. As long as the CIA never became a truly central intelligence agency, they were satisfied. Tellingly, bureaucratic actors leaped into action only once—in 1996, at the first hint of serious organizational reform. Legislators, for their part, stayed out of the intelligence business as long as they possibly could. When press revelations in the 1970s, 1980s, and 1990s drew the public's attention to the CIA, Congress followed suit—investigating but not seriously restricting CIA covert operations and instituting only modest changes to intelligence analysis and coordination. Driven by electoral concerns, legislators had little reason to tackle the agency's management problems. The Central Intelligence Agency developed in a way that suited the interests of key political players.

EVENTS

As in the NSC system case, critical developments in American politics and foreign policy had a reinforcing effect, entrenching the CIA in its evolutionary trajectory. We can see this by examining more closely two types of incidents: positive events—those that nudged the CIA along its path of lopsided development—and negative events—those that could have prompted reversal of this trend but did not.

Three major positive events helped to expand the CIA's covert operations. The first was Soviet aggression in Europe during the late 1940s. U.S. officials became preoccupied with the Soviet threat almost immediately after the war's end (U.S. Senate 1976; Karalekas 1984). Their fears were well founded. By the end of 1948, Communist regimes had been established in Poland, Romania, Bulgaria, Hungary, and Czechoslovakia. Soviet domination threatened Western Europe as well. With Soviet pressure on Berlin, with Soviet troops massed on the borders of Eastern Europe, and with Soviet-backed Communist movements in Italy, Greece, and France, many American officials believed an outright military attack on Europe to be imminent (Cline 1981). "For U.S. policymakers," Karalekas concludes, "international events seemed to be a sequence of Soviet incursions" (Karalekas 1984, 38).

These incursions helped catalyze the creation of CIA covert capabilities. Indeed, covert operations in the late 1940s became one weapon in an arsenal of new American foreign policy initiatives ranging from massive economic aid programs (the Marshall Plan) to regional military alliances (NATO).

Just how crucial were these early Soviet actions to developing the CIA's covert arm? Or, to pose the counterfactual, would the CIA's clandestine service have arisen without the Cold War? Given presidential incentives for responsive and flexible foreign policy tools, the odds appear about even. The absence of a clear threat might have provided even greater incentive to cultivate a sophisticated covert capability. Presidents need more intelligence, not less, when they are unsure where the danger lies. In recent years, policy makers have used this very argument to justify the CIA's continuation after the Cold War.

The Korean war also contributed to the growth of covert operations. The requirements of war led to a fourfold expansion of the CIA and a new emphasis on paramilitary activities (U.S. Senate 1976, 23). By 1953, the agency's covert operations had become far-flung and well funded. As former CIA Deputy Director Ray Cline concludes, "The CIA began to get the authority, the funds, and the staff to operate as a real central intelligence machine only under the impetus of the War in Korea in 1950" (Cline 1981, 103).

Communist aggression came to the agency's aid once more in the late 1970s. Besieged by congressional investigations, negative press reports, and a hostile president, the Central Intelligence Agency's covert directorate appeared to be in trouble. Yet a series of Soviet-backed Communist incursions, culminating in the invasion of Afghanistan, helped silence the agency's critics and transform the president into a supporter of clandestine operations. By 1979, even the American press was urging policy makers to revitalize the agency.

These three episodes worked in the same direction; Communist offensives in Europe during the late 1940s, in Asia during the early

1950s, and in the Middle East and Africa during the late 1970s all bolstered policy makers' support for clandestine operations.

But these threatening actions by the Soviet Union and its proxies did not exist in isolation. For all the major episodes of Soviet aggression, there were equally major incidents of American clandestine activities gone awry, of dirty tricks discovered and scandals exposed. Three events in particular—the Bay of Pigs, the 1970s scandals, and Iran-Contra—raised serious questions about the usefulness and ethics of CIA covert operations. And yet none of these events stemmed the growing tide of covert activity. As noted earlier, the CIA's failed invasion of Cuba in 1961 prompted Kennedy and his advisers to use covert actions more, not less; in fact, the number and scope of clandestine operations peaked later in the decade. Similarly, press reports of CIA assassination plots, subversive operations, and illegal domestic activities in the mid-1970s created a scare for agency officials. But calls for severely limiting and even banning covert activities soon gave way to a renewed emphasis on them. During the Reagan administration, intelligence budgets skyrocketed and covert actions flourished (Prados 1996; Woodward 1987; Andrew 1995). One Reagan-era initiative—a training and armament program for the Afghan Mujahideen—ranks among the largest and most successful covert operations ever undertaken by the United States (Blechman 1990, 137). Even Iran-Contra appeared to have little effect. In 1988, the CIA's Directorate of Operations still garnered half the agency's budget. Scandalous moments, it seems, have not seriously harmed or diminished the CIA's covert activity.

Finally, no account of the CIA would be complete without consideration of the end of the Cold War. Indeed, if one had to choose a single event with the greatest chance of transforming the Central Intelligence Agency, the Soviet Union's collapse would be it. And yet the Central Intelligence Agency looks remarkably unchanged. Certainly, the "new world order" has shifted intelligence priorities to new areas. But the agency's basic organization, its operations, its powerful covert side and ineffectual coordination/analysis side have remained intact.

Whether scandalous moments or massive changes in the international environment, external shocks have been unable to move the CIA off its developmental course. Communism may have sustained the agency's covert branch, but its absence has not led to the agency's demise.

SUMMARY

The CIA's fate was not preordained, but it was highly determined. Structural choices made in 1947 allowed presidents to house clandestine capabilities in the new intelligence agency. Using vague clauses in the National Security Act, presidents were able to develop, expand, and order covert operations by themselves, without congressional interference or involvement. At the same time, the CIA's initial design made it difficult for the agency to perform its clearinghouse role. This was no accident. Weak centralization was the price for the CIA's creation.

Self-interest also goes a long way toward explaining why the Central Intelligence Agency's covert side flourished and its coordination side stagnated. The National Security Act created a range of developmental paths for the CIA. Presidential, bureaucratic, and legislative interests determined which path the new agency would take. Natural incentives and Cold War imperatives gave presidents good reason to bolster the CIA's clandestine unit. However, improving the CIA's coordination side has always been politically problematic. From 1947 on, bureaucrats in other intelligence agencies have adopted a live-and-let-live attitude, turning a blind eye to the CIA's increasing involvement in clandestine affairs so long as the agency did not interfere with their own collection, analysis, and dissemination of intelligence. Presidents have not been in the dark about this; they have long known that righting the wrongs of the National Security Act required massive organizational change, which existing agencies would vigorously oppose. This they could not afford. Legislators, for their part, had little reason to oversee covert operations and even less reason to delve into the details of management reform.

Finally, events helped propel the CIA along its evolutionary path. Threatening actions by the Soviet Union helped sustain the CIA's covert arm, while other events—CIA scandals and the Soviet Union's demise—seemed unable to shake the agency from its course.

Conclusions

Like the National Security Council system and Joint Chiefs of Staff, the Central Intelligence Agency case provides empirical support for the National Security Agency Model. Consider for a moment realism's ideal intelligence agency. Such an agency would effectively cull and distill raw intelligence from an array of other organizations and distribute insightful analyses to top decision makers in a timely fashion. If realists are right, the security imperatives and intelligence needs of the Cold War should have fostered the development of a CIA whose analysis branch at least equaled its covert side in strength, independence, and general capabilities. But this is not at all what we find in 1947 or in any subsequent period. On the analysis side, agency design and operations have been more resistant than responsive to American Cold War intelligence needs.

By contrast, the Central Intelligence Agency case fits nicely with the three evolutionary hypotheses developed in the National Security Agency Model. First, CIA evolution has been shaped primarily by the executive branch. Postwar presidents have had a natural affinity for clandestine operations. Every president since Truman has protected and relied on the Central Intelligence Agency to wage shadow wars across the globe. Clandestine activities offered presidents flexible, responsive, and secret foreign policy weapons at a time when Cold War combat made these attributes more desirable than ever before. Yet presidents have refrained from tackling the agency's coordination problems. Their reluctance has stemmed more from fears of bureaucratic resistance than from congressional intervention. As Lieutenant General William E. Odom, former chief of the NSA, put it, "It's painfully simple. The president, secretary of defense, director of central intelligence and perhaps the secretary of state, these guys have to be committed to get these reforms done. If not, it won't be done" (quoted in Pincus 1996b).

Second, like the National Security Council system and the Joint Chiefs of Staff, the CIA developed without much congressional involvement. Oversight of covert intelligence activities proved minimal before 1974 and ineffectual after that. Meanwhile, Congress has never paid much heed to the CIA's coordination/analysis side. The decentralized intelligence system that soldiers, diplomats, and G-men fought so hard to achieve in 1947 has remained largely untouched.

Third, the CIA's evolutionary course can be better understood by examining its initial design, the rational motives of political players, and a handful of focusing events. As in our other cases, structural choices made at the agency's birth had lasting implications for its development. While vague clauses opened the door for covert operations, specific management provisions prevented the agency from fulfilling its coordination responsibilities. The interests and capabilities of presidents, bureaucrats, and legislators also influenced the CIA's schizophrenic evolution. No one, it seems, had strong incentives to stem the growth of the CIA's covert side or to reform its coordination side. Finally, the CIA has proved remarkably resistant to the force of events. The Cold War Communist threat helped justify the creation and growth of clandestine operations, but its disappearance has not yet reversed the trend. Similarly, CIA imbroglios and failures may have damaged the agency's morale but they have not led to major changes in its mission, design, or operations.

CHAPTER 8

Conclusion

Anyone who has ever filed a tax return or stood in line at the Department of Motor Vehicles will tell you that government agencies are far from perfect. No doubt some agencies function better than others, and all have individual employees who are dedicated professionals. But it is fair to say that U.S. domestic programs are not formulated and implemented by crack outfits working together as a well-oiled machine.

We expect more when it comes to foreign affairs. There the stakes are higher. As citizens, we may be asked to endure financial hardship, to cede some degree of our civil liberties, and even to put our children in harm's way—all in pursuit of the greater national good. When the state can compel such supreme sacrifice, we hope and expect that government organs will be well made, that they will do a good job.

Unfortunately, this is not the case. Domestic and foreign policy agencies differ in fundamental ways, but they all arise from an American political system that hinders effective design. Ironically, the most cherished features of American democracy are to blame. Frequent elections and geographic districts keep legislators responsive to the popular will, but they also provide strong incentives for members to favor local interests over national ones. Separation of powers may guard against despotism, but it often prevents presidents from acting unilaterally. This is especially problematic when we consider that presidents are the only officials with powerful incentives to consider national concerns and are surrounded by bureaucrats who resist them at every turn. Majority rule tempers extreme ideas and sweeping proposals through political compromise. But compromise also dilutes legislation when bold change is needed. These enduring elements of our political system have given rise to a national security apparatus that is poorly equipped to perform. Like their domestic policy counterparts, American national security agencies are irrationally designed for rational reasons.

We can see the process at work in all three of the case studies. Historical evidence suggests that most political players did not consider broad national concerns when they designed the National Security Council system, the Joint Chiefs of Staff, or the Central Intelligence Agency in the 1947 National Security Act. Policy makers were not sitting around a table dreaming up the ideal postwar foreign policy apparatus. They were waging full-scale political warfare. They were fighting to protect their own interests. President Truman tried to get a system that would work well to serve the nation's needs. But he was surrounded by self-interested bureaucrats and abandoned by self-interested legislators.

The results were far from the bureaucratic ideal. The National Security Council and its staff landed in the legislation by accident. They were political by-products, artifacts of compromise that no one much considered in the end. JCS design was more deliberate; the Navy set out to cripple the agency at birth. Secretary Forrestal and his colleagues infused the Joint Chiefs of Staff with conflicting interests at all levels. They guaranteed interservice gridlock by insisting on unanimous decision rules. And they made sure the JCS had no authority over service budgets. The Navy demanded these things because they were good for the Navy. Navy leaders intentionally created a JCS that was incapable of producing coherent military strategy, coordinating military operations, or offering useful military advice. The Central Intelligence Agency also was not destined for success. Existing intelligence services within the Navy, War, Justice, and State departments had no interest in relinquishing autonomy and power to a new central intelligence authority. Instead, they set out to undermine the CIA's powers at the outset. They succeeded. The Central Intelligence Agency was bereft of any statutory authority to do its job well. It could not compel interdepartmental intelligence cooperation or coordination. It could not determine the budgets, priorities, or activities of other intelligence units. It became a central authority in name only. In short, all three of these agencies were poorly designed because bureaucrats would not stand down and legislators would not stand up. President Truman may have had the nation's interests at heart, but he had to settle. For him, something was better than nothing. The National Security Act was the best he could do.

Not surprisingly, these agencies have worked poorly through the decades. Institutional birthmarks have had lasting effects. Only one of the three agencies, the NSC staff, has been able to overcome its initial handicaps soon enough to make a real difference. And this was accidental. Using a few loopholes in the National Security Act, presidents were able to reinvent the NSC staff and discard the more formal statutory National Security Council. Timing was key: they began making these changes almost immediately, before the newly created and still fragmented Defense Department could mount a united opposition. In this one instance, presidents had a unique opportunity to start over. Unfortunately, the NSC staff appears to be the exception, not the rule.

Some may take issue with these findings, objecting to the idea that we can say what constitutes effective agency design. To some extent they are right. Rarely is there universal agreement on the single best organizational alternative. Theories of organization are not nearly that sophisticated or complete. That, however, is no reason to give up. We may not know what agency design is best, but we certainly know what is bad and what is better. Even a cursory glimpse at history suggests that the national security agencies examined here have suffered from serious organizational defects. When the initial NSC system could not produce useful policy advice for the president, when the Joint Chiefs could not conduct well-coordinated military maneuvers or offer an integrated military perspective, when an organization named the Central Intelligence Agency could not provide centralized intelligence, we know things are not as they should be. The fact is that the JCS, the CIA, and for a time even the NSC staff have not met minimal standards of agency performance.

Additional Findings

The empirical cases point to two additional findings that are worth highlighting. First, *the Congress appears to be much weaker and more insignificant than most political scientists generally admit.*

To put this claim into some perspective, it is worth taking a step back and asking, "If the proverbial Martian were to land in Washington, how would she know an ineffectual Congress when she saw one?"

For starters, our Martian should find a weak Congress having a hard time getting its views and desires written into law. Whether for lack of interest or lack of capabilities, it lets others take the lead. Initiative—or more precisely its absence—is the key indicator. Legislators are unlikely to call for hearings, to insist on playing a part in the executive branch's drafting process, or to amend legislation once it is introduced. Such a Congress is more of a political stage than a political actor in its own right. It is a forum in which others fight their battles and publicly air their views.

Congress's behavior during the National Security Act debates fits this description well. From the opening salvos in 1944 until Truman's signature in 1947, legislators stood outside the political battlefield. Hearings were held, but always at the request of executive branch players. The purpose of these hearings was not so much to sway others within the House and Senate: everyone knew most members were waiting for the War and Navy departments to work out a deal. Rather, the hearings were a way for each side to communicate its views and objections to the president, the press, and the public. In addition, draft bills were always written according to the specific instructions of the president and his warring military departments. In June 1946, the Senate Military Affairs Committee took rubber-stamping to new heights when it simply stapled the most recent War-Navy compromise plan to its current draft bill. Finally, provisions of the National Security Act bore an uncanny resemblance to the Truman administration's proposal. NSC and JCS provisions copied the administration's language literally word for word. Although House members insisted on including more detailed language for the CIA, they did not look far; instead of drafting their own provisions, they simply copied the wording of Truman's original intelligence executive directive of 1946. Congress may have passed the National Security Act, but it did not have a strong hand in shaping the bill.

An outside observer also would expect a weak Congress to shy away from overseeing national security agencies once they arise. On a daily basis, legislators should pay little attention to agency activities. In the longer term, they should produce little in the way of reform legislation, even when agency problems and abuses are well known.

This is exactly what we find in the NSC, JCS, and CIA cases. For over 25 years, Congress refused to set up an intelligence oversight committee at all. Only in 1974, after press reports of CIA *domestic* surveillance activities, did the House and Senate begin to create an oversight infrastructure. The JCS and NSC staff have received even less attention on a daily basis. As for reform legislation, the historical record speaks for itself: in more than 150 years of CIA, JCS, and NSC staff history, Congress has succeeded in passing just one piece of major reform legislation—the Goldwater-Nichols Defense Reorganization Act of 1986. This despite the fact that members have known about JCS flaws ever since the late 1940s and about CIA management problems at least since the 1970s. In sum, congressional oversight initiatives have been rarely undertaken, poorly directed, and easily overcome.

The second major finding is that *national security agencies appear remarkably impervious to external events.* Escalating Cold War tensions in the 1950s and 1960s did nothing to generate improvements to either the Joint Chiefs of Staff or the CIA's management capabilities. Nor did outright policy failures, fiascoes, or scandals. The Bay of Pigs led Kennedy to use covert operations more, not less. It did prompt the president to appoint a special White House military adviser, but did not lead to any more thoroughgoing efforts to fix either the CIA or the JCS. Twenty more years of military misadventures still did not do the trick for the Joint Chiefs of Staff. Fundamental reform required nothing less than a harmonic convergence of prolonged pressure, sudden events, individual leadership, and good fortune. The Central Intelligence Agency has not been so lucky. Today, years after the end of the Cold War and Aldrich Ames's arrest as a Soviet mole, the agency has yet to undergo anything resembling an organizational overhaul. Though the NSC staff has had a better overall track record, Oliver North's shady schemes show that even this agency can go awry. And when it does, little can be done. Nothing prevents today's NSC staff from repeating the mistakes of Iran-Contra. National security agencies appear to be well insulated indeed.

How can this be? How can such critical organs of government be so far out of reach? Why are they not held accountable for the bad outcomes they produce? There appear to be two answers. The first has to do with initial agency design. I have argued that founding moments loom large for national security agencies because the American political system stacks the deck in favor of the legislative status quo. Separation of powers, the congressional committee system, majority voting rules—all these things make new laws difficult to pass. Consequently, laws that do manage to get through the system are hard to change. Given these political facts of life, major agency overhauls should be rare, even in the face of agency scandal or poor performance. It turns out they are.

The second reason has to do with presidents. Presidents have strong incentives to develop national security organs that are effective, responsive, and responsible; of all the actors in American politics, presidents are most likely to have national interests at heart. The problem is that their capabilities are weak. Only at rare moments can they undertake fundamental agency reforms on their own. The NSC staff appears to be such an example. Usually, however, presidents are not so fortunate. They must contend with powerful bureaucratic opponents and self-interested legislators. In addition, presidents always have full plates. They face more competing claims and demands on their time than anyone else in government. Their most valuable assets—political capital and attention—are in shortest supply. Though CIA management reform may be important, there is always a more immediate crisis on the day's agenda or another issue that offers potentially greater political rewards for lower political risk. It is no coincidence that every president since Truman has developed coping mechanisms to circumvent JCS and CIA deficiencies. With so much to do and so little time to do it, they have few other options.

The upshot is that agencies do not respond naturally or easily to changing international events, conditions, and problems. They do not adapt to their environment. National security agencies are likely to be poorly designed and built to stay that way.

This is especially bad news for today's post–Cold War policy makers. For if America's national security apparatus was inadequately designed to face old, familiar threats, how can we expect it to be any better at facing new, unfamiliar ones? However flawed these Cold War organizations were in the past, they are likely to be even more so now. What's more, starting over and creating new organizations from scratch is not a realistic option. In 1947, American officials had the luxury of a relatively clean slate. New agencies could be created because few were already on the scene. Even so, we have seen how existing bureaucratic actors fought tooth and nail to protect themselves against encroachments by newcomers. Thanks to the National Security Act and presidential coping maneuvers, there are more organizational players today. Consequently, a 21st-century version of the National Security Act would probably face even more fierce bureaucratic battles and more disappointing results. Policy makers will likely have to make do with what we have.

The Cost of Agency Design

Suboptimal agency design is not without costs. These can be classified in three types. First, badly designed agencies can produce bad policy outcomes; they can cause policy setbacks, diplomatic failures, and military disasters that hurt American interests and American citizens. For instance, JCS design ensured that top American military officers would be kept out of the loop on major military issues. The agency was structurally incapable of offering a comprehensive military point of view on basic matters of planning, strategy, and operations. As John Kester commented in 1982, "The present JCS system makes the chiefs irrelevant much of the time. I recall many occasions on which the Secretary of Defense would try to get the advice of professional officers on pending issues. He could talk to the Chiefs alone sometimes, and he daily consulted with the Chairman. . . . But that did not take the place of well thought out and developed positions by a staff looking at issues from the point of view of the armed forces as a whole" (U.S. House 1982, 509). Instead, policy makers have relied on civilian defense officials for basic advice on military matters—and this practice has led to trouble. Many defense experts attribute the Vietnam war to the unwise counsel of uninformed Defense Department civilians. As former JCS chairman David Jones put it, "Vietnam was perhaps our worst example of confused objectives and unclear responsibilities" (U.S. House 1982, 53).[1] The ill-fated Bay of Pigs invasion was also concocted without substantive input from the JCS; the chiefs discovered the plan by accident (Korb 1976, 134).

Disaster has also stemmed from the JCS's inability to coordinate interservice operations in the field. The attempt to rescue the American hostages in Iran in 1980 is a textbook case. The mission was doomed from the start when each service insisted on its piece of the action. Responding to service interests, the rescue plan called for Marines to launch their helicopters from Navy ships and rendezvous in the desert with Army commandos transported by Air Force planes. Despite the plan's obvious complexity and reliance on inter-service coordination, no joint training was ever conducted. Instead, each service practiced its own part in isolation. When the rescue day arrived, many of the team members had never met. There weren't even any arrangements for the service commanders to communicate with each other. On April 24, 1980, the mission was aborted just hours after it began—but not before eight men had burned to death when a helicopter collided with a transport plane.

Similarly, poor coordination and confused lines of command led to the 1983 bombing of a Marine barracks in Beirut, killing 241 American Marines. Investigations revealed that the U.S. unified commander in Lebanon had expressed concerns over lax security months before the blast but had lacked the power to order the necessary changes (Boo 1991).

CIA organizational deficiencies also have led to missteps and misadventures. The agency's inability to coordinate intelligence from the rest of the community produced major intelligence failures in Korea and at the Bay of Pigs. Moreover, the CIA's focus on covert activity has borne little fruit at considerable expense. Of the five major paramilitary activities examined by the Church Committee in 1976, four failed to achieve their stated objectives and further undermined U.S. credibility. The committee concluded that such covert activity not only "limited the foreign policy options available to the United States by creating ties to groups and causes" but proved "increasingly costly to America's interests and reputation" (U.S. Senate 1976, 156, 425).

As these examples suggest, there is a connection between agency structure and policy outcomes. Vietnam, the Bay of Pigs, Iran, Beirut, Korea—all of these episodes might not have occurred had the Joint Chiefs of Staff and Central Intelligence Agency been able to do their jobs better. Certainly, even the best organizations make mistakes, and even the most irrationally constructed agencies can produce results. Poor agency design is not a surefire recipe for failure, but it does make policy setbacks more likely and more frequent.

The second type of cost associated with faulty agency design has to do with success. Ill-suited agencies may still end up producing positive outcomes, but they exact a high price in the process. U.S.

troops may have successfully invaded Grenada in 1983, but they suffered a surprising number of casualties because of interservice coordination problems. Jimmy Carter eventually secured the release of
the American hostages in Iran. If the rescue attempt had succeeded,
however, the hostages would have come home nine months earlier.
In 1950, Truman's police action in Korea successfully repelled the
communist advance. But had the Central Intelligence Agency been
better able to read the situation, our military involvement there
might well have been avoided altogether. In all of these cases, the
results were good. They could have been better.

Third, design flaws impose all sorts of opportunity costs. How
much time do presidents waste and how much capital do they needlessly expend to overcome the shortcomings of their own national
security agencies? What would Lyndon Johnson have accomplished
without the Vietnam war? What policies would Carter have pursued
if he had not been incapacitated by the hostage crisis for so long? If
Kennedy had not gone forward with the Bay of Pigs, would
Khrushchev have dared place nuclear missiles in Cuba and brought
us to the brink of nuclear war? Seen in this light, agency design
hardly appears trivial. Because of the way they are structured,
American national security agencies ensure that both policy failures
and successes will be costly.

Implications for Theory and Practice

The evidence spells bad theoretical news for realism and good news
for new institutionalist approaches. Though realists do not profess to
offer a theory of domestic-level organization, they do make rather
strong unspoken logical assertions about it. If realists are right and
the international distribution of power compels states to behave in
the ways they do, then subnational factors such as foreign policy
agencies cannot exercise much independent influence. For this to be
true, agencies must be able to translate national interests into
action. At some base level, all national security organizations should
be well designed and able to adapt to major changes in the international system.

Applied to the three cases, realism tells us the NSC system, the
JCS, and the CIA should have worked moderately well from the out-
set and should have stayed pretty much the same until the Cold
War's end, when dramatic changes in the international system

demanded the creation of a new or modified American national security apparatus. This is not what we find. None of the agencies emerged from the National Security Act of 1947 in good shape. While the NSC system and the CIA's covert side adapted to Cold War needs in relatively short order, the JCS and the CIA's analysis side did not. Instead, the Joint Chiefs of Staff organization was continually plagued by organizational problems for 40 years, and the CIA's analytical branch never recovered from its initial deficiencies. Moreover, not one of these agencies has been significantly altered or replaced since the Cold War's end. It appears that realism cannot account for even the broad outlines of agency origins and evolution.

New institutionalism appears more promising. Although the three case studies cannot prove the theory true in any scientific sense, they do illustrate its explanatory power. Alone, each agency examined here lends support to the National Security Agency Model. Taken together, they provide even more compelling evidence.

Variation is the key. Forged in the same law by the same people against the same Cold War backdrop, the NSC system, JCS, and CIA have not developed in similar ways. The NSC system began as a throwaway legislative provision but rapidly became the president's most trusted and influential foreign policy unit. The JCS, by contrast, started out as the centerpiece of the bill but was hobbled from birth until its reform in 1986. Meanwhile, the CIA developed along two tracks at once, with the covert side rapidly and unexpectedly overshadowing the coordination and analysis branch. Transformation, stagnation, and bifurcation have been the respective evolutionary patterns of these agencies.

The ability of a single approach to explain different outcomes is always a positive sign. It indicates that the model's variables are the critical ones, that we have separated what matters from what does not. National security agencies may develop in a variety of ways, but they do so for similar reasons.

That said, much remains to be done. For starters, it makes sense to expand the scope of the National Security Agency Model, to see just how broadly the framework applies. What does this approach have to say about the origins and evolution of foreign economic policy organizations such as the United States Trade Representative or the National Economic Council? How can it account for large bureaucracies such as the Defense and State departments? And what of the

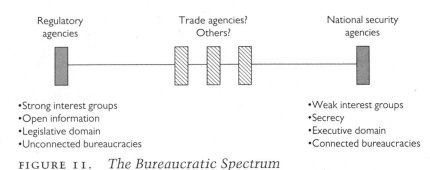

FIGURE 11. *The Bureaucratic Spectrum*

myriad other unexplored agencies in the domestic policy arena? All of these questions beg a larger and more important one: Is this the beginning of a general theory of bureaucracy?

I believe that it is. I have argued that we get analytic leverage by transporting new institutionalism from American politics to international relations. While the approach needs some serious adjustment, the logic suggests a way to understand why national security agencies look and behave the way they do. New institutionalists have made a convincing case that domestic regulatory agencies are handicapped at birth. The same appears to be true for national security agencies. Equally important, we now know four critical variables that distinguish national security agencies from their regulatory counterparts: the interest group environment, the availability of information, the policy domain, and the degree of bureaucratic connectedness. Indeed, it makes sense to think of regulatory agencies at one end of the bureaucratic spectrum and national security agencies at the other, as in Figure 11. On the one side, regulatory agencies live in a world where interest groups are plentiful and powerful, information is readily available, issues lie in the legislative domain, and bureaucracies are loosely connected to one another. The politics is distributive in nature. National security agencies lie at the opposite extreme, with weak interest groups, extreme secrecy, issues that lie in the executive domain, and tightly connected bureaucracies. The political game is played over public goods.

This is encouraging. If these two types of agencies mark the ends of the spectrum, then all other government organizations should lie somewhere in the middle. We can move inward by systematically adjusting the values of the four variables and testing their influence on agency design. The prospect exists for developing a richer picture of American bureaucracy using a single theoretical framework.

A second and even more challenging task lies ahead: understanding more fully the relationship between agency structure and policy outcomes. This project has taken agencies themselves as the object of study. In the long run, however, it is not enough to know why government organizations arise and develop in the ways they do. We need a better understanding of how design choices affect policy making and international relations in general. Such connections are murky. Current approaches, including this one, have a hard time going beyond the basic intuition that organization matters. We need to do better.

The building blocks are there. With a firm grasp of agency origins and evolution, we can now begin to design comparable cases that test the influence of agency design on policy making. To say that JCS design led to policy failure in case X at time Y means little unless we know how this organization arose and what it looked like at different points in time. Indeed, the JCS of 1946 is a far cry from the JCS of 1996. By isolating design changes, we can compare different JCS structures in similar crises. We can, for example, test the influence of Goldwater-Nichols provisions by comparing the Joint Chiefs' performance in the Korean war to their performance in the Persian Gulf war of 1991. Ultimately, treating agencies as dependent variables has the potential to illuminate their influence as independent variables.

For practitioners, the National Security Agency Model provides no silver bullets, but it does offer some takeaways for presidents and for organizational reformers more generally. First, this research suggests the counterintuitive finding that when it comes to organizational reform, presidents should avoid taking the moderate road. It is no secret that American presidents must pick their political battles with care. In business terms, they need to maximize the return on their resource investment. Unfortunately, as we have seen, major reorganizations of national security agencies almost invariably have a low probability of success. That being the case, presidents should steer clear of such overhauls whenever possible. If reform is in the air, however, then chief executives should not waste time considering proposals unless they are willing to lend the full weight of their office to the effort. They should either pound the table—vehemence still offers low short-term political dividends but at least improves the chances of success—or leave the room, investing instead in other initiatives that offer higher potential returns. The middle road of moderate presidential support only appears pragmatic. In reality, it both jeopardizes reform efforts and needlessly uses valuable presidential resources that could be put to better use elsewhere.

Second, presidents would do well to take a closer look at organizational history to gain an understanding of the birthmarks of their national security agencies and the coping mechanisms other presidents have used to overcome them. As Ann Richards, former governor of Texas, once said, fools rush in where fools have been before. This does not have to be the case. Future presidents can and should borrow from the innovations of their predecessors. Coping mechanisms such as Truman's creation of the National Security Agency by executive order and Kennedy's appointment of a special White House military adviser provide a ready-made menu of options to mitigate the effects of poor agency design.

Third, chief executives need to beware of organizational pitfalls. Better management requires a better knowledge of dangerous organizational weaknesses. For example, Jimmy Carter should have been keenly aware that the hostage rescue effort in Iran was likely to be dogged by poor interservice coordination and a me-too attitude that would give each service a piece of the action regardless of operational demands. Had such issues been in the foreground, he could have countered them, insisting on such things as joint rescue team training drills. Knowledge here is power. Recognizing organizational weaknesses can help presidents thwart their most pernicious effects.

Lessons for organizational reformers follow along similar lines. Like presidents, others who desire more effective national security agencies would benefit from a closer examination of agency origins, of the statutory birthmarks that make some government organizations inherently easier to change than others. Indeed, it is not enough to develop brilliant new ideas about agency design. The right ideas in the wrong political environment will never amount to much. To succeed, reformers need to have a better sense of which agencies are the hardest targets and why. More homework at the beginning of the process should lead to reform proposals that have a better chance of becoming reality.

Second, the three case studies suggest that reformers need to get bureaucrats' support early on if improvements are to stand a chance. The claim that this is more easily said than done is a gross understatement. As we have seen, entrenched bureaucrats in existing agencies pose the most serious obstacles to reform. However, gaining the support of at least a few enlightened officials can help resist the opposing tides later. This tack worked well in JCS reform; with two of the chiefs out in front pressing for change, the military services found it more difficult to wage a rear-guard action.

Third and finally, to navigate the shoals of Congress, major reform legislation must have the unwavering support of a few venerated congressional leaders. These members have to be willing to call in their chits and to stake their reputations to overcome the resistance of committees that stand to lose power and average members who have no good reason to cooperate. Although many factors contributed to the success of Goldwater-Nichols, there is no doubt that Barry Goldwater was one of them. It was only by making the bill his congressional swan song, his last major battle, that Goldwater marshaled the votes he needed to win. If history is any guide, the leadership factor will be of equal importance in the future.

Of course, none of these things will guarantee results or make reform easy. If the case studies have shown anything, it is that organizational reformers inside and outside the government face a daunting task. But these lessons can help at the margins. It is the best we can do for now. In the long run, the challenge for practitioners and academics alike is to discover the underlying regularities that shape government agencies, and through them policy choices. It is to find a useful, meaningful middle ground between grand theory and ad hoc reality. It is, in short, to start with politics.

Appendixes

Notes on Tabulation of Foreign Policy
Interest Groups

The breakdown of foreign policy/domestic policy interest groups is based on the following numbers:

Domestic policy interest groups	
Business	3,469
Transport/energy	1,377
Public interest	1,256
Health	1,054
Local government	540
Miscellaneous	520
All domestic policy interest groups	8,216
Foreign policy interest groups	922
All interest groups	9,138

These tabulations are based on raw data found in the "Selected Subjects Index" (pp. 721–63) of *Washington Representatives, 1990*. Containing a comprehensive listing of interest groups in the United States, *Washington Representatives* includes law firms, professional lobbying organizations, national and professional associations, corporations, foundations, foreign governments, issue-specific lobbies, political action committees (PACs), and other special interest groups. The "Selected Subjects Index" lists individual organizations under 140 headings according to "significant or timely legislative, manufacturing or professional interest." A few of the headings: "Sugar," "Marine," "Health Care," "Environment," "Religion."

The original data suffered from two problems. First, they underestimated foreign policy–related interest groups. Of the 140 subject headings, only two—"Foreign Relations" and "Foreign Trade"—explicitly covered foreign affairs. Thus such organizations as defense contractors, veterans' groups, and religious relief organizations were left out. To get a better estimate of foreign policy–related interest groups, I included ten additional headings with a strong foreign policy orientation: "Aerospace," "Aircraft Industry," "Arab," "Conservation," "Copyrights," "Defense," "Military," "Naval," "Nuclear Energy," and "Veterans."

Next, I turned to headings that contained a significant but not overwhelming number of foreign policy organizations: "Civil Rights," "Economic Development," "Environment," "Foundations," "Government," "Law," "Minorities," "Natural Resources," "Political Science," "Pollution," "Population," "Religion," "Social Welfare," and "Women." Organizations under these headings were recoded and data were reaggregated to separate foreign policy from domestic policy groups. Thus "Civil Rights" became two headings: "Civil Rights—Domestic" and "Civil Rights—Foreign."

The second data problem was that many groups appeared under multiple headings. One defense contractor, for example, was listed under "Aerospace," "Aircraft Industry," and "Defense." To clean the data, I grouped headings into twelve broader area clusters and then eliminated duplicate entries within each cluster. For example:

Cluster	Headings
Agriculture	Agriculture, Beverage, Cocoa, Coffee, Dairy, Food, Fruit, Grain, Feed, Livestock, Meat, Poultry, Pesticides, Sugar, Tobacco

New York Times *Coverage of National Security Advisers, 1947–1998*

Average number of entries per year in the *New York Times Index* under each national security adviser's name:

National Security Adviser	Administration	Average number of entries
Sidney Souers*	Truman	2
James S. Lay, Jr.*	Truman	1
Robert Cutler†	Eisenhower	15
Dillon Anderson	Eisenhower	17
Gordon Gray	Eisenhower	6
McGeorge Bundy	Kennedy/Johnson	39
Walt Rostow	Johnson	35
Henry Kissinger	Nixon (1969 – 72)	295
Brent Scowcroft	Ford	16

continued

*Since the position of national security adviser was not created until 1953, corresponding figures from 1947 through 1952 have been tabulated on the basis of entries for the NSC executive secretary.
†Robert Cutler served as Eisenhower's national security adviser twice, from 1953 to 1955 and from 1957 to 1958. The number of his *New York Times* entries reflects the combined average of both periods.
SOURCE: 1961–79 figures based on I. M. Destler, "National Security Management: What Presidents Have Wrought," *Political Science Quarterly* 95 (Winter): 582; other figures tabulated by author from *New York Times Index*.

New York Times Coverage of National Security Advisors (*continued*)

National Security Adviser	Administration	Average number of entries
Zbigniew Brzezinski	Carter	135
Richard Allen	Reagan	75
William Clark	Reagan	55
Robert McFarlane	Reagan	47
John Poindexter	Reagan	46
Frank Carlucci	Reagan	49
Colin Powell	Reagan	22
Brent Scowcroft	Bush	17
Anthony Lake	Clinton	14
Samuel (Sandy) Berger	Clinton (through April 1998)	22

Legislative Changes
to the Joint Chiefs of Staff

Legislation	Provisions
1949 Amendments to National Security Act	• JCS chairman created • Joint Staff increased from 100 to 210 • JCS made "principal military advisers" to NSC
1953 Reorganization Plan no. 6	• JCS chair given more authority: chair approves appointments of Joint Staff officers, manages work of Joint Staff and its director • JCS removed from executive agent status; i.e., handling day-to-day communications and supervision over unified commands
1958 Defense Reorganization Act	• JSC chair strengthened: chair allowed to vote in deliberations; chair selects Joint Staff director with approval of secretary of defense; control of Joint Staff transferred from JCS corporate body to JCS chair; chair must, however, act "on behalf of" corporate JCS • Joint Staff increased from 210 to 400 • Chiefs directed to concentrate on joint duties and delegate service management to newly created vice chiefs

continued

Legislative Changes to the Joint Chiefs of Staff *(continued)*

Legislation	*Provisions*
1986 Goldwater-Nichols Defense Reorganization Act	• Military departments removed as executive agents; chain of command now runs from president to secretary of defense "through" JCS to unified commands • JCS chair strengthened: chairman, not corporate JCS, is made "principal military adviser" to president; vice chair created to handle daily work • Joint Staff parochialism reduced: joint posting now required for promotion; JCS chair can promote Joint Staff officers even if parent service chief objects; Joint Staff increased from 400 to 1,627 • CINCs granted greater autonomy, authority; specified operational chain of command runs from president to secretary of defense to unified and specified combatant commanders

Value of Defense Contracts Awarded, FY 1994, by Region (millions of dollars)

Region	Value	Percent
Northeast	$18,752	17.00%
Midwest	16,593	15.04
South	42,741	38.74
West	32,229	29.22
ALL REGIONS	$110,315	100.00%

SOURCE: *Statistical Abstract of the United States, 1995* (Washington: U.S. Department of Commerce, 1995), 358.

Notes

Introduction

1. I define "national security" in the traditional geostrategic, military sense. Although the end of the Cold War has brought increased attention to the economic aspects of national security, these issues still fit only tenuously in the policy-making process. We can see this clearly in the changing, experimental character of economic security organizations that have appeared alongside the National Security Council system in both the Bush and Clinton administrations. As one senior foreign policy observer put it, "it's still hard to put economic interests into national security. It's coming, but it's embryonic" (confidential, interview by author, July 20, 1995).

2. Barry Blechman, interview by author, Feb. 10, 1995. For more, see Korb 1976; Locher 1985; Perry 1989.

3. Two types of domestic-level arguments do address domestic structure as dependent variables: decision-making theories and work on Congress and foreign policy. Unfortunately, both literatures describe more than they explain. Decision theorists such as Alexander George (1980) reduce agency origins and evolution to the particular choices of individual presidents. According to George, it does not make much sense for presidents—or scholars, for that matter—to dwell on the deeper underlying factors that influence agency design and development; presidents are relatively free to choose whatever policy-making structures and processes they wish.

Work on Congress and U.S. foreign policy tends to be atheoretical, anecdotal, and normative. As James Lindsay notes (1994), this vein of research is less interested in building theory than in debating the extent of congressional resurgence (Franck and Weisband 1979; Cronin 1980; Deering 1989; Destler 1981a; Stockton 1991) or discussing the vices and virtues of con-

247

gressional foreign policy activism (Mann 1990; Friedberg 1991; Pastor 1991). Systematic studies examining oversight of the Pentagon or the intelligence community are few and far between (Art 1985; Blechman 1990; Heginbotham 1984; Lindsay 1990; Johnson 1980, 1985b, 1989; Smist 1994).

4. See Krasner 1978, 1991; Waltz 1979; Thucydides 1980; Gilpin 1981; Morgenthau 1985; Mearsheimer 1990.

5. By national interest, I mean an objective that is expected to contribute to the national security or general welfare of the nation (Clark and Legere 1969, 266). See also Krasner 1978.

Chapter 1

1. For review, see Moe 1984; Wood 1988; Shepsle 1989b; Wood 1990; Milgrom and Roberts 1992; Rothenberg 1994.

2. Early work attributed the surprising stability of policy choices to congressional institutions such as committees, the seniority system, and monopoly jurisdiction. Such institutions did not magically appear. They arose because they promised to make every legislator better off—by enforcing bargains, providing information, and monitoring agreements. See Shepsle 1979, 1986, 1989b; Weingast 1981, 1984; Rohde and Shepsle 1987; Weingast and Marshall 1988; Krehbiel 1991; Cox and McCubbins 1993.

3. This is not to say that presidents are irrelevant. Indeed, much of the debate between the McNollgast and Moe camps centers on how much presidents influence agency design. See Moe 1985, 1987a, 1989; Moe and Wilson 1994.

4. Senate aide, confidential telephone interview by author, May 12, 1994.

5. Congress may expend substantial effort to oversee the bureaucracy, but typically only when interest groups make it worthwhile to do so. Interest groups both raise the incentives and lower the costs of congressional oversight. On the incentive side, groups fuel the electoral connection. They possess both the interest and political resources to make their voices count (Schattschneider 1935; Latham 1952; McConnell 1966; Truman 1971; Lowi 1979). On the cost side, groups serve as ready-made, user-friendly information sources. They monitor agency activities extensively, keep in close, frequent contact with legislators, and pull the appropriate fire alarms—issuing formal complaints, filing suit, and publishing press releases—when agencies appear to stray too far (McCubbins and Schwartz 1984). Joel Aberbach found interest groups to be a major source of information for congressional oversight committees. He writes, "Twenty-seven percent of the respondents reported that group representatives provide their committee units with intelligence about programs and agencies in the form of complaints, and 20 percent just give information. Slightly over 40 percent of the total reported receiving complaints, information, or

both from groups, and this feedback is helpful in tracking agency or programs" (Aberbach 1990, 90).

6. According to Moe, bureaucracies are inevitably the creatures of others. They are secondary actors, forged out of the interests of legislators and presidents. But as we shall see, when it comes to foreign policy, existing bureaucrats have quite a large investment in the creation and development of agencies other than their own.

7. In 1990, the array of domestic policy interest groups—which included political action committees, corporations, issue-specific lobbies, trade and professional associations, foundations, and professional lobbying firms—numbered 8,216. (My tabulations from *Washington Representatives, 1990.*) For more, see Appendix A.

8. Domestic policy public interest groups, which arose largely in the 1960s and 1970s, are one obvious and important exception to this pattern. The point, however, is that an underlying, stable set of powerful lobbies that has long existed in the domestic arena has been relatively absent in the foreign policy realm.

9. In fact, defense contractors in the 1940s and early 1950s *opposed* large peacetime military budgets, fearing such government spending would take valuable resources away from the private sector and cripple the postwar economic recovery (Hill 1979). Moreover, as Aaron Wildavsky argues, there is little reason to believe that the military-industrial complex has ever had an interest in shaping U.S. foreign policy outcomes. "There is an important distinction between the questions 'Who will get a given contract?' and 'What will our defense policy be?' " (Wildavsky 1991, 40).

10. This figure is a liberal estimate. The source defines "Washington representatives" broadly. It includes foreign governments, other registered foreign agents, major national associations and labor unions, U.S. companies, professional lobbyists, law firms, and special interest groups. Moreover, my analysis reaggregated the raw data to include organizations— such as veterans' groups, aerospace firms, religious relief organizations, and environmental protection groups—that did not originally appear under the source's "foreign relations" and "foreign trade" primary headings. In total, foreign policy–related organizations numbered 922 out of a total of 9,138 interest groups. The tabulation of foreign policy interest groups is explained in Appendix A.

11. I am indebted to Brent Scowcroft for this point.

12. I conducted these interviews from May 1994 to February 1999. For a breakdown of interviews, see the Bibliography.

13. Confidential interview by author, July 12, 1995.

14. Confidential interview by author, July 7, 1995.

15. Douglas Paal, interview by author, July 25, 1995.

16. Confidential telephone interview by author, July 10, 1995.

17. The most obvious case is the Israeli lobby—the American Israel Public Affairs Committee (AIPAC). One senior-level executive branch offi-

cial remarked, "I don't think there is anybody who would deny that in the long run, they can carry the whole foreign aid bill. Because if they will agree, if the funding is there, they will get on board, and if it has got the other stuff that you wanted, they will help push it through. They have got the lobby to do it. They have got the strength to do it" (confidential interview by author, July 7, 1995).

18. Certainly this is not true of all legislators. In every Congress, there are a few who stake their reputations and devote much of their time to foreign policy issues. I refer to these as the "national security intellectuals." More on them below.

19. Senior Senate staffer, confidential telephone interview by author, Aug. 7, 1995. This view was shared by NSC staff as well. Geoffrey Kemp, Mideast senior NSC official in the Reagan administration, told me, "I think by and large, foreign policy lobby groups . . . are not as well informed as you are [in the NSC staff]. I don't think that's true in domestic affairs; I think that at the domestic level, in many cases they [interest groups] are *better* informed about the issues than the administration, so they have no compunction about feeling very strongly and persisting" (interview by author, July 11, 1995; emphasis Kemp's).

20. During the Cuban missile crisis, the president informed Congress of the situation and his planned naval blockade just hours before announcing the decision on national television (Kennedy 1969, 53–55).

21. The CIA's secret mining of Nicaraguan harbors in 1983 and the Iran-Contra arms-for-hostages deal are two prominent examples of executive branch violations.

22. See Jay 1987.

23. Anthony Lewis makes the point even more strongly. In a *New York Times* editorial on May 26, 1995, he wrote, "The Articles of Confederation, which joined the American states together in 1781, assigned the running of foreign affairs to Congress. The idea was such a dismal failure that in 1787 the Framers of the Constitution made the President the principal voice of the United States abroad."

24. Most political scientists would agree that since 1965, voters have increasingly cast their ballots on the basis of personal considerations of the candidates rather than party affiliation. Such personal voting, in turn, has reinforced district-centered behavior within Congress. Knowing the party label gets them only so far at the ballot box, the post-1965 members have worked hard to enhance their personal reputations as "our representative in Washington." They pay ever more attention to local needs, interests, and constituency casework, and spend increasing time in the district to maintain personal contacts with constituents and key supporters. Such a climate leaves them little time or incentive to take the lead on broader foreign policy issues. See Fenno 1978; Jacobson 1987; Alford and Brady 1993.

25. Claiming that "the safety of the nation is the supreme law,"

Jefferson responded to a British attack on the U.S. frigate *Chesapeake* by ordering arms purchases without congressional approval or appropriation (Sofaer 1976, 22).

26. For more on the rise of presidential power, see Patterson 1976; Fisher 1995.

27. The War Powers Act makes this point clearly. Drafted in reaction to America's undeclared war in Vietnam, the act sought to limit the president's ability to engage the United States in armed conflict without express congressional consent. Yet the War Powers Act has been more significant in the breach than in practice. Since 1973 there have been 25 instances in which the act could have been applied but wasn't. To give just a few examples: In 1980, President Carter refused to consult with Congress before launching a rescue operation for American hostages in Iran, claiming the mission was "humanitarian" and therefore outside the act's provisions. In 1986, President Reagan informed congressional leaders of American air strikes against Libya after the F-111 bombers had already left their bases in Britain. And in 1991, President Bush threatened to take military action against Iraq on the basis of United Nations Security Council resolutions alone. Though he ultimately received congressional authorization to take offensive action against Iraq at the eleventh hour, Bush made clear that he could and would have acted without it. In signing the legislation, he noted, "As I made clear to Congressional leaders at the outset, my request for Congressional support did not, and my signing of this resolution does not, constitute any change in the long-standing positions of the executive branch on either the President's constitutional authority to use the Armed Forces to defend vital U.S. interests or the constitutionality of the War Powers resolution" (quoted in Fisher 1995, 150–51). Fisher concludes:

> The drift of the war power from Congress to the President after World War II is unmistakable. . . . Presidents now regularly claim that the commander-in-chief clause empowers them to send American troops anywhere in the world, including into hostilities, without first seeking legislative approval. Congress has made repeated efforts since the 1970s to restore legislative prerogatives, with only moderate success. Presidents continue to wield military power single-handedly, agreeing only to consult with legislators and notify them of completed actions. (Fisher 1995, 185)

See also Jordan, Taylor, and Korb 1993, 129; Spitzer 1993, 149–92. For a sampling of the debate about the effectiveness of the War Powers Act, see Scigliano 1981; Carter 1984; Franklin 1986; Casper 1989; Cohen 1989; Katzmann 1990.

28. The American politics literature distinguishes between two types of oversight: (1) ex ante, by which Congress controls agency behavior by placing structural and procedural features into the enacting legislation; and (2) ex post, by which Congress controls agency behavior after the agency aris-

es through monitoring and through a system of rewards and punishments. In this discussion, I refer only to the second type.

29. Whether presidents gain or lose public approval points depends on the tone of opinion leaders or political elites quoted in the media.

30. Before most district-focused, reelection-seeking members will get actively involved in a foreign policy issue, two things need to occur. First, the issue itself must become "domesticated"—transformed into a domestic policy concern. This can happen when, for example, there is high potential for the loss of American lives, when domestic budget constraints are perceived to be serious, when concern arises that a foreign threat (such as communism) lurks at home, or when foreign policy agencies engage in disturbing domestic activities, such as CIA wiretapping of American citizens. Second, the president must be taken out of the foreign policy equation. He must either come to some agreement with congressional majority opinion or be too weak or distracted by other political issues to mount an effective opposition. In the words of one veteran Senate committee staffer, "If the Congress tries to do it without the president, you end up with what you've got now, which is the president and his allies on Capitol Hill opposing whatever proposals are being made by the outside party" (confidential interview by author, July 26, 1995).

31. This is the classic principal-agent problem.

32. See also Fiorina 1981.

33. The Senate's "advise and consent" power over political appointments has often been mentioned as a third major oversight mechanism. But as Moe argues, "the power of appointment is fundamentally presidential. Congress can and does influence the president's personnel choices in various ways, but its role is clearly secondary" (Moe 1987a, 489). Moreover, even here, congressional activism seems significantly greater in domestic policy than in foreign policy. Seventy-five percent of all Cabinet nominations rejected by the Senate were domestic policy positions. No secretary of state has ever failed to receive Senate confirmation (Congressional Quarterly 1993a, 16).

34. For more, see Moe 1987a.

35. Senior Senate committee staffer, confidential interview by author, July 26, 1995.

36. Leslie Gelb, telephone interview by author, Aug. 8, 1995.

37. See Moe 1984; Kiewiet and McCubbins 1991; Milgrom and Roberts 1992.

38. McGeorge Bundy, interview by author, June 13, 1995.

39. Jimmy Carter captures this problem in his memoirs, describing his run-in with Congressman Jack Brooks (D-Tex.) over a special procedural bill designed to facilitate executive branch reorganization. Carter writes of their meeting:

> [Brooks] had a grin on his face and a briefcase full of records of the Kennedy and Johnson years. He said, "Governor, Lyndon Johnson was

the greatest arm-twister Washington has ever seen, and he did not like to get beat on Capitol Hill. Look at this list! He was never successful in getting more than one-third of his proposed reorganization plans through Congress, even with this special procedure. If you win this argument on the legislation, you still won't have anything to show for it." (Carter 1995, 74)

40. Brent Scowcroft, interview by author, July 7, 1995.

41. In this case, State Department foot-dragging came back to haunt the president. During the Cuban missile crisis, Nikita Khrushchev offered Kennedy a quid pro quo withdrawal of the Jupiters for the Soviet missiles in Cuba—a deal that backed Kennedy into a corner. Faced with capitulation or escalation to potential nuclear war, Kennedy became furious. "Get those frigging missiles off the board!" he reportedly shouted during a meeting (Allison 1971, 142). This was not an isolated incident. Just one year earlier, CIA officials ignored the president's direction to plan the Bay of Pigs invasion without American air support. According to National Security Adviser McGeorge Bundy, CIA officials assured Kennedy that their invasion force "could disappear into the woodwork. But what they really thought was that when they needed air, because the operation would be wrecked without it, that he would give it" (McGeorge Bundy, interview by author, June 13, 1995).

Chapter 2

1. The NSC, the NSC staff, and the NSC system are not the same. The National Security *Council* is the formal, statutory body currently consisting of the president, the vice president, the secretary of defense, and the secretary of state. The National Security Council *staff* consists of the national security adviser and the 50 or so area and functional specialists who are appointed at the pleasure of the president and who are charged with coordinating analysis, offering policy recommendations for the president, and providing the staffwork for formal council meetings. The NSC *system* includes both the formal council and the informal staff.

2. For more, see Sander 1972; Destler 1977; Endicott 1982; Hoxie 1982; Melbourne 1983; Brzezinski 1987; Hess 1988; Lord 1988; Stevens 1989; Burke 1990.

3. See, for example, Hall 1975; Destler 1977; Endicott 1982; Hess 1988; Stevens 1989; Shoemaker 1991; Kemp 1993; Nathan and Oliver 1994.

4. The National Security Act did a number of things besides create the NSC system. It established a Department of the Air Force separate from the departments of the Army and Navy, it granted statutory authority to the informal World War II–era Joint Chiefs of Staff, it created the Central Intelligence Agency, and it also provided for a number of other coordinating committees and structures. They included a National Security

Resources Board to coordinate military, industrial, and civilian mobilization; a War Council composed of the secretary of defense and the secretaries and chiefs of staff of the Army, Navy, and Air Force; a Munitions Board; and a Research and Development Board to advise the secretary of defense on scientific research relating to national security. See *U.S. Statutes at Large* 1948, 495–510.

5. Until the 1947 National Security Act, the departments of War and the Navy had no common superior except the president. At the end of World War II, the War Department consisted of the Army ground and air forces, while the Navy Department oversaw the Navy, the Marine Corps, and its own aviation unit. Note that before the National Security Act, there was no separate Department of the Air Force. In fact, the autonomy of U.S. air forces proved to be a major issue in the National Security Act debates.

6. This chapter draws on five sets of congressional hearings: (1) 1944 hearings before the House Select Committee on Post-War Military Policy (the Woodrum Committee); (2) 1945 hearings before the Senate Military Affairs Committee; (3) 1946 hearings before the Senate Naval Affairs Committee; (4) 1947 hearings before the House Committee on Expenditures in the Executive Departments; and (5) 1947 hearings before the Senate Armed Services Committee.

7. For more, see U.S. Senate 1946, 228.

8. See also Donovan 1977, 139.

9. The full JCS, however, could not agree on the terms of the report, and sent it to the president with four separate commentaries. This split ultimately prevented the JCS from exercising much influence over the unification debate. See Caraley 1966, 38.

10. Note that the report also recommended creation of a separate Air Force Department. In total, then, there would be three military services: the Army, the Navy, and the Air Force.

11. The president's mounting frustration and anger can be seen in his press conferences. On Dec. 20, 1945, the day after his unification address to Congress, Truman pointedly denied that his remarks had been meant to "muzzle" the Navy. He declared, "I want everybody to express his honest opinion on the subject, and I want to get the best results that are possible. In order to do that, I want the opinions of everybody. And nobody has been muzzled" (Truman 1961–66, 1: 565). But on Apr. 11, 1946, when asked if he considered the Navy's continued opposition to unification justified, the president replied, "No, I do not. I do not think the Navy was justified in making a fight after I announced the policy" (ibid., 2: 194). By Apr. 17 the president openly accused the Navy of lobbying and publicly assailed Rear Admiral A. S. Merrill, who had openly attacked unification in a recent press interview (ibid., 204).

12. The role of the Marines and the Navy's retention of reconnaissance

and antisubmarine land-based aircraft were the other outstanding areas of disagreement.

13. Truman's third unification plan, sent to Congress on Jan. 16, 1947, eliminated all earlier references to a Defense Department. The proposed secretary of defense would have no department to support him. He would also have no administrative responsibility or right to control the three military services. In effect, the Army, Navy, and Air Force would be autonomous, headed by their own secretaries and military chiefs. In addition, the plan assured the Navy's control over naval aviation and the Marine Corps. All and all, it was a major victory for Forrestal (Congressional Quarterly 1965, 248; Donovan 1977, 202, 265).

14. Two considerations prompted the Budget Bureau's involvement. First, the bureau was concerned that a powerful NSC might usurp its own advisory functions. Second, as Alfred Sander writes, Budget Bureau officials were "concerned that the draft delegated authority which only the President can delegate since in the American constitutional system only the President is responsible for the ultimate formulation of foreign and military policy" (Sander 1972, 379).

15. For the full text of Truman's proposal to Congress of Feb. 26, 1947, see U.S. House 1947b.

16. To give two examples, in March 1944, Adolph J. Sabath (D-Ill.), chairman of the House Rules Committee, held up a resolution establishing a Select Committee on Post-War Military Policy until he received assurances that President Roosevelt and the secretaries of War and the Navy did not object (Caraley 1966, 25); in the spring of 1946, Navy Secretary Forrestal persuaded David I. Walsh (D-Mass.), chairman of the Senate Naval Affairs Committee, to hold additional unification hearings for the sole purpose of publicizing the Navy's opposition (Congressional Quarterly 1965, 245).

17. See also Senate and House floor debates in the *Congressional Record*, 1947, 8291–320, 8489–528, 9396–457.

18. In the fall of 1946, Democratic representatives campaigned without mentioning Truman's name, the Republicans gained control of Congress for the first time since the Depression, and the president's popularity hit 32 percent—a record low that would remain unbroken for over 25 years; only in October 1973, at the height of the Watergate scandal, did a president's public approval score dip lower (McCullough 1992, 470–75, 504, 520, 523; Edwards and Gallup 1990, 153–63).

19. Witnesses included the chief of naval operations, Fleet Admiral Chester W. Nimitz, and the Pacific Fleet commander, Admiral John H. Towers.

20. See the press conferences of Mar. 28, Apr. 11, and Apr. 17, 1946, in Truman 1961–66, 2: 174, 194, 204.

Chapter 3

1. See Hall 1975; George 1980; Endicott 1982; Melbourne 1983; *Tower Commission Report* 1987; Hess 1988; Lord 1988; Stevens 1989.

2. Between June 1950 and January 1953, the president missed only 9 of 71 NSC meetings.

3. The Executive Office of the President has never come under financial attack by Congress. As Wildavsky argues, the reason is not simply that the size of the budget is relatively small. "After all," he wrote in 1988, "Congress has become involved in budgetary disputes over much smaller items" than the EOP's $100 million budget. Instead, it appears that Congress has restrained itself out of a "tradition of comity"—out of the sense that the president has the right to spend funds for his personal expenses as he wishes, so long as he does not question what Congress spends on itself. As a result, Congress's purse strings have not proved particularly useful in efforts to oversee this part of the executive branch (Wildavsky 1988, 162–63).

4. Between 1953 and 1961, Eisenhower's National Security Council held 346 regular meetings—nearly one each week. On average, the meetings ran two and a half hours. Perhaps most important, over 90 percent of those sessions were attended by the president (Destler, Gelb, and Lake 1984, 172–73).

5. This oft-used term was coined by Eisenhower's first national security adviser, Robert Cutler (Cutler 1956).

6. The position was originally recommended by a study of the NSC system prepared by Robert Cutler. It was officially established on Mar. 17, 1953, when the president approved Cutler's report in writing.

7. In a revealing diary entry on May 14, 1953, Eisenhower refers to Cutler as "*my* administrative assistant and director of the National Security Council" (Eisenhower 1981, 238; emphasis mine).

8. Later the president put his special assistant in charge of implementation as well, appointing him chairman of the Operations Coordinating Board.

9. According to the presidential directive that set up the NSC system, the board was to "facilitate the formulation of policies, during the process of drafting policy recommendations, by marshaling the resources of the respective departments and agencies; by identifying the possible alternatives; by endeavoring to achieve acceptable agreements; by discussing differences; by avoiding undesirable compromises which conceal or gloss over real differences; and by reducing differences to as clearly defined and narrow an area as possible prior to reference to the Council" (Lay 1953).

10. Kennedy made clear the breadth and importance of Bundy's job in an April 1961 interview with the NBC correspondent Ray Scherer. Describing his relationship with his national security adviser, the president remarked, "All matters of international security go through McGeorge Bundy. . . . He

is now my assistant on national security matters. . . . On every meeting that we have with those dealing with problems such as Laos, Mr. Bundy is there. He then follows for me the implementation of our decisions here so that we don't decide something and then have it fall between departments" (Smith 1987, 17).

11. According to Arthur M. Schlesinger's account of the administration, "Kennedy told friends that, next to David Ormsby Gore, Bundy was the brightest man he had ever known" (1965, 197).

12. Bundy himself alluded to this expanded role in a letter to Senator Henry Jackson in September 1961. "The business of the National Security Council staff goes well beyond what is treated in formal meetings of the National Security Council," he wrote. "It is our purpose, in cooperation with other Presidential staff officers, to meet the president's staff needs throughout the national security area" (quoted in Smith 1987, 40).

13. Calculations based on NSC meeting data found in Falk 1964; Destler, Gelb, and Lake 1984, 172–73; and Smith 1987, 31, 39.

14. The one exception here is Richard Allen, Reagan's first national security adviser. I discuss the Reagan experiment in Cabinet government in more detail later.

15. Even Brent Scowcroft, who as national security adviser during the Ford and Bush administrations was widely regarded as the closest modern example of the pre-Kennedy "honest broker" model, saw his job as "helping the president." He gave fair airing to department views, but he added his own voice to the chorus—advocating specific policies and courses of action, going on presidential diplomatic missions abroad, and helping to develop the administration's overarching foreign policy architecture. Scowcroft described his role in the Bush administration in this way: "The president had a clear idea of what he wanted to do on foreign policy. I could anticipate where he'd come down on an issue. He would let me go with things. I would go into his office and say, 'Here's what I'd like to do on these issues, unless you tell me differently' " (Brent Scowcroft, interview by author, Feb. 8, 1995). For more on his style and role in the Bush administration, see John Barry, "The Jim and Brent Show," *Newsweek*, Feb. 27, 1989; Priscilla Painton, "Brent Scowcroft: Mr. Behind-the-Scenes," *Time*, Oct. 7, 1991; Strobe Talbott, "Toward a Safer World," *Time*, Oct. 7, 1991; Ann Reilly Dowd, "A Business Guide to Bush Country," *Fortune*, July 17, 1989.

16. Leslie Gelb writes, "It has been my experience that the same staffer behaves very differently in the White House than in the State Department, Defense Department, or CIA; one is far more conscious of presidential stakes and interests when in residence in Pennsylvania Avenue" (Gelb 1980, 27).

17. Before then, the White House had a difficult time acquiring even routine information. Eisenhower's staff secretary, Andrew Goodpaster, had to force a showdown with CIA Director Allen Dulles in front of the president

to get Dulles's cooperation in forwarding basic agency information (Destler, Gelb, and Lake 1984, 243).

18. For a detailed account of the creation of the Situation Room, see Destler, Gelb, and Lake 1984; Smith 1987.

19. We get a striking image of the two men from their own memoirs. Responding to news of the Watergate break-in, Nixon seems to take the seamy side of politics for granted: "I had been in politics too long, and seen everything from dirty tricks to vote fraud. I could not muster much moral outrage over a political bugging" (Nixon 1990, 628). Carter, by contrast, takes great pride in his anti-Watergate, populist stance during his presidential campaign: "As an American, I had been embarrassed by the Watergate scandal and the forced resignation of the President. I realized that my own election had been aided by a deep desire among the people for open government, based on a new and fresh commitment to changing some of the Washington habits which had made it possible for the American people to be misled. . . . I told supporters, if I ever lie to you, if I ever make a misleading statement, don't vote for me. I would not deserve to be your President" (Carter 1995, 29, 69).

20. Tabulations by author based on Destler 1980b and *New York Times Index*. Kissinger and Brzezinski are the only two national security advisers ever to appear in the *New York Times* more than 100 times in a given year. See Appendix B.

21. For details on the Carter and Nixon administrations, including the NSC system, see Crocker 1975; Kissinger 1979; Vance 1983; Destler, Gelb, and Lake 1984; Brzezinski 1985; Nixon 1990; Shoemaker 1991; Isaacson 1992; Haldeman 1994; Carter 1995. Information about the operation of the NSC system was also obtained from personal interviews with Nixon and Carter NSC staffers.

22. The concordance between the president and his two foreign policy players on this point is well illustrated in their memoirs and in subsequent interviews. Brzezinski remarked in 1982, for example, "My expectation [had] been that [the president and I] would be working very closely as a team with the secretary of state being, as I said earlier, the initiator and principal adviser on policy and I coordinating the workings of the national security machinery" (*Washington Quarterly* 1982, 71–72). See also Vance 1983; Brzezinski 1985; Carter 1995.

23. The directive established a Policy Review Committee, chaired by the secretary of state, to deal with major policy reviews, with a separate Special Coordinating Committee, chaired by Brzezinski, to handle crisis management, sensitive intelligence issues, and arms control talks.

24. "My own preference," Carter admits in his memoirs, "was that one of the roles of the Secretary of State be the education of the American public about foreign policy. Secretary Vance was not particularly inclined to assume this task on a sustained basis. . . . Zbigniew Brzezinski was always ready and willing to explain our position on international matters, analyze

a basic strategic interrelationship, or comment on a current event" (Carter 1995, 56). See also Vance 1983, 34–35.

25. It is undoubtedly true that Brzezinski quickly took advantage of opportunities to increase his influence with the president. The national security adviser made sure to control the paper flow to the president and used his chairmanship of the interagency Special Coordinating Committee to shape U.S. policy on a range of substantive issues beyond its original mandate (Vance 1983, 37; Brzezinski 1985, 66). Nevertheless, Carter did not object. "After all, why did [the president] keep me for four years?" Brzezinski asked in an interview. "I mean, he could have fired me. I certainly advocated policies with which he very often disagreed. It isn't that he liked me. . . . He knew two things about me. . . . One, he valued my loyalty. Two, he knew that I was advocating what I really thought. And he needed that. . . . And three, he increasingly lost confidence in Vance" (Zbigniew Brzezinski, interview by author, July 24, 1995).

26. Vesting principal authority in the departments and agencies had worked well during Reagan's governorship of California. More important, it offered a possible way to prevent a repeat of the Carter administration's foreign policy feuding and confusion. By strengthening the secretary of state's role and stemming the rising influence of the national security adviser, the Reagan inner circle sought to give greater coherence to U.S. foreign policy (Ty Cobb, interview by author, July 28, 1995; Geoffrey Kemp, interview by author, July 11, 1995; Paul Stevens, interview by author, July 25, 1995; Brent Scowcroft, interview by author, July 7, 1995).

27. Brent Scowcroft, interview by author, July 7, 1995.

28. Geoffrey Kemp, interview by author, July 11, 1995.

29. Brent Scowcroft, interview by author, July 7, 1995.

30. For good accounts of post–Iran-Contra reforms of the NSC system, see *Tower Commission Report* 1987; Powell 1989; Stevens 1990.

31. McGeorge Bundy, interview by author, June 13, 1995.

32. Dick Cheney made this point in an interview. Having served as a member of Congress, as a presidential chief of staff, and as secretary of defense, Cheney concluded, "I think if there is a bad [foreign policy] disaster they will blame the President. That's how come he gets paid so much money and gets to live in that fancy house. It is very hard to hold Congress accountable for anything. I *was* one" (Dick Cheney, interview by author, July 31, 1995).

33. Bush NSC staff aide, confidential interview by author, July 13, 1995.

34. Curiously, the vast majority of scholarly studies have found fault with the modern National Security Council system, arguing that foreign policy authority should return to the Department of State. See, for example, Sapin 1966; Clark and Legere 1969; Destler 1972b; Allison and Szanton 1976; Gelb 1980.

35. Several former members of NSC staffs emphasized the derivative nature of their power—and their resulting dependence on the president. As

Reagan's NSC executive secretary, Paul Stevens, put it, "At the end of the day . . . you are playing with the President's political capital when you are in a critically important function that close to him or her. [You need to be] conscious that political capital is a wasting asset. Once you lose it, you don't get it back very easily. . . . The NSC essentially, because of the nature of foreign policy and security policy and the way it's looked at now, can either make the returns on the investment extraordinarily great for a president or they can deplete it just as easily with equal and opposite results. So you have to run an NSC that is highly conscious of that and accountable to the president" (Paul Stevens, interview by author, July 25, 1995).

36. McGeorge Bundy, interview by author, June 13, 1995. Bundy's sentiment was shared by all the NSC staffers I interviewed, regardless of the administration in which they served.

37. In 1949, at President Truman's request, Congress amended the National Security Act. Among other things, the amendments reconstituted the statutory membership of the National Security Council by dropping the secretaries of the Navy, Army, and Air Force and adding the vice president.

38. See also Forrestal 1951, 315–16.

39. See also Sander 1972.

40. This mission also deprives the department of key domestic political allies to push its programs and help it withstand bureaucratic battles. While most domestic departments, and even the Department of Defense, have strong interest group and constituency ties, the State Department by and large does not.

41. Richard Garon, interview by author, July 14, 1995.

42. It is worth noting that Nelson (1981) believes the Jackson Committee substantially influenced Kennedy's decision to change the NSC system. But her evidence seems inconclusive at best. She argues that the committee's report received wide attention among political scientists and served as the topic of a Council on Foreign Relations seminar. But exposure does not equal influence. Certainly we do not know what went through the president's mind. But both explanations of the NSC system's evolution cast doubt on the influence of this report. For traditionalists, Kennedy's personality and leadership style made him inclined to favor a looser, more ad hoc NSC system. The logic of this argument suggests that Kennedy would have made the changes he did with or without the Jackson Committee report. My explanation leads to the same conclusion, but for a different reason: Kennedy—like all presidents—was compelled to act by the demands and capabilities of his office. Indeed, two of the most important Kennedy innovations in the NSC system—creating the Situation Room and moving McGeorge Bundy's office to the White House—occurred in reaction to the Bay of Pigs. Given this fact, it seems reasonable to conclude that events themselves—the exigencies of office—played a much stronger role in making up Kennedy's mind than the report of a congressional investigation.

43. Paul Stevens, interview by author, July 25, 1995.

44. House member, confidential interview by author, Aug. 2, 1995.

45. Legislative aide, confidential interview by author, July 14, 1995. The Foreign Affairs Committee is now called the Committee on International Relations.

46. Note that official names of the congressional committees dealing with foreign policy have fluctuated in recent years.

47. Legislative aide, confidential interview by author, July 14, 1995.

48. Based on figures obtained for the FY 1990 Bush administration NSC staff budget. Collection of Ty Cobb.

49. Tower Commission staff member, confidential telephone interview, July 10, 1995.

Chapter 4

1. Note that despite having representation on the JCS, the Army Air Forces were still housed within the War Department.

2. At the time, the Department of War included both the Army and its air arm, the Army Air Forces. In fact, creation of a separate Department of the Air Force was one of the few provisions that all sides accepted early in the unification conflict.

3. This summary is based on the two principal War Department plans that dominated the unification debate. The first of these, drafted by General Joseph T. McNarney, deputy chief of staff of the Army, was presented to the House Select Committee on Post-War Military Policy (the Woodrum Committee) in the spring of 1944. The second was drafted by Lieutenant General Lawton Collins and submitted to the Senate Military Affairs Committee in the fall of 1945. For a good overview of the plans, see Legere [1951] 1988; Caraley 1966; JCS 1980.

4. See also U.S. Senate 1945, 9–22, 49–61, 155–80, 359–80; testimony of War Department officials in U.S. House 1944a.

5. In the same vein, General Marshall remarked: "Under the present system, or lack of system, two separate executive departments compete for annual appropriations. Each asserts its independent viewpoint before separate committees and subcommittees of the Congress. And each tends to seek the maximum appropriations for itself. Such a procedure offers no assurance that each dollar appropriated buys the largest measure of protection for the nation" (U.S. Senate 1945, 51–52).

6. Lest there be any doubt about whether Navy autonomy threatened the future of the Army or the Air Force, consider the remarks of Admiral William Halsey: "We have everything in the Navy—sea, air—and the marines are our ground troops. If they want to build up from there, okay. Otherwise I'm against unification" (quoted by Assistant Secretary of War John J. McCloy, in U.S. Senate 1945, 460).

7. At the time of the hearings, Forrestal still technically held the post of

under secretary of the Navy. Because of the illness of Secretary Frank Knox, however, he became the most senior naval official to testify before Congress. In any event, Forrestal was sworn in as secretary two months later, in May 1944.

8. See Eberstadt 1945, 35–36; testimony of Secretary James Forrestal and Rear Admiral Thomas Robbins, in U.S. Senate 1945, 575–604; testimony of Admiral Forrest Sherman, deputy chief of naval operations, in U.S. House 1947a, 238.

9. See Eberstadt 1945, 38, 79; Pratt 1947; naval witness testimony in U.S. Senate 1945 and 1946.

10. See Eberstadt 1945; U.S. Senate 1945; Pratt 1947; testimony by Admiral Forrest Sherman in U.S. Senate 1947, 154–235.

11. See testimony by Admiral Charles M. Cooke in U.S. Senate 1945, 274–75, 281.

12. This conclusion is based on the congressional testimony of War and Navy department officials. The clearest exposition of the War Department's position comes from Assistant Secretary of War John J. McCloy. He states in the 1945 Senate Military Affairs Committee hearings:

> The view advanced by the Secretary of the Navy is that the top authority should be the Joint Chiefs of Staff, a group of four or five senior officers who can reach decisions only by unanimous agreement. . . . I think those words "unanimous agreement" must be emphasized. . . . My understanding from the Eberstadt report (p. 82) and from the position taken by all witnesses who have opposed current unification proposals, is that the Joint Chiefs of Staff must continue as a nonvoting body which can act only by unanimous agreement. . . . [But] the Constitution grew out of the conviction that committee government by unanimous consent was unsound. (U.S. Senate 1945, 444)

13. For more, see U.S. House 1944a; U.S. Senate 1945; Legere [1951] 1988; Caraley 1966; JCS 1980.

14. The Eberstadt Report did provide for a "Chief of Staff to the President" to serve on the JCS, should the president desire one. It is clear in the report and in subsequent congressional testimony, however, that this "Chief of Staff" was not meant to "head" the JCS in any way or to exercise any sort of operational command over the armed forces. Indeed, the Navy's model appeared to be the wartime JCS "chairman," Admiral William Leahy, who served as the president's military liaison. In Admiral Ernest King's words, the wartime Joint Chiefs of Staff considered Leahy more of a "spokesman" than a "chairman" (U.S. Senate 1946, 129).

15. One need only scan the committee's witness list to see the pro-Navy bias of these hearings. Altogether, the committee heard from 23 witnesses. Twenty of them held official positions in the Navy, two were senators, and one represented General Electric. Not a single witness testified on behalf of the War Department or the White House (U.S. Senate 1946, iii).

16. As Forrestal recalled, "The President said that while he would not be too much concerned if the nation could always count on having someone like Admiral Leahy in the position, he felt nevertheless that the idea was a dangerous one, that it was too much along the lines of the 'man on horseback' philosophy, and that he had finally made up his own mind against it" (Forrestal 1951, 161).

17. The letter is printed in U.S. Senate 1946, 203–7.

18. Truman's plan also gave the president the option of appointing a fourth JCS member—the "Chief of Staff to the Commander in Chief." Despite the title, this chief of staff was expected to function as a presidential military liaison rather than as a supreme military commander or JCS chairman.

19. The full text of Truman's proposal to Congress of Feb. 26, 1947, is found in U.S. House 1947b. For a summary of provisions, see also U.S. Senate 1946, 11–12.

20. There is reason to believe that Royall was expressing his sincere beliefs here, rather than presenting the official War Department line. His remarks were made in private, to the White House aide Clark Clifford, *after* the passage of the National Security Act.

21. Congressional support came mostly from members of the old Naval Affairs Committee, many of whom had personally served in the Navy and whose districts benefited from the Navy's shipbuilding programs.

Chapter 5

1. My analysis draws principally on William Lynn's treatment (1985, 174–81). Other useful sources for the Eisenhower reforms include Ries 1964; Congressional Quarterly 1965, 276–77, 299–300; Korb 1976; JCS 1980; Kester 1982; Lynn and Posen 1985. See also Eisenhower's State of the Union Message of Jan. 9, 1958, and his Special Message to the Congress on Reorganization of the Defense Establishment of Apr. 3, 1958 (Eisenhower 1958–61, 6: 2–15 and 274–90); and *U.S. Statutes at Large* 1959, 514–22.

2. The testimony of such key Navy witnesses as Chief of Naval Operations Arleigh Burke was said to have "pointed up the Navy's long-standing opposition to unification moves, and its success in maintaining support for its views" (Congressional Quarterly 1965, 300). Navy pressures proved particularly influential in defeating three of Eisenhower's most radical proposals: (1) to repeal restrictions on transfer or reassignment of combatant functions assigned to the services; (2) to grant the secretary of defense full authority to initiate or end service research and development projects; (3) to appropriate all defense funds to the secretary of defense rather than to the military departments. Note that these provisions did not directly deal with the Joint Chiefs of Staff, suggesting that Eisenhower felt

he had more room to push through stronger measures centralizing military organization on the civilian side than he did on the military JCS side.

3. The president remarked in a special message to Congress in April 1958:

> I have long been aware that the Joint Chiefs' burdens are so heavy that they find it very difficult to spend adequate time on their duties as members of the Joint Chiefs of Staff. This situation is produced by their having the dual responsibilities of chiefs of the military services and members of the Joint Chiefs of Staff. . . . I therefore propose that present law be changed to make it clear that each chief of a military service may delegate major portions of his service responsibilities to his vice chief. Once this change is made, the Secretary of Defense will require the chiefs to use their power of delegation to enable them to make their Joint Chiefs of Staff duties their principal duties. (Eisenhower 1958–61, 6: 282–83)

4. These were the Aerospace Defense Command, the Military Airlift Command, and the Strategic Air Command.

5. The only legislative change made to the JCS during this time was a minor one: in 1978 the commandant of the Marine Corps was made a full JCS member, codifying what had existed in practice since 1952.

6. The committee, chaired by Gilbert W. Fitzhugh, was officially called the Blue Ribbon Defense Panel.

7. These are only the presidentially commissioned reports; numerous other studies of the defense apparatus have been produced by executive agencies, as well as by outside defense analysts and observers. In a 1982 article in *Armed Forces Journal International*, General Edward "Shy" Meyer counted at least nine such critical reports between 1970 and 1982. "Almost from its inception the JCS has been a magnet for critical studies," he notes. "Each new Administration customarily revisits the national security apparatus and its decision-making process . . . [but] change targeted at fundamental shortcomings of the JCS has been absent" (Meyer 1982, 82–90).

8. Truman's first executive secretary, Sidney Souers, was an admiral in the Navy. Ford's national security adviser, Brent Scowcroft, held a Ph.D. in international relations and had risen to the rank of brigadier general in the Air Force. Reagan appointed three military men to serve as national security adviser during his tenure: Marine Lieutenant Colonel Robert "Bud" McFarlane, Navy Admiral John Poindexter, and Army Lieutenant General Colin Powell.

9. Brent Scowcroft echoed this view of Taylor's appointment: "The Bay of Pigs was a huge embarrassment to the president, and I think one of the things he felt as a result of it was that he didn't get the kind of military analysis that he wanted and that it was too hard to get from the JCS, too cumbersome, and not as useful, and so what he wanted was a real military expert answerable just to him" (interview by author, July 7, 1995).

10. I owe Ty Cobb and Paul Stevens a great debt for providing information about the organization and personnel of the NSC staffs before 1982. Such information about post-1982 NSC staffs can be found in the *Federal Staff Directory* and the *Federal Yellow Book*.

11. Vincent Davis notes, "There was no question that the OSD [Office of the Secretary of Defense] civilian hierarchy gained new bureaucratic strength, and it is largely correct that the overall JCS apparatus, in comparison to the growing clout on the civilian side within the OSD, remained generally weak and ineffective." However, Davis goes on to conclude that this did not mean "the services were somehow withering on the vine." Indeed, it was precisely because the JCS remained weak that the services could continue their internecine warfare and exert centrifugal pressures on U.S. defense policy (Davis 1985, 153–54).

12. There can be little doubt about the connection between JCS ineffectiveness and the increasing power of civilian analysts within the Department of Defense. Philip Odeen, a long-time organization expert, notes, "The McNamara defense management revolution in the 1960s was in no small part the result of shoddy cross-service coordination, poor or nonexistent analytic support for military department budgets, programs, and weapons choices, and the failure of the services and JCS to do long-range planning" (in Art, Davis, and Huntington 1985, 299). Along the same lines, John Kester observes: "Secretary Robert S. McNamara's broadening of the role of the assistant secretary of defense for international security affairs reflected in some part a need for help in political-military activities which the chiefs were not supplying. McNamara's expansion of his civilian staff and designation of an assistant secretary for systems analysis clearly were designed to supply him with alternatives to programs urged by the services—alternatives he could not get from JCS" (Kester 1982, 531).

13. Note, however, that the bill expressly prohibited the JCS chairman from having any command authority over combat forces.

14. During the Vietnam war, for example, American armed forces conducted five separate air wars so that each military service could get its own piece of the action. Even the evacuation of Saigon in 1975 was split between two commands—one at sea, one on land. As a result, each command determined its own H-hour for evacuation, leading to serious confusion and delay (Jones 1984, 276).

15. For example, Marine pilots were chosen to fly Navy helicopters on the six-hour flight, even though Air Force pilots were far better suited for such a lengthy low-altitude mission (Goldwater 1988, 344).

16. For more, see Beckwith and Knox 1983; Sick 1985; Perry 1989; Boo 1991.

17. For more on waste and abuse during this period, see Richard Halloran, "Why Defense Costs So Much," *New York Times*, Jan. 11, 1981; George C. Wilson, "Even Senate Hard-Liners Find Rich Pentagon Diet Difficult to Swallow," *Washington Post*, Apr. 17, 1981; Richard Halloran,

"Aide Acknowledges Waste in Pentagon Spending," *New York Times*, July 13, 1983; Charles Mohr, "Pentagon Expert Cites More Waste," *New York Times*, Sept. 30, 1983.

18. At the same time that House hearings got under way, a new Washington think tank, the Roosevelt Center for American Policy Studies, began an independent assessment of the defense establishment. The study was headed by two well-known insiders, Barry Blechman and Douglas Bennett.

19. See also testimony by Admiral Thomas H. Moorer and Admiral James L. Holloway III in U.S. House 1982; Perry 1989. Caspar Weinberger concurred (telephone interview by author, Mar. 11, 1996).

20. Two other factors contributed to the setback: first, in an effort to placate Secretary Weinberger (whom he hoped to replace), John Tower, chairman of the Senate Armed Services Committee, obstructed all reform efforts in the Senate. Second, the Roosevelt Center's independent study collapsed, removing any alternative forum for studying and advancing the reform issue (Perry 1989).

21. Reagan administration officials hotly contest this assessment of military failure. As Caspar Weinberger, then secretary of defense, noted in an interview, "We did exactly what we meant to do in Grenada, and did it in nine days. Grenada was an outstanding success. Combat is a messy thing. I'll never see a flawless combat operation" (telephone interview by author, Mar. 11, 1996). See also Weinberger 1990; Meese 1992; Shultz 1993.

22. For more on the military aspects of the invasion, see Duffy 1984; Goldwater 1988; Perry 1989; Allard 1990.

23. I am grateful to Dick Cheney for raising this point. When asked what would prompt the average, district-oriented legislator to press for major defense reorganization, Cheney noted, "The average member doesn't. That's the reason why it's called Goldwater-Nichols. Barry Goldwater took it on as his last crusade, his last really significant thing he did as a member of the Senate. He . . . [and] Bill Nichols . . . were very well respected members and had distinguished military careers in their own right, years before" (interview by author, July 31, 1995).

24. Committee members who supported the plan were Strom Thurmond (S.C.), William Cohen (Me.), Gary Hart (Colo.), James Exon (Neb.), Carl Levin (Mich.), Edward Kennedy (Mass.), Jeff Bingaman (N.M.), Alan Dixon (Ill.), Sam Nunn (Ga.), and Barry Goldwater (Ariz.). Those against it were John Warner (Va.), Pete Wilson (Calif.), Jeremiah Denton (Ala.), Phil Gramm (Tex.), John Stennis (Miss.), and John Glenn (Ohio). Three senators leaning against reform were Gordon Humphrey (N.H.), Dan Quayle (Ind.), and John East (N.C.) (Goldwater 1988, 339).

25. Caspar Weinberger, telephone interview by author, Mar. 11, 1996.

26. At best, the president stalled for time, appointing a blue-ribbon commission, led by former Deputy Secretary of Defense David Packard, to study reform in depth.

27. This original setup made even the 1949 addition of a JCS chairman irrelevant. As one Air Force officer described it, "The chair was in effect a eunuch unless the JCS concurred" (confidential interview by author, Feb. 8, 1995).

28. More on the relationship between service rivalry and civilian control can be found in Ginsburgh 1964; Ries 1964; Kanter 1975; CSIS 1985; Davis 1985; and Huntington 1985.

29. Colin Powell, telephone interview by author, Feb. 3, 1999.

30. Brent Scowcroft, interview by author, July 7, 1995.

31. Colin Powell, telephone interview by author, Feb. 3, 1999.

Chapter 6

1. The term "rogue elephant" was first applied to the CIA by Senator Frank Church in his 1976 review of the agency's history and activities (U.S. Senate 1976).

2. This point is hotly contested. Many experts believe that Harry Truman intentionally created a central intelligence agency with covert capabilities and insulation from congressional control. At the very least, they argue, Truman deliberately included two elastic clauses in the National Security Act that could be used to justify covert CIA operations (see, for example, Cline 1981; Clifford 1991). However, Truman's insertion of these clauses was merely a response to congressional enumeration of the CIA's authority. As the following discussion shows, Truman did not seek a CIA with wide discretionary powers.

3. The complete text of Donovan's memo to the president of Nov. 18, 1944, can be found in Troy 1981, 445–47; and Leary 1984, 123–25.

4. A full copy of Truman's CIG directive can be found in Troy 1981, 464–65; Leary 1984, 126–27; and CIA 1994, 29–31.

5. Truman's special message to Congress of Dec. 19, 1945, is quite revealing on this count. In his most important address on foreign policy organization, his remarks focus almost exclusively on the need for consolidating the military services. Intelligence issues are mentioned only obliquely, almost in passing. In more than fourteen pages of comments, the president refers to postwar intelligence organization only three times. In the first reference, Truman notes generally that "our military policy . . . should reflect our fullest knowledge of the capabilities and intentions of other powers." The second reference comes when he emphasizes the need for "other major aspects" of a total security program. Even here, Truman seems far more concerned with industrial mobilization and the development of scientific research programs than with a peacetime intelligence system. At the end of the paragraph, he adds, "The findings of our intelligence service must be applied to all of these." In the third reference, Truman notes that "the development of a coordinated, government-wide

intelligence system is in progress," but gives no hint about how the system should be organized or what it might do (Truman 1961–66, 1: 546–60).

6. The president's personal beliefs also contributed to his position. Evidence suggests that Truman harbored "Gestapo" fears about concentrating intelligence authority in one organization. Presidential aide George M. Elsey recalled that Truman "wanted to be certain that *no single* unit or agency of the Federal Government would have so much power that we would find ourselves, perhaps inadvertently, slipping in the direction of . . . a police state" (transcript, George M. Elsey oral history interview by Jerry N. Hess, July 10, 1970, quoted in Jeffreys-Jones 1989, 29; emphasis Elsey's). The Budget Bureau director, Harold Smith, agreed. In his diaries, Smith notes that the president repeatedly expressed concern about "building up a gestapo" (Harold D. Smith Papers, Truman Library, quoted ibid.).

7. The OSS was disbanded by executive order and CIG was created by an executive directive.

8. The administration did present a separate CIA bill to Congress two years later. The Central Intelligence Agency Act of 1949 regularized the CIA's budget and enabled the director of central intelligence to spend funds on covert operations without notifying Congress. However, it did not specify the agency's functions, jurisdiction, or restrictions in any greater detail. See *U.S. Statutes at Large* 1950a, 208–13.

9. The OSS wartime experience had been an exercise in frustration and bureaucratic competition. Karalekas notes, "Although by the end of the war OSS had expanded dramatically, the organization encountered considerable resistance to the execution of its mission. From the outset the military were reluctant to provide OSS with information for its research and analysis role and restricted its operations" (Karalekas 1984, 17).

10. The complete text of JIC 239/5 can be found in Troy 1981, 451–54.

11. It should be noted that Truman originally requested a review of the intelligence debate. It is unclear, however, whether the president directly asked that Souers, a Navy officer and author of the Eberstadt Report's intelligence sections, be charged with the task. Souers's memo can be found in CIA 1994, 17–19. See also Troy 1981, 339–40.

12. The documentary evidence on this point is striking. From May 1946 to January 1947, Truman and the military consistently included intelligence provisions in their unification proposals—intelligence provisions that clearly meant to grant CIG statutory authority without changing its design or operation in any way. On May 31, 1946, the secretaries of war and the Navy drafted a letter outlining their points of agreement and outstanding differences on all aspects of military unification. Creation of a Central Intelligence Agency was listed among the eight agreed-upon points. The letter makes clear that this new CIA would differ in no way from the existing Central Intelligence Group. Like CIG, the CIA would "compile, analyze, and evaluate information gathered by various Government agencies" but would not collect information or conduct its own operations. Like CIG,

the CIA would operate under a superintending authority of the secretaries of state, war, the Navy, and others. To remove any doubt, the letter noted that "an organization along these lines, established by Executive order, already exists" (*Congressional Record* 1946, 7425–26). President Truman used identical CIA language in the draft unification proposal he sent to Congress on June 15, 1946. On January 16, 1947, the War and Navy departments finally agreed to an entire unification bill. Sending a letter of transmittal to the president, they again noted: "There shall be a . . . Central Intelligence Agency (which already exists) as agreed by the Secretary of War and the Secretary of the Navy in their letter to the President of May 31, 1946" (U.S. Senate 1947, 2–3).

13. Specifically, the NIA authorized CIG to carry out independent research and analysis, and gave the agency its own clandestine collection capability. With these changes, CIG moved from coordinating intelligence to producing its own intelligence estimates for the president.

14. First, the committee voted to make the president a statutory member of the National Security Council. Since the CIA reported to the NSC, this move theoretically gave the CIA greater access to the president than originally planned. However, it still fell far short of granting the agency a private channel to the president, especially since the president was not required to attend NSC meetings. Second, the committee made clear that civilians, as well as military officers, were eligible for appointment as director of central intelligence; the president's bill did not rule out civilian appointments but did not specifically mention them (Troy 1981).

15. U.S. House 1947a. Tabulations conducted by author. Note that the committee also went into executive session to discuss intelligence issues. But these sessions appear to have been brief and focused on press leaks of CIG operational activities. For more, see Darling [1953] 1990; Troy 1981.

16. Truman's diary suggests the president intended to grant CIG statutory legitimacy without changing its substantive functions or operations in any way. See also U.S. Senate 1976, 71; Karalekas 1984; Lowenthal 1992.

17. The most vocal legislators were Representatives Clarence Brown (R-Ohio), James Wadsworth (R-N.Y.), Fred Busbey (R-Ill.), and Senator Millard E. Tydings (D-Md.).

Chapter 7

1. The clandestine service has performed two distinct types of activities. The first—*covert intelligence collection*—involves obtaining secret information about a foreign country without that country's knowledge. The second type of activity is *covert action*, defined by the CIA as "any clandestine operation or activity designed to influence foreign governments, organizations, persons or events in support of United States foreign policy" (U.S. Senate 1976, 141). Action can range from low-level propaganda to coup

attempts to paramilitary activities. For purposes of simplicity, I have grouped both types of activities together when I discuss the CIA's covert side.

2. Presidents contend that two sources give them legal authority to order CIA covert operations: (1) constitutional guarantees of executive power in foreign affairs; (2) vague provisions of the National Security Act that direct the Central Intelligence Agency to perform "additional services of common concern" and "such other functions and duties related to intelligence affecting the national security as the National Security Council may from time to time direct" (*U.S. Statutes at Large* 1948, 498). More on this below.

3. The JCS plan was JIC 239/5, issued on Jan. 1, 1945.

4. Truman's CIG directive was issued on Jan. 22, 1946. Its text is in Leary 1984, 464–65.

5. The Church Committee is the popular or more widely known name of the Senate Select Committee to Study Governmental Operations with Respect to Intelligence Activities. For the Church Committee Report, see U.S. Senate 1976.

6. See also Truman 1956, 52, 58; Reichard 1986, 262; Lowenthal 1992, 17.

7. The authorization officially came in NSC 4/A. Activities included broadcasting propaganda by radio and by leaflet drops (Breckinridge 1986, 32).

8. For details about these reform efforts, see Karalekas 1984; Jeffreys-Jones 1989; Blechman 1990; Smist 1994.

9. Budget allocations provide a good illustration of how U.S. intelligence priorities have shifted since the Soviet Union's fall. In 1980, 60 percent of the American intelligence budget was directed toward the Soviet republics. By 1993, that figure had declined to less than 20 percent (Hedley 1995, 27).

10. In February 1975, the House created its own Select Committee on Intelligence, chaired by Representative Otis Pike. For a number of reasons, however, including massive leaks of classified intelligence information, the committee never got off the ground. Spending most of its effort investigating its own security breaches, the Pike Committee did not influence CIA reform proposals or debates. For more, see Smist 1994 and Olmsted 1996.

11. The executive branch did not sit idly by. On Jan. 14 1975, President Gerald Ford established a blue ribbon panel headed by Vice President Nelson Rockefeller to investigate charges of illegal domestic CIA activities. Many observers, however, have criticized the commission as a political maneuver designed to take the steam out of the congressional investigation.

12. The Church Committee itself writes that its inquiry "arose out of allegations of substantial, even massive wrong-doing within the 'national intelligence' system" (U.S. Senate 1976, 1).

13. Executive Order 12063, Jan. 24, 1978; text in Leary 1984, 153–68.

14. One explanation for such congressional restraint was the belief that legal solutions were not needed. The Iran-Contra congressional investigating committees concluded that "the Iran-Contra Affair resulted from the failure

of individuals to observe the law, not from deficiencies in existing law or in our system of governance. . . . Government officials must observe the law, even when they disagree with it" (U.S. Senate and House 1987, 423).

15. The act required only that the president inform Congress "in a timely fashion" whenever he did not give "prior notice" of covert operations (*U.S. Statutes at Large* 1992a, 443)

16. See the Intelligence Authorization Act of 1993 (*U.S. Statutes at Large* 1992b).

17. The commission's final chairman was Harold Brown, former defense secretary.

18. The report (IC21) is "The Intelligence Community in the 21st Century." See U.S. House 1996.

19. Others were more blunt. David Wise wrote in the *Washington Post*, "The panel labored mightily and came up with a mouse" (Wise 1996).

20. The plan also called for redefining the role of the existing deputy director of central intelligence to focus more explicitly on daily management of the CIA (U.S. House 1996, "Overview and Summary," 10–11).

21. Instead, the law allowed the defense secretary's nominations for top posts in the NSA, NRO, and National Imagery and Mapping Agency (NIMA) to go forward even over the DCI's objections (*U.S. Statutes at Large* 1997).

22. See in particular Woodward 1987.

23. "Major" covert operations are defined as programs that cost at least $5 million, aim to overthrow a foreign government, or both (Jeffreys-Jones 1989, 235).

24. Representative Lee Hamilton (D-Ind.), chairman of the House Intelligence Committee during 1985–86, put it this way: "The advantage of covert action is that the action can be done without the approval of Congress. A covert action 'finding' doesn't need the approval of Congress. This is the big attraction of covert action to the executive branch" (quoted in Smist 1994, 257–58).

25. See also Cline 1981, 125.

26. Karalekas attributes the rapid growth of the CIA's covert activities in late 1940s and early 1950s to four factors: (1) the Korean war; (2) vague policy directives from the National Security Council; (3) conflicting policy needs of the State and Defense departments, which generated additional clandestine activities; (4) internal CIA organizational arrangements that provided incentives to expand the number and scope of covert operations (Karalekas 1984, 43–45).

Chapter 8

1. See also Powell 1995.

Bibliography

Interviews

Forty-eight members of the national security community were interviewed between May 1994 and February 1999. These included current and former Cabinet members, National Security Council staff members, senior military officers, legislators, congressional staffers, and other foreign policy watchers such as journalists, academics, and public policy experts. Executive branch respondents represented every presidential administration from Kennedy to Clinton.

All interviews were conducted in person, unless otherwise noted. Many people were interviewed more than once. Attribution was determined at the beginning of each interview. Those listed below agreed to be quoted on the record. The remainder — 28 in all — asked that their names be kept confidential.

Name	Affiliation
Francis Bator*	NSC staff (Johnson)
Zbigniew Brzezinski	National security adviser (Carter)
McGeorge Bundy	National security adviser (Kennedy/Johnson)

Name	Affiliation
Frank Carlucci	National security adviser (Reagan); secretary of defense (Reagan)
Richard Cheney	Secretary of defense (Bush)
Tyrus Cobb	NSC staff (Reagan)
Chester Crocker	NSC staff (Nixon)
Norm Dicks	Representative (D-Wash.)
Tom Duesterberg	Chief of staff, Representative Chris Cox (R-Calif.)
Richard Garon	Majority chief of staff, House International Relations Committee
Geoffrey Kemp	NSC staff (Reagan)
Robert McFarlane	National security adviser (Reagan)
Douglas Paal	NSC staff (Bush)
Colin Powell*	National security adviser (Reagan); JCS chairman (Bush)
Brent Scowcroft	National security adviser (Ford, Bush)
Paul Stevens	NSC staff (Reagan)
Gregory Treverton	NSC staff (Carter)
Victor Utgoff	NSC staff (Carter)
Michael Ward	Representative (D-Ky.)
Caspar Weinberger*	Secretary of defense (Reagan)

*Interviewed by telephone.

Primary and Secondary Sources

Aberbach, Joel D. 1990. *Keeping a Watchful Eye.* Washington: Brookings.

Acheson, Dean. 1969. *Present at the Creation: My Years in the State Department.* New York: W. W. Norton.

Alford, John R., and David W. Brady. 1993. "Personal and Partisan Advantage in U.S. Congressional Elections." In *Congress Reconsidered*, edited by Lawrence C. Dodd and Bruce I. Oppenheimer, 5th ed. Washington: Congressional Quarterly Press.

Allard, C. Kenneth. 1990. *Command, Control, and the Common Defense.* New Haven: Yale University Press.

Allison, Graham T. 1969. "Conceptual Models of the Cuban Missile Crisis." *American Political Science Review* 63: 689–718.

———. 1971. *Essence of Decision: Explaining the Cuban Missile Crisis.* Boston: Little, Brown.

Allison, Graham T., and Morton H. Halperin. 1989. "Bureaucratic Politics: A Paradigm and Some Policy Implications." In *American Foreign Policy: Theoretical Essays,* edited by G. John Ikenberry. New York: HarperCollins.

Allison, Graham T., and Peter Szanton. 1976. *Remaking Foreign Policy.* New York: Basic Books.

Ambrose, Stephen E. 1981. *Ike's Spies: Eisenhower and the Espionage Establishment.* Garden City, N.Y.: Doubleday.

Anderson, Perry. 1974. *Passages from Antiquity to Feudalism and Lineages of the Absolutist State.* London: New Left Books.

Andrew, Christopher. 1995. *For the President's Eyes Only: Secret Intelligence and the American Presidency from Washington to Bush.* New York: HarperCollins.

Arias, Ron. 1991. "A Man to Take to the Well: Who's the Chief Gonna Call in a Crisis? Brent Scowcroft." *People,* Nov. 25.

Art, Robert J. 1973. "Bureaucratic Politics and American Foreign Policy: A Critique." *Policy Sciences* 4 (December): 467–90.

———. 1985. "Congress and the Defense Budget: Enhancing Policy Oversight." *Political Science Quarterly* 100: 227–48.

Art, Robert J., Vincent Davis, and Samuel P. Huntington, eds. 1985. *Reorganizing America's Defenses: Leadership in War and Peace.* Washington: Pergamon-Brassey's.

Aspin, Les. 1975. "The Defense Budget and Foreign Policy: The Role of Congress." *Daedalus* 104, no. 3: 155–74.

Axelrod, Robert. 1983. *The Evolution of Cooperation.* New York: Basic Books.

Bachrach, Peter, and Morton S. Baratz. 1962. "Two Faces of Power." *American Political Science Review* 56: 947–52.

Baker, James Addison, III, with Thomas M. DeFrank. 1995. *The Politics of Diplomacy: Revolution, War, and Peace, 1989–1992.* New York: Putnam.

Barrett, Archie D. 1983. *Reappraising Defense Organization: An Analysis Based on the Defense Organization Study of 1977–1980.* Washington: National Defense University Press.

Barry, John M. 1989. *The Ambition and the Power.* New York: Penguin.

Bawn, Kathleen. 1994. "Political Control Versus Expertise: Congressional Choices About Administrative Procedures." *American Political Science Review* 89, no. 1: 62–73.

Beck, Robert J. 1993. *The Grenada Invasion.* Boulder: Westview Press.

Becker, Gary. 1983. "A Theory of Competition Among Pressure Groups for Political Influence." *Quarterly Journal of Economics* 98: 329–47.

Beckwith, Charlie A., and Donald Knox. 1983. *Delta Force*. New York: Harcourt Brace Jovanovich.

Bendor, Jonathan, and Thomas H. Hammond. 1992. "Rethinking Allison's Models." *American Political Science Review* 86, no. 2: 301–22.

Berry, Clifton, Jr., and Deborah Kyle. 1977. "The 'Other Cabinet': The National Security Council Staff." *Armed Forces Journal* 114, no. 11: 12–20.

Bessette, Joseph M., and Jeffrey Tulis, eds. 1981. *The Presidency and the Constitutional Order*. Baton Rouge: Louisiana State University Press.

Blackwell, James A., and Barry M. Blechman, eds. 1990. *Making Defense Reform Work*. Washington: Brassey's.

Blechman, Barry M. 1990. *The Politics of National Security: Congress and U.S. Defense Policy*. New York: Oxford University Press.

Blechman, Barry M., and William J. Lynn, eds. 1985. *Toward a More Effective Defense: The Final Report of the CSIS Defense Organization Project*. Washington: Center for Strategic and International Studies, Georgetown University.

Boatman, John. 1994. "The Long Road to Jointness." *Jane's Defence Weekly* 22, no. 23: 18.

Bock, Joseph G., and Duncan L. Clarke. 1986. "The National Security Assistant and the White House Staff: National Security Policy Decisionmaking and Domestic Political Considerations, 1947–1984." *Presidential Studies Quarterly* 16, no. 2: 258–79.

Boo, Katherine. 1991. "How Congress Won the War in the Gulf: Implementing the Goldwater-Nichols Defense Reorganization Act in the Persian Gulf War." *Washington Monthly* 23, no. 10: 31.

Boren, David L. 1992. "The Intelligence Community: How Crucial?" *Foreign Affairs* 71, no. 3: 52–62.

Borkund, C. W. 1991. *U.S Defense and Military Fact Book*. Santa Barbara: ABC-CLIO.

Braden, Tom. 1977. "The Birth of the CIA." *American Heritage* 28, no. 2: 4–13.

Breckinridge, Scott D. 1986. *The CIA and the U.S. Intelligence System*. Boulder: Westview Press.

Brody, Richard A. 1991. *Assessing the President: The Media, Elite Opinion, and Public Support*. Stanford: Stanford University Press.

Brown, Harold. 1983. *Thinking About National Security: Defense and Foreign Policy in a Dangerous World*. Boulder: Westview Press.

———. (Chairman). 1996. Commission on the Roles and Capabilities of the United States Intelligence Community [Brown Commission]. *Preparing for the 21st Century: An Appraisal of U.S. Intelligence* (March). Available at http://www.gpo.gov/su_docs/dpos/epubs/int/index.html/

Brzezinski, Zbigniew. 1985. *Power and Principle*. 2d ed. New York: Farrar, Straus & Giroux.

———. 1987. "The NSC's Midlife Crisis." *Foreign Policy* 69 (Winter): 80–99.

Bundy, William P. 1982. "The National Security Process: Plus Ça Change . . . ?" *International Security* 7, no. 3: 94–109.

Burgin, Eileen. 1993. "Congress and Foreign Policy: The Misperceptions." In *Congress Reconsidered*, edited by Lawrence C. Dodd and Bruce I. Oppenheimer, 5th ed. Washington: Congressional Quarterly Press.

Burke, John P. 1990. "The Institutional Presidency." In *The Presidency and the Political System*, edited by Michael Nelson. Washington: Congressional Quarterly Press.

Burke, John P., and Fred I. Greenstein. 1989. *How Presidents Test Reality: Decisions on Vietnam, 1954 and 1965*. New York: Russell Sage Foundation.

Cain, Bruce, John Ferejohn, and Morris Fiorina. 1987. *The Personal Vote: Constituency Service and Electoral Independence*. Cambridge: Harvard University Press.

Caldwell, Dan. 1977. "Bureaucratic Foreign Policy-making." *American Behavioral Scientist* 21: 87–110.

Campbell, Colin S. J., and Bert A. Rockman. 1991. *The Bush Presidency: First Appraisals*. Chatham, N.J.: Chatham House.

Campbell, John F. 1971. *The Foreign Affairs Fudge Factory*. New York: Basic Books.

Caraley, Demetrios. 1966. *The Politics of Military Unification: A Study of Conflict and the Policy Process*. New York: Columbia University Press.

Carter, Jimmy. 1977a. "Establishment of Presidential Review and Directive Series/NSC." Presidential Directive NSC-1 (January 20). Mimeograph. Collection of Paul Stevens.

———. 1977b. "The National Security Council System." Presidential Directive/NSC-2 (January 20). Mimeograph. Collection of Paul Stevens.

———. 1995. *Keeping Faith: Memoirs of a President*. 3d ed. Fayetteville: University of Arkansas Press.

Carter, Stephen. 1984. "The Constitutionality of the War Powers Resolution." *Virginia Law Review* 70 (February): 101–34.

Casper, Gerhard. 1985. "The Constitutional Organization of Government." *William and Mary Law Review* 26: 177–98.

———. 1989. "An Essay in Separation of Powers: Some Early Versions and Practices." *William and Mary Law Review* 30, no. 2: 211–61.

———. 1990. "Appropriations of Power." *University of Arkansas Law Journal* 13 (Fall): 1–23.

Central Intelligence Agency (CIA). 1976. *Intelligence in the War of Independence*. Washington: Central Intelligence Agency.

———. 1994. *The CIA Under Harry Truman*. Edited by Michael Warner. Washington: History Staff, Center for the Study of Intelligence, Central Intelligence Agency.

Challener, Richard D. 1986. "The National Security Policy from Truman

to Eisenhower: Did the 'Hidden Hand' Leadership Make Any
Difference?" In *The National Security: Its Theory and Practice,
1945–1960*, edited by Norman A. Graebner. New York: Oxford
University Press.

Chomsky, Noam. 1972. "The Pentagon Papers and U.S. Imperialism in
South East Asia." In *Spheres of Influence in the Age of Imperialism*.
Linz, Austria: Spokesman Books.

Christopher, Warren. 1995. Letter to Senator Jesse Helms, Chairman,
Committee on Foreign Relations, United States Senate, about S. 908,
the Foreign Relations Revitalization Act of 1995 (July 25). Mimeograph.
Author's collection.

Church, George. 1994. "Taking His Show on the Road: Clinton's New
Success in Juggling Foreign Problems Is More than Just Good Luck."
Time, October 31.

Clark, Asa A., IV, Peter W. Chiarelli, Jeffrey S. McKitrick, and James W.
Reed, eds. 1984. *The Defense Reform Debate: Issues and Analysis*.
Baltimore: Johns Hopkins University Press.

Clark, Keith C., and Laurence J. Legere, eds. 1969. *The President and the
Management of National Security*. New York: Praeger.

Clifford, Clark, with Richard Holbrooke. 1991. *Counsel to the President*.
New York: Random House.

Cline, Ray S. 1981. *The CIA Under Reagan, Bush, and Casey*.
Washington: Acropolis Books.

Clinton, Bill. 1995. The Foreign Relations Revitalization Act of 1995 (S.
908). Statement by the President (July 16). Washington: Office of the
Press Secretary, the White House.

Coase, R. H. 1937. "The Nature of the Firm." *Economica* 4: 386–405.

Cohen, Richard E. 1989. "Marching Through the War Powers Act."
National Journal, December 30.

Congressional Quarterly. 1965. *Congress and the Nation, 1945–1965*.
Washington: Congressional Quarterly Press.

———. 1969. *Congress and the Nation, 1965–1968*. Washington:
Congressional Quarterly Press.

———. 1971. *Guide to the U.S. Congress*. Washington: Congressional
Quarterly Press.

———. 1973. *Congress and the Nation, 1969–1972*. Washington:
Congressional Quarterly Press.

———. 1977. *Congress and the Nation, 1973–1976*. Washington:
Congressional Quarterly Press.

———. 1981. *Congress and the Nation, 1977–1980*. Washington:
Congressional Quarterly Press.

———. 1985a. *Congress and the Nation, 1981–1984*. Washington:
Congressional Quarterly Press.

———. 1985b. "Intelligence Panels: Fresh Faces, Familiar Issues."
Congressional Quarterly, January 19. Quoted in Barry M. Blechman,

The Politics of National Security: Congress and U.S. Defense Policy,
155–56 (New York: Oxford University Press, 1990).

———. 1990. *Congress and the Nation, 1985–1988*. Washington:
Congressional Quarterly Press.

———. 1993a. *Congress A to Z: CQ's Encyclopedia of American
Government*. Washington: Congressional Quarterly Press.

———. 1993b. *Congress and the Nation, 1989–1992*. Washington:
Congressional Quarterly Press.

———. 1998. *Congress and the Nation, 1993–1996*. Washington:
Congressional Quarterly Press.

Congressional Record. 1946. Washington.

———. 1947. Washington.

———. 1956. Washington.

———. 1995. Washington.

Cooper, Richard. 1972. "Economic Interdependence and Foreign Policy in
the Seventies." *World Politics* 24, no. 2: 159–81.

Corwin, Edward S. 1957. *The President: Office and Powers*. 4th ed. New
York: New York University Press.

Council on Foreign Relations. 1996. *Making Intelligence Smarter: The
Future of U.S. Intelligence*. New York: Council on Foreign Relations.

Cox, Gary W., and Mathew D. McCubbins. 1993. *Legislative Leviathan:
Party Government in the House*. Berkeley: University of California
Press.

Crabb, Cecil V., Jr., and Pat M. Holt, eds. 1984. *Invitation to Struggle:
Congress, the President, and Foreign Policy*. 2d ed. Washington:
Congressional Quarterly Press.

Crocker, Chester A. 1975. "The Nixon-Kissinger National Security
Council System, 1969–1972: A Study in Foreign Policy Management."
In *Report of the Commission on the Organization of the Government
for the Conduct of Foreign Policy* (Murphy Commission Report), vol. 6,
app. O (June), 79–99. Washington: GPO.

Cronin, Thomas E. 1980. "A Resurgent Congress and the Imperial
Presidency." *Political Science Quarterly* 95 (Summer): 209–37.

Crowe, William J., Jr. 1993. *The Line of Fire*. New York: Simon &
Schuster.

Cutler, Robert. 1956. "The Development of the National Security
Council." *Foreign Affairs* 34: 441–58.

Dahl, Robert A. 1961. *Who Governs?* New Haven: Yale University Press.

Daly, John Charles. 1978. *The Joint Chiefs of Staff in National Policy*.
Washington: American Enterprise Institute.

Darling, Arthur B. [1953] 1990. *The Central Intelligence Agency: An
Instrument of Government, to 1950*. University Park: Pennsylvania
State University Press.

Davis, Vincent. 1985. "The Evolution of Central U.S. Defense
Management." In *Reorganizing America's Defense: Leadership in War*

and Peace, edited by Robert J. Art, Vincent Davis, and Samuel P. Huntington. Washington: Pergamon-Brassey's.

Deering, Christopher J. 1989. "National Security Policy and Congress." In *Congressional Politics*, edited by Christopher J. Deering. Homewood, Ill.: Dorsey Press.

Derthick, Martha. 1990. *Agency Under Stress: The Social Security Administration in American Government*. Washington: Brookings.

Destler, I. M. 1971. "Can One Man Do?" *Foreign Policy* 5 (Winter): 28–40.

———. 1972a. "Making Foreign Policy: Comment." *American Political Science Review* 66: 786–90.

———. 1972b. *Presidents, Bureaucrats, and Foreign Policy: The Politics of Organizational Reform*. Princeton: Princeton University Press.

———. 1977. "National Security Advice to U.S. Presidents: Some Lessons from Thirty Years." *World Politics* 29 (January): 143–76.

———. 1980a. "A Job That Doesn't Work." *Foreign Policy* 38 (Spring): 80–88.

———. 1980b. "National Security Management: What Presidents Have Wrought." *Political Science Quarterly* 95 (Winter): 573–88.

———. 1981a. "Dateline Washington: Congress as Boss?" *Foreign Policy* 42: 167– 80.

———. 1981b. "Executive-Congressional Conflict in Foreign Policy: Explaining It; Coping with It." In *Congress Reconsidered*, edited by Lawrence C. Dodd and Bruce I. Oppenheimer, 2d ed. Washington: Congressional Quarterly Press.

———. 1981c. "National Security II: The Rise of the Assistant (1961– 1981)." In *The Illusion of Presidential Government*, edited by Hugh Heclo and Lester M. Salamon. Boulder: Westview Press.

———. 1986. "The Presidency and National Security Organization." In *The National Security: Its Theory and Practice, 1945–1960*, edited by Norman A. Graebner. New York: Oxford University Press.

Destler, I. M., Leslie H. Gelb, and Anthony Lake. 1984. *Our Own Worst Enemy: The Unmaking of American Foreign Policy*. New York: Simon & Schuster.

Dickson, Brian. 1983. "The JCS: Impressionistic Reform." *Washington Quarterly* 6, no. 1: 78.

Dodd, Lawrence C., and Richard L. Schott. 1979. *Congress and the Administrative State*. New York: John Wiley.

Donovan, Robert J. 1977. *Conflict and Crisis: The Presidency of Harry S. Truman, 1945–1948*. New York: W. W. Norton.

Dowd, Maureen. 1983. "The Man with the President's Ear." *Time*, August 8.

Doyle, Michael. 1983. "Kant, Liberal Legacies, and Foreign Affairs." *Philosophy and Public Affairs* 12, no. 3: 205–35; and no. 4: 323–53.

Drew, Elizabeth. 1995. *On the Edge: The Clinton Presidency*. New York: Touchstone.

Duffy, Michel. 1984. "Caucus Chief Reveals Faults of Grenada Invasion: Incompatible Radios and Tourist Maps." *Defense Week*, January 30.

Eberstadt, Ferdinand. 1945. *Unification of the War and Navy Departments and Postwar Organization for National Security: Report to Hon. James Forrestal, Secretary of the Navy*. Printed for use of the U.S. Senate, Committee on Naval Affairs, 79th Cong., 1st sess. (October 22). Committee print S1281.

Edwards, George C., III, and Alec M. Gallup. 1990. *Presidential Approval*. Baltimore: Johns Hopkins University Press.

Edwards, George C., III, John H. Kessel, and Bert A. Rockman, eds. 1993. *Researching the Presidency: Vital Questions, New Approaches*. Pittsburgh: University of Pittsburgh Press.

Eisenhower, Dwight D. 1953. Letter to Robert Cutler approving James S. Lay's National Security Council memorandum (March 17). Mimeograph. Collection of Paul Stevens.

———. 1958–61. *Public Papers of the Presidents of the United States: Dwight D. Eisenhower, 1953–1961*. 8 vols. Washington: GPO

———. 1963. *Mandate for Change*. New York: Doubleday.

———. 1981. *The Eisenhower Diaries*. Edited by Robert H. Ferrell. New York: W. W. Norton.

Elsey, George M. Papers. Harry S Truman Library. Quoted in Demetrios Caraley, *The Politics of Military Unification: A Study of Conflict and the Policy Process* (New York: Columbia University Press, 1966).

Endicott, John E. 1982. "The National Security Council." In *American Defense Policy*, edited by John F. Reichard and Steven R. Sturm, 5th ed. Baltimore: Johns Hopkins University Press.

Fain, Tyrus G., Katharine C. Plant, and Ross Milloy, eds. 1977. *The Intelligence Community: History, Organization, and Issues*. New York: R. R. Bowker.

Fairfield, William S. 1958. *The Reporter* 18 (May 15). Quoted in Samuel P. Huntington, *The Common Defense: Strategic Programs in National Politics*, 399–400 (New York: Columbia University Press, 1961).

Falk, Stanley L. 1964. "The National Security Council Under Truman, Eisenhower, and Kennedy." *Political Science Quarterly* 79 (September): 403–34.

Fenno, Richard F., Jr. 1973. *Congressmen in Committees*. Boston: Little, Brown.

———. 1978. *Home Style: House Members in Their Districts*. New York: HarperCollins.

Fiorina, Morris P. 1981. "Congressional Control of the Bureaucracy: A Mismatch of Incentives and Capabilities." In *Congress Reconsidered*, edited by Lawrence C. Dodd and Bruce I. Oppenheimer, 2d ed. Washington: Congressional Quarterly Press.

———. 1982a. "Legislative Choice of Regulatory Forms: Legal Process or Administrative Process?" *Public Choice* 39 (September): 33–66.

———. 1982b. "Group Concentration and the Delegation of Legislative Authority." Social Science Working Paper no. 112, California Institute of Technology.

Fisher, Louis. 1995. *Presidential War Power*. Lawrence: University Press of Kansas.

Fitzhugh, Gilbert W. (Chairman). 1970. Blue Ribbon Defense Panel. *Report to the President and the Secretary of Defense on the Department of Defense*. Washington: GPO.

Ford, Gerald R. 1974. "The National Security Council System." National Security Decision Memorandum 265 (August 9). Mimeograph. Collection of Paul Stevens.

———. 1976. "Functions and Organizations of National Security Council Sub-groups." National Security Decision Memorandum 326 (April 21). Mimeograph. Collection of Paul Stevens.

———. 1979. *A Time to Heal*. New York: Harper & Row.

Forrestal, James. 1951. *The Forrestal Diaries*. Edited by Walter Millis. New York: Viking.

Franck, Thomas M., and Edward Weisband. 1979. *Foreign Policy by Congress*. New York: Oxford University Press.

Franklin, Daile P. 1986. "Why the Legislative Veto Isn't Dead." *Presidential Studies Quarterly* 16 (Summer): 491–502.

Freedman, Lawrence. 1976. "Logic, Politics, and Foreign Policy Processes: A Critique of the Bureaucratic Politics Model." *International Affairs* 52: 434–49.

Friedberg, Aaron L. 1991. "Is the United States Capable of Acting Strategically?" *Washington Quarterly* 14 (Winter): 5–23.

Frye, William. 1947. *Marshall, Citizen Soldier*. Indianapolis: Bobbs-Merrill. Quoted in Demetrios Caraley, *The Politics of Military Unification: A Study of Conflict and the Policy Process*, 19 (New York: Columbia University Press, 1966).

Fulbright, J. William. 1962. "American Foreign Policy in the 20th Century Under an 18th-Century Constitution." *Cornell Law Quarterly* 47 (Fall): 7.

Gates, Robert M. 1996. *From the Shadows: The Ultimate Insider's Story of Five Presidents and How They Won the Cold War*. New York: Simon & Schuster.

Gelb, Leslie H. 1980. "Why Not the State Department?" *Washington Quarterly* (Autumn): 25–40.

Gelb, Leslie H., and Richard K. Betts. 1979. *The Irony of Vietnam: The System Worked*. Washington: Brookings.

George, Alexander L. 1972. "The Case for Multiple Advocacy in Making Foreign Policy." *American Political Science Review* 66: 751–85.

———. 1980. *Presidential Decisionmaking in Foreign Policy: The Effective Use of Information and Advice*. Boulder: Westview Press.

Gerschenkron, Alexander. 1963. "Economic Backwardness in Historical Perspective." In *Economic Backwardness in Historical Perspective*. Cambridge: Harvard University Press.

Gilligan, Thomas W., William J. Marshall, and Barry R. Weingast. 1989. "Regulation and the Theory of Legislative Choice: The Interstate Commerce Act of 1887." *Journal of Law and Economics* 32 (April): 35–61.

Gilpin, Robert. 1981. *War and Change in World Politics*. New York: Cambridge University Press.

Ginsburgh, Robert N. 1964. "The Challenge to Military Professionalism." *Foreign Affairs* 42: 255–68.

Goldberg, David Howard. 1990. *Foreign Policy and Ethnic Interest Groups: American and Canadian Jews Lobby for Israel*. New York: Greenwood Press.

Goldwater, Barry. 1988. *Goldwater*. New York: Doubleday.

Goodpaster, Andrew J. 1977. "Four Presidents and the Conduct of National Security." *Journal of International Relations* 2, no. 1: 26–37.

Gourevitch, Peter. 1978. "The Second Image Reversed: The International Sources of Domestic Politics." *International Organization* 32 (Autumn): 881–912.

Gowa, Joanne. 1986. "Anarchy, Egoism, and Third Images: The Evolution of Cooperation and International Relations." *International Organization* 40 (Winter): 167–86.

Graebner, Norman A., ed. 1986. *The National Security: Its Theory and Practice, 1945–1960*. New York: Oxford University Press.

Greenstein, Fred I. 1978. "Change and Continuity in the Modern Presidency." In *The New American Political System*, edited by Anthony King. Washington: American Enterprise Institute.

———. 1982. *The Hidden-Hand Presidency: Eisenhower as Leader*. New York: Basic Books.

Grieco, Joseph M. 1988. "Anarchy and the Limits of Cooperation: A Realist Critique of the Newest Liberal Institutionalism." *International Organization* 42, no. 3: 485–507.

Grier, Peter. 1995. "Looking Back, Looking Ahead." *Air Force Magazine*, November.

Gunther, Gerald. 1991. *Constitutional Law*. 12th ed. Westbury, N.Y.: Foundation Press.

Haas, Ernst B. 1980. "Why Cooperate? Issue-Linkage and International Regimes." *World Politics* 32, no. 3: 357–405.

———. 1982. "Words Can Hurt You; or, Who Said What to Whom About Regimes." *International Organization* 36, no. 2: 207–43.

———. 1986. *Why We Still Need the United Nations: The Collective*

Management of International Conflict, 1945–1984. Berkeley: Institute of International Studies.

Haass, Richard. 1982. "The Role of the Congress in American Security Policy." In *American Defense Policy*, edited by John F. Reichart and Steven R. Sturm, 5th ed. Baltimore: Johns Hopkins University Press.

Haig, Alexander M., Jr. 1984. *Caveat: Realism, Reagan, and Foreign Policy*. New York: Macmillan.

Haldeman, H. R. 1994. *The Haldeman Diaries: Inside the Nixon White House*. New York: Putnam.

Hall, David K. 1975. "The 'Custodian-Manager' of the Policymaking Process." In *Report of the Commission on the Organization of the Government for the Conduct of Foreign Policy* (Murphy Commission Report). Vol. 2, app. D (June): 100–119. Washington: GPO.

Hall, Richard. 1993. "Participation, Abdication, and Representation in Congressional Committees." In *Congress Reconsidered*, edited by Lawrence C. Dodd and Bruce I. Oppenheimer, 5th ed. Washington: Congressional Quarterly Press.

Halloran, Richard. 1981. "Why Defense Costs So Much." *New York Times*, January 11.

Halperin, Morton H. 1974. *Bureaucratic Politics and Foreign Policy*. Washington: Brookings.

Hammond, Paul Y. 1961. "The National Security Council as a Device for Interdepartmental Coordination: An Interpretation and Appraisal." *American Political Science Review* (December): 899–910.

Hansen, John Mark. 1991. *Gaining Access: Congress and the Farm Lobby, 1919–1981*. Chicago: University of Chicago Press.

Hart, John. 1995. *The Presidential Branch from Washington to Clinton*. 2d ed. Chatham, N.J.: Chatham House.

Hartmann, Susan M. 1971. *Truman and the 80th Congress*. Columbia: University of Missouri Press.

Hartz, Louis. 1955. *The Liberal Tradition in America*. New York: Harcourt, Brace.

Hedley, John Hollister. 1995. *Checklist for the Future of Intelligence*. Washington: Georgetown University Institute for the Study of Diplomacy. Quoted in Gregory F. Treverton, "Intelligence Since Cold War's End," in Twentieth Century Fund, *In from the Cold: Report of the Twentieth Century Fund Task Force*, 112 (New York: Twentieth Century Fund Press, 1996).

Heginbotham, Stanley J. 1984. "Congress and Defense Policymaking: Toward Realistic Expectations in a System of Countervailing Parochialism." In *National Security Policy: The Decision-Making Process*, edited by Robert L. Pfaltzgraff, Jr., and Uri Ra'anan. Hamden, Conn.: Archon Books.

Henderson, Phillip G. 1984. "Advice and Decision: The Eisenhower National Security Council Reappraised." In *The Presidency and*

National Security Policy, edited by R. Gordon Hoxie. New York: Center for the Study of the Presidency.

Henkin, Louis. 1972. *Foreign Affairs and the Constitution*. Mineola, N.Y.: Foundation Press.

Hess, Stephen. 1988. *Organizing the Presidency*. 2d ed. Washington: Brookings.

Hiatt, Fred. 1983. "Weinberger Blames Congress for Pentagon Mismanagement Problems." *Washington Post*, July 29.

Hill, William Steinert. 1979. "The Business Community and National Defense: Corporate Leaders and the Military, 1943–1950." Ph.D. diss., Department of History, Stanford University.

Hilsman, Roger. 1967. *To Move a Nation*. New York: Doubleday.

———. 1995. "Does the CIA Still Have a Role?" *Foreign Affairs* 74, no. 5: 104–16.

Hintze, Otto. 1975. "Military Organization and the Organization of the State." In *The Historical Essays of Otto Hintze*, edited by Felix Gilbert. New York: Oxford University Press.

Houston Journal of International Law. 1988. "Symposium: Legal and Policy Issues in the Iran-Contra Affair: Intelligence Oversight in a Democracy." *Houston Journal of International Law* 11, no. 1 (Fall).

Hoxie, R. Gordon. 1982. "The National Security Council." *Presidential Studies Quarterly* (Winter): 108–13.

———. 1984, ed. *The Presidency and National Security Policy*. New York: Center for the Study of the Presidency.

Humphrey, David C. 1984. "Tuesday Lunch at the Johnson White House: A Preliminary Assessment." *Diplomatic History* 8 (Winter): 81–101.

———. 1994. "NSC Meetings During the Johnson Presidency." *Diplomatic History* 18 (Winter): 29–45.

Huntington, Samuel P. 1953. "The Marasmus of the ICC: The Commission, the Railroads, and the Public Interest." *Yale Law Journal* 61: 467–509.

———. 1961. *The Common Defense: Strategic Programs in National Politics*. New York: Columbia University Press.

———. 1983. "Introduction to National Security Decision Making in the White House and Its Organization." *World Affairs* 146, no. 2: 124–26.

———. 1985. *The Soldier and the State: The Theory and Politics of Civil-Military Relations*. 2d ed. Cambridge: Harvard University Press.

Inderfurth, Karl F., and Loch K. Johnson, eds. 1988. *Decisions of the Highest Order: Perspectives on the National Security Council*. Pacific Grove, Calif.: Brooks/Cole.

Isaacson, Walter. 1983. "Disappearing Act at Foggy Bottom." *Time*, August 8.

———. 1992. *Kissinger*. New York: Simon & Schuster.

Iyengar, Shanto, and Donald R. Kinder. 1987. *News That Matters*. Chicago: University of Chicago Press.

Jackson, Henry M. 1959. "How Shall We Forge a Strategy for Survival?" Address before the National War College (April 16), Washington. In *Decisions of the Highest Order: Perspectives on the National Security Council,* edited by Karl F. Inderfurth and Loch K. Johnson, 78–81 (Pacific Grove, Calif.: Brooks/Cole, 1988).

——, ed. 1965. *The National Security Council: Jackson Subcommittee Papers on Policy-Making at the Presidential Level.* New York: Praeger.

Jacobson, Gary. 1987. "Running Scared: Elections and Congressional Politics in the 1980s." In *Congress: Structure and Policy,* edited by Mathew D. McCubbins and Terry Sullivan. New York: Cambridge University Press.

Janus, Irving L. 1972. *Victims of Groupthink.* Boston: Houghton Mifflin.

Jay, John. 1987. "Federalist no. 64." In *The Federalist Papers,* by James Madison, Alexander Hamilton, and John Jay. Edited by Isaac Kramnick. Harmondsworth: Penguin.

Jeffreys-Jones, Rhodri. 1989. *The CIA and American Democracy.* New Haven: Yale University Press.

Jervis, Robert. 1976. *Perception and Misperception in International Politics.* Princeton: Princeton University Press.

——. 1986. "Intelligence and Foreign Policy: A Review Essay." *International Security* 11, no. 3: 141–61.

——. 1988. "Realism, Game Theory, and Cooperation." *World Politics* 40, no. 3: 317–49.

Johnson, Loch K. 1980. "The U.S. Congress and the CIA: Monitoring the Dark Side of Government." *Legislative Studies Quarterly* 5: 477–500.

——. 1985a. *A Season of Inquiry: The Senate Intelligence Investigation.* Lexington: University Press of Kentucky.

——. 1985b. "Legislative Reform and Intelligence Policy." *Polity* 17: 549–73.

——. 1989. *America's Secret Power: The CIA in a Democratic Society.* New York: Oxford University Press.

——. 1994. "Playing Hardball with the CIA." In *The President, the Congress, and the Making of Foreign Policy,* edited by Paul E. Peterson. Norman: University of Oklahoma Press.

——. 1996. *U.S. Intelligence in a Hostile World: Secret Agencies.* New Haven: Yale University Press.

Johnson, Lyndon Baines. 1971. *The Vantage Point: Perspectives of the Presidency, 1963–1969.* New York: Holt, Rinehart & Winston.

Joint Chiefs of Staff (JCS), Joint Secretariat, Historical Division. 1980. "A Concise History of the Joint Chiefs of Staff, 1942–1979." Mimeograph.

——. 1987. "Role and Functions of the Joint Chiefs of Staff: A Chronology." Mimeograph.

Joint Chiefs of Staff, Special Operations Review Group (Admiral James L. Holloway III, USN ret., chairman). 1980. *Rescue Mission Report.* Washington: Joint Chiefs of Staff.

Jones, David C. 1982. "Why the Joint Chiefs of Staff Must Change." *Directors and Boards* 6 (Winter): 4–13

———. 1984. "What's Wrong with the Defense Establishment." In *The Defense Reform Debate: Issues and Analysis,* edited by Asa A. Clark IV, Peter W. Chiarelli, Jeffrey S. McKitrick, and James W. Reed. Baltimore: Johns Hopkins University Press.

Jordan, Amos A., William J. Taylor, Jr., and Lawrence J. Korb. 1993. *American National Security: Policy and Process.* 4th ed. Baltimore: Johns Hopkins University Press.

Kaiser, Karl. 1968. *German Foreign Policy in Transition.* London: Oxford University Press.

Kalb, Marvin, and Bernard Kalb. 1974. *Kissinger.* Boston: Little, Brown.

Kanter, Arnold. 1975. *Defense Politics: A Budgetary Perspective.* Chicago: University of Chicago Press.

Karalekas, Anne. 1984. "History of the Central Intelligence Agency." In *The Central Intelligence Agency: History and Documents,* edited by William M. Leary. University: University of Alabama Press. Originally published in U.S. Senate, Select Committee to Study Governmental Operations with Respect to Intelligence Activities of the United States [Church Committee], *Final Report.* 94th Cong., 2d sess. (April 26, 1976). S. Rept. 94-755, Serial 13133-6.

Katzenstein, Peter J., ed. 1978. *Between Power and Plenty: Foreign Economic Policies of Advanced Industrial States.* Madison: University of Wisconsin Press.

Katzmann, Robert A. 1990. "War Powers: Toward a New Accommodation." In *A Question of Balance: The President, the Congress, and Foreign Policy,* edited by Thomas E. Mann. Washington: Brookings.

Kemp, Geoffrey. 1993. "Presidential Management of the Executive Bureaucracy." In *U.S. Foreign Policy: The Search for a New Role,* edited by Robert J. Art and Seyom Brown. New York: Macmillan.

Kennedy, Robert F. 1969. *Thirteen Days: A Memoir of the Cuban Missile Crisis.* New York: W. W. Norton.

Keohane, Robert O. 1980. "The Theory of Hegemonic Stability and Changes in International Economic Regimes, 1967–1977." In *Changes in the International System,* edited by Ole R. Holsti, Randolph M. Siverson, and Alexander L. George. Boulder: Westview Press.

———. 1984. *After Hegemony: Cooperation and Discord in the World Political Economy.* Princeton: Princeton University Press.

———, ed. 1986. *Neorealism and Its Critics.* New York: Columbia University Press.

Keohane, Robert O., and Joseph S. Nye. 1977. *Power and Interdependence.* Boston: Little, Brown.

Kernell, Samuel H. 1978. "Explaining Presidential Popularity." *American Political Science Review* 72: 506–22.

————. 1989. "The Evolution of the White House Staff." In *Can the Government Govern?* edited by John E. Chubb and Paul E. Peterson. Washington: Brookings.

————. 1993. *Going Public: New Strategies of Presidential Leadership.* 2d ed. Washington: Congressional Quarterly Press.

Kester, John G. 1980. "The Future of the Joint Chiefs of Staff." *American Enterprise Institute Foreign and Defense Policy Review* 2, no. 1: 18.

————. 1982. "The Role of the Joint Chiefs of Staff." In *American Defense Policy,* edited by John F. Reichart and Steven R. Sturm, 5th ed. Baltimore: Johns Hopkins University Press.

Key, V. O. 1948. *Politics, Parties, and Pressure Groups.* 2d ed. New York: Thomas Y. Crowell.

Kiewiet, D. Roderick, and Mathew D. McCubbins. 1991. *The Logic of Delegation: Congressional Parties and the Appropriations Process.* Chicago: University of Chicago Press.

Kinnard, Douglas. 1977. *President Eisenhower and Strategy Management: A Study in Defense Politics.* Lexington.: University Press of Kentucky.

Kirschten, Dick. 1980. "Beyond the Vance-Brzezinski Clash Lurks an NSC Under Fire." *National Journal,* May 17.

————. 1982. "Clark Emerges as a Tough Manager, Not a Rival to the Secretary of State." *National Journal,* July 17.

Kissinger, Henry A. 1969. *American Foreign Policy: Three Essays.* New York: W. W. Norton.

————. 1970. Letter to Senator Henry Jackson describing the current approach to the NSC and its use in presidential decision-making (March 3). Mimeograph. Collection of Paul Stevens.

————. 1979. *White House Years.* Boston: Little, Brown.

————. 1986. "Not Its Power, but Its Weakness." *Washington Post,* December 21.

Klein, Joe. 1993. "The Hidden Lake." *Newsweek,* July 19.

Knorr, Klaus Eugen, and Sidney Verba, eds. 1961. *The International System: Theoretical Essays.* Princeton: Princeton University Press.

Koh, Harold Hongju. 1990. *The National Security Constitution: Sharing Power After the Iran-Contra Affair.* New Haven: Yale University Press.

Korb, Lawrence J. 1976. *The Joint Chiefs of Staff: The First Twenty-five Years.* Bloomington: Indiana University Press.

————. 1995. "Our Overstuffed Armed Forces." *Foreign Affairs* 74, no. 6 (November/December): 22–34.

Krasner, Stephen D. 1971. "Are Bureaucracies Important? (or Allison Wonderland)." *Foreign Policy* 7 (Summer): 159–79.

————. 1976. "State Power and the Structure of International Trade." *World Politics* 28, no. 3: 317–47.

————. 1978. *Defending the National Interest.* Princeton: Princeton University Press.

———. 1991. "National Power and Global Communications, or, Life at the Pareto Frontier." *World Politics* 43: 336–66.

———, ed. 1983. *International Regimes*. Ithaca: Cornell University Press.

Krehbiel, Keith. 1991. *Information and Legislative Organization*. Ann Arbor: University of Michigan Press.

Latham, Earl. 1952. *The Group Basis of Politics: A Study in Base Point Legislation*. Ithaca: Cornell University Press.

Lawson, Chappell. 1994. "The Export-Import Bank and the Politics of Bureaucratic Structure." Unpublished paper (October), Stanford University.

Lay, James. S. 1953. "Recommendations Regarding the National Security Council." Memorandum for the National Security Council (March 17). Mimeograph. Collection of Paul Stevens.

Leacacos, John P. 1971. "Kissinger's Apparat." *Foreign Policy* 5 (Winter): 3–27.

Leary, William M., ed. 1984. *The Central Intelligence Agency: History and Documents*. University: University of Alabama Press.

Leffler, Melvyn P. 1992. *A Preponderance of Power: National Security, the Truman Administration, and the Cold War*. Stanford: Stanford University Press.

Legere, Laurence J. [1951] 1988. *Unification of the Armed Forces*. Harvard Dissertations in American History and Political Science. New York: Garland.

Lenin, V. I. [1917] 1939. *Imperialism: The Highest Stages of Capitalism*. New York: International Publishers.

Levy, Jack. 1988. "Domestic Politics and War." *Journal of Interdisciplinary History* (Spring): 653–73.

Light, Paul C. 1991. *The President's Agenda: Domestic Policy Choice from Kennedy to Reagan*. Rev. ed. Baltimore: Johns Hopkins University Press.

Lindsay, James M. 1990. "Congressional Oversight of the Department of Defense: Reconsidering the Conventional Wisdom." *Armed Forces and Society* 16: 7–33.

———. 1994. *Congress and the Politics of U.S. Foreign Policy*. Baltimore: Johns Hopkins University Press.

Lindsay, James M., and Randall B. Ripley. 1992. "Foreign and Defense Policy in Congress: A Research Agenda for the 1990s." *Legislative Studies Quarterly* 17 (Aug.): 417–49.

Locher, James R., III. 1985. "Defense Organization: The Need for Change." *Staff Report Prepared for the Senate Committee on Armed Services*. 99th Cong., 1st sess. S. Rept. 99-86.

———. 1988. "Organization and Management." In *American Defense Annual*, edited by Joseph Kruzel. Lexington, Mass.: D. C. Heath.

Long, Admiral Robert L. J., Chairman. 1983. "Report of the Department of

Defense Commission on Beirut International Airport Terrorist Act."
Mimeograph (December 20).

Lord, Carnes. 1988. *The Presidency and the Management of National
Security*. New York: Free Press.

Lowenthal, Mark M. 1992. *U.S. Intelligence: Evolution and Anatomy*. 2d
ed. Westport, Conn.: Praeger.

Lowi, Theodore J. 1979. *The End of Liberalism*. 2d ed. New York: W. W.
Norton.

Lynn, William J. 1985. "The Wars Within: The Joint Military Structure
and Its Critics." In *Reorganizing America's Defense: Leadership in War
and Peace*, edited by Robert J. Art, Vincent Davis, and Samuel P.
Huntington. Washington: Pergamon-Brassey's.

Lynn, William J., and Barry R. Posen. 1985. "The Case for JCS Reform."
International Security 10, no. 3: 69–97.

Mackenzie, G. Calvin. 1981. "The Paradox of Presidential Personnel
Management." In *The Illusion of Presidential Government*, edited by
Hugh Heclo and Lester M. Salamon. Boulder: Westview Press.

Madison, James. 1987. "Federalist no. 10." In *The Federalist Papers*, by
James Madison, Alexander Hamilton, and John Jay. Edited by Isaac
Kramnick. Harmondsworth: Penguin.

Maechling, Charles, Jr. 1976. "Foreign Policy-Makers: The Weakest
Link?" *Virginia Quarterly Review* 52: 1–23.

Makinson, Larry, and Joshua Goldstein. 1994. *Open Secrets: The
Encyclopedia of Congressional Money and Politics*. Washington:
Congressional Quarterly Press.

Mann, Thomas E., ed. 1990. *A Question of Balance: The President, the
Congress, and Foreign Policy*. Washington: Brookings.

Marcus, Ruth. 1994. "Clinton's Very Private Adviser: Tony Lake Delivers
His Counsel on National Security out of the Limelight." *Washington
Post Magazine*, January 2.

May, Ernest R. 1955. "The Development of Political-Military
Consultation in the United States." *Political Science Quarterly* 70
(June): 161–80.

———. 1992. "Intelligence: Backing into the Future." *Foreign Affairs* 71,
no. 3: 63–72.

Mayhew, David. 1974. *Congress: The Electoral Connection*. New Haven:
Yale University Press.

McConnell, Grant. 1966. *Private Power and American Democracy*. New
York: Knopf.

McCubbins, Mathew D. 1985. "The Legislative Design of Regulatory
Structure." *American Journal of Political Science* 29, no. 4: 721–48.

McCubbins, Mathew D., Roger G. Noll, and Barry R. Weingast
[McNollgast]. 1987. "Administrative Procedures as Instruments of
Political Control." *Journal of Law, Economics, and Organization* 3:
243–77.

McCubbins, Mathew D., and Talbot Page. 1987. "A Theory of Congressional Delegation." In *Congress: Structure and Policy*, edited by Mathew D. McCubbins and Terry Sullivan. New York: Cambridge University Press.

McCubbins, Mathew D., and Thomas Schwartz. 1984. "Congressional Oversight Overlooked: Police Patrols Versus Fire Alarms." *American Journal of Political Science* 28: 165–79.

McCullough, David. 1992. *Truman*. New York: Simon & Schuster.

McFarlane, Robert C., Richard Saunders, and Thomas C. Shull. 1984. "The National Security Council: Organization for Policy Making." In *The Presidency and National Security Policy*, edited by R. Gordon Hoxie. New York: Center for the Study of the Presidency.

McFarlane, Robert C., with Zofia Smardz. 1994. *Special Trust*. New York: Cadell & Davies.

McNamara, Robert S., with Brian VanDeMark. 1995. *In Retrospect: The Tragedy and Lessons of Vietnam*. New York: Times Books.

Mearsheimer, John. 1990. "Back to the Future: Instability in Europe After the Cold War." *International Security* 15, no. 1: 5–56.

Meese, Edwin, III. 1992. *With Reagan: The Inside Story*. Washington: Regnery Gateway.

Melbourne, Roy M. 1983. "Odyssey of the NSC." *Strategic Review* 11 (Summer): 51–64.

Menges, Constantine C. 1988. *Inside the National Security Council: The True Story of the Making and Unmaking of Reagan's Foreign Policy*. New York: Simon & Schuster.

Meyer, Edward C. 1982. "The JCS—How Much Reform Is Needed?" In U.S. House, Committee on Armed Services, Subcommittee on Investigations, *Reorganization Proposals for the Joint Chiefs of Staff: Hearings on H.R. 6828, Joint Chiefs of Staff Reorganization Act of 1982*, 97th Cong., 2d sess. (April 21). Originally published in *Armed Forces Journal International* (April 1982): 82–90.

Milgrom, Paul, and John Roberts. 1992. *Economics, Organization, and Management*. Englewood Cliffs, N.J.: Prentice Hall.

Milkis, Sidney M., and Michael Nelson. 1990. *The American Presidency*. Washington: Congressional Quarterly Press.

Moe, Terry M. 1984. "The New Economics of Organization." *American Journal of Political Science* 28 (November): 739–77.

———. 1985. "The Politicized Presidency." In *The New Direction in American Politics*, edited by John E. Chubb and Paul E. Peterson. Washington: Brookings.

———. 1987a. "An Assessment of the Positive Theory of 'Congressional Dominance.' " *Legislative Studies Quarterly* 12, no. 4: 475–520.

———. 1987b. "Interests, Institutions, and Positive Theory: The Politics of the NLRB." *Studies in American Political Development* 2: 236–99.

———. 1989. "The Politics of Bureaucratic Structure." In *Can the*

Government Govern? edited by John E. Chubb and Paul E. Peterson.
Washington: Brookings.

———. 1990a. "Political Institutions: The Neglected Side of the Story."
Journal of Law, Economics, and Organization 6 (special issue): 213–53.

———. 1990b. "The Politics of Structural Choice: Toward a Theory of
Public Bureaucracy." In *Organization Theory: From Chester Barnard to
the Present and Beyond*, edited by Oliver E. Williamson. New York:
Oxford University Press.

———. 1991. "Politics and the Theory of Organization." *Journal of Law,
Economics, and Organization* 7 (special issue): 106–29.

Moe, Terry M., and Scott A. Wilson. 1994. "Presidents and the Politics of
Structure." *Law and Contemporary Problems* 57 (Winter–Spring):1–44.

Moore, Barrington, Jr. 1966. *Social Origins of Dictatorship and
Democracy*. Boston: Little, Brown.

Morgan, Dan. 1982. "How Much for Defense?" *Washington Post*,
December 2.

Morgenthau, Hans J. 1985. *Politics Among Nations*. 6th ed. Rev. by
Kenneth W. Thompson. New York: Knopf.

Mueller, John E. 1970. "Presidential Popularity from Truman to Johnson."
American Political Science Review 64: 18–34.

———. 1973. *War, Presidents, and Public Opinion*. New York: John
Wiley.

Mulcahy, Kevin V. 1986. "The Secretary of State and the National
Security Adviser: Foreign Policy Making in the Carter and Reagan
Administrations." *Presidential Studies Quarterly* 16, no. 2 (Spring):
280–99.

Murphy, Robert D. (Chairman). 1975. Commission on the Organization of
the Government for the Conduct of Foreign Policy [Murphy
Commission]. *Report* (June). Washington: GPO.

Nathan, James A., and James K. Oliver. 1994. *Foreign Policy Making and
the American Political System*. 3d ed. Baltimore: Johns Hopkins
University Press.

National Defense University, Armed Forces Staff College. 1991. *The Joint
Staff Officer's Guide, 1991*. Norfolk, Va.: National Defense University.

National Security Council Staff. 1988. "Reagan-Bush Transition Briefing
Book: Background on NSC Organization and Administration.
Declassified Sections Only." Mimeograph. Collection of Paul Stevens.

Nelson, Anna Kasten. 1981. "National Security I: Inventing a Process,
1945–1960." In *Illusion of Presidential Government*, edited by Hugh
Heclo and Lester M. Salamon. Boulder: Westview Press.

———. 1983. "The 'Top of Policy Hill': President Eisenhower and the
National Security Council." *Diplomatic History* 7 (Fall): 307–26.

Neustadt, Richard E. 1960. *Presidential Power*. New York: Wiley.

———. 1970. *Alliance Politics*. New York: Columbia University Press.

Nixon, Richard. 1969a. "Establishment of NSC Decision and Study

Memoranda Series." National Security Decision Memorandum 1 (January 20). Mimeograph. Collection of Paul Stevens.

———. 1969b. "Reorganization of the National Security Council System." National Security Decision Memorandum 2 (January 20). Mimeograph. Collection of Paul Stevens.

———. 1990. *The Memoirs of Richard Nixon.* 2d ed. New York: Simon & Schuster.

Nunn, Sam. 1991. "Military Reform Paved Way for Gulf Triumph; Changes Ordered by U.S. Congress Helped Pentagon." *Atlanta Journal and Constitution,* March 31.

Odeen, Philip A. 1980. "Organizing for National Security." *International Security* 5 (Summer): 111–29.

Ogden, Christopher. 1989. "Vision Problems at State . . . ; Critics say James Baker Has No Consistent Policies." *Time,* September 25.

Olmsted, Kathryn S. 1996. *Challenging the Secret Government: The Post-Watergate Investigations of the CIA and FBI.* Chapel Hill: University of North Carolina Press.

Olson, Mancur. 1965. *The Logic of Collective Action: Public Goods and the Theory of Groups.* Cambridge: Harvard University Press.

Ornstein, Norman J., and Shirley Elder. 1978. *Interest Groups, Lobbying, and Policymaking.* Washington: Congressional Quarterly Press.

Oseth, John M. 1985. *Regulating U.S. Intelligence Operations: A Study in the Definition of the National Interest.* Lexington: University Press of Kentucky.

Owen, John M. 1994. "How Liberalism Produces Democratic Peace." *International Security* 19, no. 2: 87–125.

Owens, MacKubin Thomas. 1985. "The Hollow Promise of JCS Reform." *International Security* 10, no. 3: 98–111.

Oye, Kenneth A., ed. 1986. *Cooperation Under Anarchy.* Princeton: Princeton University Press.

Pastor, Robert A. 1991. "Congress and U.S. Foreign Policy: Comparative Advantage or Disadvantage?" *Washington Quarterly* 14: 101–14.

Patterson, James T. 1976. "The Rise of Presidential Power Before World War II." *Law and Contemporary Problems* 40, no. 2: 39–57.

Peltzman, Sam. 1976. "Toward a More General Theory of Regulation." *Journal of Law and Economics* 19: 211–40.

Pennypacker, Morton. 1939. *General Washington's Spies on Long Island and in New York.* Brooklyn: Long Island Historical Society.

Perlmutter, Amos. 1974. "The Presidential Political Center and Foreign Policy: A Critique of the Revisionist and Bureaucratic-Political Orientations." *World Politics* 27: 87–106.

Perry, Mark. 1989. *Four Stars.* Boston: Houghton Mifflin.

———. 1992. *Eclipse: The Last Days of the CIA.* New York: William Morrow.

Peterson, Mark A. 1992a. "Interest Mobilization and the President." In

The Politics of Interests: Interest Groups Transformed, edited by Mark P. Petracca. Boulder: Westview Press.

———. 1992b. "The President and Organized Interests—White House Patterns." *American Political Science Review* 86: 612–25.

Petracca, Mark P., ed. 1992. *The Politics of Interests: Interest Groups Transformed*. Boulder: Westview Press.

Pincus, Walter. 1996a. "Clinton Approves Disclosure of Intelligence Budget Figure." *Washington Post*, April 24.

———. 1996b. "Curtain Is Falling on Another Intelligence Drama: Reform." *Washington Post*, July 8.

———. 1996c. "Intelligence Battleground: Reform Bill." *Washington Post*, May 30.

———. 1996d. "Panels Continue Impasse on Intelligence; Senate Armed Services Bars Plan to Strengthen Role of CIA Head." *Washington Post*, June 7.

———. 1996e. "Spy Chief's Grasp Reaches Other Pockets; Senate Panel Hands DCI Budget Power in Pentagon." *Washington Post*, April 25.

———. 1996f. "Untangling the Spy Network's Webs; Rep. Combest Wants CIA Clandestine Operations Separate and NRO Split." *Washington Post*, March 5.

Powell, Colin L. 1989. "The NSC System in the Last Two Years of the Reagan Administration." In *The Presidency in Transition*, edited by R. Gordon Hoxie. New York: Center for the Study of the Presidency.

———. 1995. *My American Journey*. New York: Random House.

Powell, Robert. 1991. "Absolute and Relative Gains in International Relations Theory." *American Political Science Review* 85, no. 4: 1303–20.

Prados, John. 1991. *Keepers of the Keys: A History of the National Security Council from Truman to Bush*. New York: William Morrow.

———. 1996. *Presidents' Secret Wars: CIA and Pentagon Covert Operations from World War II Through the Persian Gulf War*. Rev. ed. Chicago: Ivan R. Dee.

Pratt, Fletcher. 1947. "The Case Against Unification." In U.S. House, Committee on Expenditures in the Executive Departments, *National Security Act of 1947: Hearings on H.R. 2319*, 80th Cong., 1st sess. (June 19). Originally published in *Sea Power* (1945).

Rakove, Jack N. 1984. "Solving a Constitutional Puzzle: The Treatymaking Clause as a Case Study." *Perspectives in American History* 1: 233–81.

Ranelaugh, John. 1986. *The Agency: The Rise and Decline of the CIA*. London: Weidenfeld & Nicolson.

———. 1992. *CIA: A History*. London: BBC Books.

Ransom, Harry Howe. 1987. "The Politicization of Intelligence." In *Intelligence and Intelligence Policy in a Democratic Society*, edited by Stephen J. Cimbala. Dobbs Ferry, N.Y.: Transnational Publishers.

Reagan, Ronald. 1981. "National Security Council Directives." National Security Decision Directive Number 1 (February 25). Mimeograph. Collection of Paul Stevens.

——. 1982. "National Security Council Structure." National Security Decision Directive Number 2 (January 12). Mimeograph. Collection of Paul Stevens.

——. 1987a. "Implementation of the Recommendations of the President's Special Review Board." National Security Decision Directive 266 (March 31). Mimeograph. Collection of Paul Stevens.

——. 1987b. "National Security Council Interagency Process." National Security Decision Directive 276 (June 9). Mimeograph. Collection of Paul Stevens.

Regan, Donald T. 1988. *For the Record: From Wall Street to Washington.* New York: Harcourt Brace Jovanovich.

Reichard, Gary W. 1986. "The Domestic Politics of National Security." In *The National Security: Its Theory and Practice, 1945–1960,* edited by Norman A. Graebner. New York: Oxford University Press.

Reveley, W. Taylor, III. 1981. *War Powers of the President and Congress.* Charlottesville: University Press of Virginia.

Richelson, Jeffrey T. 1989. *The U.S. Intelligence Community.* 2d ed. Cambridge, Mass.: Ballinger.

Ries, John C. 1964. *The Management of Defense.* Baltimore: Johns Hopkins University Press.

Roberts, Steven V. 1982. "Even Pentagon Pals Find Its Budget Too Fat." *New York Times,* December 5.

Rockman, Bert A. 1981. "America's Departments of State: Irregular and Regular Syndromes of Policy Making." *American Political Science Review* 75 (December): 911–27.

Rohde, David W., and Kenneth A. Shepsle. 1987. "Democratic Committee Assignments in the House of Representatives: Strategic Aspects of a Social Choice Process." In *Congress: Structure and Policy,* edited by Mathew D. McCubbins and Terry Sullivan. New York: Cambridge University Press.

Rosecrance, Richard. 1985. *The Rise of the Trading State.* New York: Basic Books.

Rostow, W. W. 1972. *The Diffusion of Power: An Essay in Recent History.* New York: Macmillan.

Rothenberg, Lawrence S. 1994. *Regulation, Organizations, and Politics: Motor Freight Policy at the Interstate Commerce Commission.* Ann Arbor: University of Michigan Press.

Sander, Alfred D. 1972. "Truman and the National Security Council: 1945–1947." *Journal of American History* 59 (September): 369–88.

Sapin, Burton M. 1966. *The Making of United States Foreign Policy.* New York: Praeger.

Sayle, Edward F. 1986. "The Historical Underpinning of the U.S.

Intelligence Community." *International Journal of Intelligence and Counterintelligence* 1, no. 1.

Schattschneider, E. E. 1935. *Politics, Pressures, and the Tariff*. New York: Prentice-Hall.

———. 1975. *The Semisovereign People: A Realist's View of Democracy in America*. Hinsdale, Ill.: Dryden Press.

Schlesinger, Arthur M., Jr. 1965. *A Thousand Days: John F. Kennedy in the White House*. New York: Fawcett Premier.

Schultz, Kenneth A. 1996. "Domestic Political Competition and Bargaining in International Crises." Ph.D. diss., Department of Political Science, Stanford University.

Scigliano, Robert. 1981. "The War Powers Resolution and the War Powers." In *The Presidency in the Constitutional Order*, edited by Joseph M. Bessette and Jeffrey Tulis. Baton Rouge: Louisiana State University Press.

Shepsle, Kenneth A. 1978. *The Giant Jigsaw Puzzle: Democratic Committee Assignments in the Modern House*. Chicago: University of Chicago Press.

———. 1979. "Institutional Arrangements and Equilibrium in Multidimensional Voting Models." *American Journal of Political Science* 23: 27–59.

———. 1986. "The Positive Theory of Legislative Institutions: An Enrichment of Social Choice and Spatial Models." *Public Choice* 50: 135–78.

———. 1989a. "The Changing Textbook Congress." In *Can the Government Govern?* edited by John E. Chubb and Paul E. Peterson. Washington: Brookings.

———. 1989b. "Studying Institutions: Some Lessons from the Rational Choice Approach." *Journal of Theoretical Politics* 1: 131–48.

Shoemaker, Christopher C. 1991. *The NSC Staff: Counseling the Council*. Boulder: Westview Press.

Shultz, George P. 1993. *Turmoil and Triumph: My Years as Secretary of State*. New York: Macmillan.

Sick, Gary. 1985. *All Fall Down: America's Tragic Encounter with Iran*. New York: Random House.

Silverstein, Gordon. 1994. "Judicial Enhancement of Executive Power." In *The President, the Congress, and the Making of Foreign Policy*, edited by Paul E. Peterson. Norman: University of Oklahoma Press.

Simon, Herbert A. 1976. *Administrative Behavior: A Study of Decision-Making Processes in Administrative Organization*. New York: Free Press.

Singer, J. David. 1961. "The Level-of-Analysis Problem in International Relations." In *The International System: Theoretical Essays*, edited by Klaus Knorr and Sidney Verba. Princeton: Princeton University Press.

Skocpol, Theda. 1979. *States and Social Revolutions: A Comparative*

Analysis of France, Russia, and China. New York: Cambridge University Press.

Smist, Frank J., Jr. 1994. *Congress Oversees the United States Intelligence Community, 1947–1994.* 2d ed. Knoxville: University of Tennessee Press.

Smith, Bromley K. 1987. "Organizational History of the National Security Council During the Kennedy and Johnson Administrations." Monograph written for the National Security Council. Mimeograph. Collection of Tyrus Cobb.

Smith, James A. 1991. *The Idea Brokers: Think Tanks and the Rise of the New Policy Elite.* New York: Free Press.

Smith, Michael Joseph. 1986. *Realist Thought from Weber to Kissinger.* Baton Rouge: Louisiana State University Press.

Smith, R. Jeffrey. 1996. "Clinton to Sign Bill Giving CIA Three New Managers; Measure Also Expands Powers of FBI, NSA." *Washington Post,* October 5.

Smith, R. Jeffrey, and Walter Pincus. 1996. "Expert Panel Wants Intelligence Director to Hold More Power." *Washington Post,* March 1.

Snidal, Duncan. 1985. "Coordination Versus Prisoners' Dilemma: Implications for International Cooperation and Regimes." *American Political Science Review* 79, no. 4: 923–42.

———. 1991. "Relative Gains and the Pattern of International Cooperation." *American Political Science Review* 85, no. 3: 701–26.

Sofaer, Abraham D. 1976. "The Presidency, War, and Foreign Affairs: Practice Under the Framers." *Law and Contemporary Problems* 40, no. 2: 12–38.

Sorensen, Theodore C. 1965. *Kennedy.* New York: Harper & Row.

———. 1987. "The President and the Secretary of State." *Foreign Affairs* 66 (Winter 1987–88): 231–48.

Souers, Sidney W. 1949. "Policy Formulation for National Security." *American Political Science Review* 43 (June): 534–43.

Spitzer, Robert J. 1993. *President and Congress: Executive Hegemony at the Crossroads of American Government.* New York: McGraw-Hill.

Steadman, Richard C. (Chairman). 1978. "The National Military Command Structure." *Report of a Study Requested by the President and Conducted in the Department of Defense.* Washington: Department of Defense.

Stein, Arthur. 1990. *Why Nations Cooperate.* Ithaca: Cornell University Press.

Stern, Philip M. 1988. *The Best Congress Money Can Buy.* New York: Pantheon.

Stevens, Paul Schott. 1989. "The National Security Council: Past and Prologue." *Strategic Review* 17 (Winter): 55–62.

———. 1990. "The Reagan NSC: Before and After." *Perspectives on Political Science* 19, no. 2: 118–22.

Stigler, George J. 1971. "The Theory of Economic Regulation." *Bell Journal of Economics and Management Science* 2: 3–21.

Stockton, Paul. 1991. "The New Game on the Hill: The Politics of Strategic Arms Control and Force Modernization." *International Security* 16: 146–70.

Sundquist, James L. 1981. *The Decline and Resurgence of Congress.* Washington: Brookings.

Symington, Stuart. 1982. "Report on Reorganization of the Department of Defense." In U.S. House, Committee on Armed Services, *Reorganization Proposals for the Joint Chiefs of Staff: Hearings on H.R. 6828, Joint Chiefs of Staff Reorganization Act of 1982*, 97th Cong., 2d sess. Originally published as *Report on Reorganization of the Department of Defense* (Washington: GPO, 1960).

Szanton, Peter. 1980. "Two Jobs, Not One." *Foreign Policy* 38 (Spring): 89–91.

Thayer, Frederick C. 1971. "Presidential Policy Processes and New Administration: A Search for Revised Paradigms." *Public Administration Review* 31 (September/October): 552–61.

Thucydides. 1980. *History of the Peloponnesian War.* Translated by Rex Warner. Notes by M. I. Finley. Baltimore: Penguin.

Tivnan, Edward. 1987. *The Lobby: Jewish Political Power and American Foreign Policy.* New York: Simon & Schuster.

The Tower Commission Report: The Full Text of the President's Special Review Board. 1987. New York: Random House.

Troy, Thomas F. 1981. *Donovan and the CIA: A History of the Establishment of the Central Intelligence Agency.* Frederick, Md.: University Publications of America.

Truman, David B. 1971. *The Governmental Process.* 2d ed. New York: Knopf.

Truman, Harry S. 1945. "Our Armed Forces Must Be United." In U.S. Senate, Committee on Military Affairs, *Department of Armed Forces, Department of Military Security: Hearings on S. 84 and S. 1482*, 97th Cong., 1st sess. (October 31). Originally published in *Collier's*, August 26, 1944.

———. 1956. *Memoirs: Years of Trial and Hope.* Vol. 2. Garden City, N.Y.: Doubleday.

———. 1961–66. *Public Papers of the Presidents of the United States: Harry S. Truman, 1945–1953.* 8 vols. Washington: GPO.

Turner, Stansfield. 1985. *Secrecy and Democracy: The CIA in Transition.* Boston: Houghton Mifflin.

U.S. Department of Commerce. 1995. *Statistical Abstract of the United States, 1995.* Washington: U.S. Department of Commerce.

———. 1997. *Statistical Abstract of the United States, 1997.* Washington: U.S. Department of Commerce.

U.S. House. 1944a. Select Committee on Post-War Military Policy

[Woodrum Committee]. *Proposal to Establish a Single Department of Armed Forces: Hearings Before the Select Committee on Post-War Military Policy.* 78th Cong., 2d sess.

———. 1944b. Select Committee on Post-War Military Policy [Woodrum Committee]. *Report.* 78th Cong., 2d sess. H. Rept. 1645.

———. 1945. *Unification of the Armed Forces of the United States: Message from the President of the United States Requesting Unification of the Armed Forces.* 79th Cong., 1st sess. H. Doc. 392. Quoted in Demetrios Caraley, *The Politics of Military Unification: A Study of Conflict and the Policy Process,* 84 (New York: Columbia University Press, 1966).

———. 1947a. Committee on Expenditures in the Executive Departments. *National Security Act of 1947: Hearings on H.R. 2319.* 80th Cong., 1st sess.

———. 1947b. *National Security Act of 1947: Communication from the President of the United States.* 80th Cong., 1st sess. H. Doc. 149.

———. 1982. Committee on Armed Services, Subcommittee on Investigations. *Reorganization Proposals for the Joint Chiefs of Staff: Hearings on H.R. 6828, Joint Chiefs of Staff Reorganization Act of 1982.* 97th Cong., 2d sess.

———. 1985. Permanent Select Committee on Intelligence. *Compilation of Intelligence Laws and Related Laws and Executive Orders of Interest to the National Intelligence Community as Amended Through March 1, 1985.* 99th Cong., 1st sess. (July).

———. 1996. Permanent Select Committee on Intelligence. *IC21: The Intelligence Community in the 21st Century.* 104th Cong., 2d sess (March). Available at http://www.gpo.gov/congress/house/intel/ic21/

U.S. Senate. 1945. Committee on Military Affairs. *Department of Armed Forces, Department of Military Security: Hearings on S. 84 and S. 1482.* 79th Cong., 1st sess.

———. 1946. Committee on Naval Affairs. *Unification of the Armed Forces: Hearings on S. 2044.* 79th Cong., 2d sess.

———. 1947. Committee on Armed Services. *National Defense Establishment (Unification of the Armed Services): Hearings on S. 758.* 80th Cong., 1st sess.

———. 1957. Committee on Armed Services. *Satellite and Missile Programs: Hearings.* 85th Cong., 1st sess. Quoted in Samuel P. Huntington, *The Common Defense: Strategic Programs in National Politics,* 400 (New York: Columbia University Press, 1961).

———. 1961. Committee on Government Operations. Subcommittee on National Policy Machinery. *Organizing for National Security: Staff Reports and Recommendations.* Vol. 3. 87th Cong., 1st sess. Quoted in Karl F. Inderfurth and Loch K. Johnson, *Decisions of the Highest Order: Perspectives on the National Security Council,* 82–87 (Pacific Grove, Calif.: Brooks/Cole, 1988).

————. 1976. Select Committee to Study Governmental Operations with Respect to Intelligence Activities of the United States [Church Committee]. *Final Report*. 94th Cong., 2d sess (April 26). S. Rept. 94-755, Serial 13133-3-8.

U.S. Senate and House. 1987. Senate Select Committee on Secret Military Assistance to Iran and the Nicaraguan Opposition and House Select Committee to Investigate Covert Arms Transactions with Iran. *Report of the Congressional Committees Investigating the Iran-Contra Affair*. 100th Cong., 1st sess (November 17).

U.S. Statutes at Large. 1948. Vol. 61, pp. 495–510. *National Security Act of 1947*.

————. 1950a. Vol. 63, pp. 208–13. *Central Intelligence Agency Act of 1949*.

————. 1950b. Vol. 63, pp. 578–92. *National Security Act Amendments of 1949*.

————. 1953. Vol. 67, pp. 638–39. *Reorganization Plan No. 6 of 1953*.

————. 1959. Vol. 72, pp. 514–22. *Defense Reorganization Act of 1958*.

————. 1976. Vol. 88, p. 1804. *Hughes-Ryan Amendment to the Foreign Assistance Act of 1961*.

————. 1981. Vol. 94, pp. 1975–82. *Intelligence Oversight Act of 1980*.

————. 1989. Vol. 100, pp. 992–1075b. *Goldwater-Nichols Department of Defense Reorganization Act of 1986*.

————. 1992a. Vol. 105, pp. 429–45. *Intelligence Authorization Act for Fiscal Year 1991*.

————. 1992b. Vol. 105, pp. 1260–77. *Intelligence Authorization Act for Fiscal Year 1992*.

————. 1993. Vol. 106, pp. 3180–254. *Intelligence Authorization Act for Fiscal Year 1993*.

————. 1995. Vol. 108, pp. 3423–61. *Intelligence Authorization Act for Fiscal Year 1995*.

————. 1997. Vol. 110, pp. 3461–87. *Intelligence Authorization Act for Fiscal Year 1997*.

Vance, Cyrus. 1983. *Hard Choices: Critical Years in America's Foreign Policy*. New York: Simon & Schuster.

Wallerstein, Immanuel. 1974. *The Modern World System*. New York: Academic Press.

Waltz, Kenneth N. 1959. *Man, the State, and War*. New York: Columbia University Press.

————. 1979. *Theory of International Politics*. New York: Random House.

Washington Quarterly. 1982. "The Best National Security System: A Conversation with Zbigniew Brzezinski." *Washington Quarterly* (Winter).

Washington Representatives, 1990. 1992. Edited by Arthur C. Close, Gregory L. Bologna, and Curtis W. McCormick. 14th ed. Washington: Columbia Books.

Webb Papers. Papers of James E. Webb. Harry S Truman Library, Independence, Mo.

Webbe, Stephen. 1981a. "Pentagon Plugs Leaks in Budget." *Christian Science Monitor*, December 10.

———. 1981b. "Study Cites 46 Abuses; 'Wasted' Dollars at the Pentagon: How Much Will Reagan Save?" *Christian Science Monitor*, February 12.

Weber, Max. 1946. *Essays in Sociology*. Translated by H. H. Gerth and C. Wright Mills. New York: Oxford University Press.

Weinberger, Caspar W. 1990. *Fighting for Peace*. New York: Warner.

———. 1995. "Keep the B-2 Program Alive." *Forbes*, November 6.

Weingast, Barry R. 1981. "Regulation, Reregulation, and Deregulation: The Political Foundations of Agency Clientele Relations." *Law and Contemporary Problems* 44: 147–77.

———. 1984. "The Congressional-Bureaucratic System: A Principal-Agent Perspective with Applications to the SEC." *Public Choice* 44: 147–92.

Weingast, Barry R., and Mark Moran. 1983. "Bureaucratic Discretion or Congressional Control? Regulatory Policymaking by the Federal Trade Commission." *Journal of Political Economy* 91: 475–520.

Weingast, Barry R., and William J. Marshall. 1988. "The Industrial Organization of Congress." *Journal of Political Economy* 96: 132–63.

Weisskopf, Thomas E. 1974. "Capitalism, Socialism, and the Sources of Imperialism." In *Testing Theories of Economic Imperialism*, edited by Steven Rosen and James Kurth. Washington: Heath.

Welch, David A. 1992. "The Organizational Process and Bureaucratic Politics Paradigms: Retrospect and Prospect." *International Security* 17 (Fall): 112–46.

Werner, Leslie Maitland. 1983. "Fraud: Deciding When to Prosecute." *New York Times*, November 7.

Wildavsky, Aaron. 1975. "The Two Presidencies." In *Perspectives on the Presidency*, edited by Aaron Wildavsky. Boston: Little, Brown.

———. 1982. "The Past and Future Presidency." In *The Power of the Presidency: Concepts and Controversy*, edited by Robert S. Hirschfield, 3d ed. New York: Aldine.

———. 1988. *The New Politics of the Budgetary Process*. Glenview, Ill.: Scott, Foresman.

———. 1991. *The Beleaguered Presidency*. New Brunswick, N.J.: Transaction Publishers.

Wilson, George C. 1986a. "Goldwater Is Right, Colleagues Say; Senate Salutes Pilot of Pentagon Reform Bill." *Washington Post*, May 10.

———. 1986b. "Mr. Reliable Becomes Mr. Fix-it; Over Pentagon Resistance, Nichols Gets Military Reform Bill Passed." *Washington Post*, August 7.

Wilson, James Q. 1980. "The Politics of Regulation." In *The Politics of Regulation*, edited by James Q. Wilson. New York: Basic Books.

———. 1989. *Bureaucracy: What Government Agencies Do and Why They Do It*. New York: Basic Books.

Wise, David. 1961. "Scholars of the Nuclear Age." In *The Kennedy Circle*, edited by Lester Tangler. New York: Sterling Lord Literistic.

———. 1996. "I Spy a Makeover; The Problem Is that U.S. Intelligence Needs More than a Cosmetic Touchup." *Washington Post*, March 24.

Wohlstetter, Roberta. 1962. *Pearl Harbor: Warning and Decision*. Stanford: Stanford University Press.

Wood, Dan B. 1988. "Principals, Bureaucrats, and Responsiveness in Clean Air Enforcement." *American Political Science Review* 82: 213–34.

———. 1990. "Does Politics Make a Difference at the EEOC?" *American Journal of Political Science* 34: 503–30.

Woodward, Bob. 1987. *Veil: The Secret Wars of the CIA, 1981–1987*. New York: Pocket Books.

———. 1991. *The Commanders*. New York: Pocket Books.

———. 1995. *The Agenda: Inside the Clinton White House*. New York: Pocket Books.

Yergin, Daniel. 1977. *Shattered Peace: The Origins of the Cold War and the National Security State*. Boston: Houghton Mifflin.

Young, Oran R. 1980. "International Regimes: Problems of Conception Formation. " *World Politics* (April): 331–56.

———. 1989. "The Politics of International Regime Formation: Managing Natural Resources and the Environment." *International Organization* (Summer): 43.

Zacharias, Ellis. 1947. "Letter to the Editor." *Washington Post*, May 27.

Index

In this index an "f" after a number indicates a separate reference on the next page, and an "ff" indicates separate references on the next two pages. A continuous discussion over two or more pages is indicated by a span of page numbers, e.g., "57–59."

Library of Congress Cataloguing-in-Publication Data

Zegart, Amy B.
　　Flawed by design : the evolution of the CIA, JCS, and
NSC / Amy B. Zegart.
　　　　p.　cm.
　　Includes bibliographical references and index.
　　ISBN 0-8047-3504-2 (cl. : alk. paper)
　　ISBN 0-8047-4131-x (pbk. : alk. paper)
　　1. United States. Central Intelligence Agency—History.
2. Intelligence service—United States.　3. United States.
Joint Chiefs of Staff—History.　4. National Security
Council (U.S.)—History.　I. Title.
　　JK468.I6Z43　1999
　　27.1273'09—dc21　　　　　　　　　　　　　99-29521

⊗ This book is printed on acid-free, archival-quality paper.

Original printing 1999

Last figure below indicates year of this printing:

08　07

Typeset in Trump Medieval by BookMatters, Richmond,
California.